ML

GEORGIAN DUBLIN

But who can vanished Time rebuild?
    When dreaming in the gloom
Sometimes at eve, when noise is stilled,
And all the middle air is filled
    With moted light and bloom,
The rose-red Georgian houses seem
To catch a glory and to gleam
    As when their lights of old
Shone out, with many a taper's blaze,
On Dublin of the bounteous days.
    Built by the liberal and the bold
In spacious street and square,
    What memories are theirs to hold
Of gallant and of fair!
Each room a house, each house a town,
    Each hall a thoroughfare!
Where feast was set and dancers swirled,
    Where bravery was seen
With beauty powdered and be-pearled,
    Where talked the lucid Dean —
A Naples of the western world,
    As fair a water's Queen!

(Oliver St John Gogarty, 1912)

KEVIN CORRIGAN KEARNS

GEORGIAN DUBLIN

Ireland's Imperilled
Architectural Heritage

DAVID & CHARLES
Newton Abbot   London   North Pomfret (Vt)

To my wife, Enita,
and children, Sean and Megan

British Library Cataloguing in Publication Data

Kearns, Kevin Corrigan
  Georgian Dublin.
  1. Architecture—Dublin (Dublin)
  2. Dublin (Dublin)—Buildings
  I. Title
  920'.9418'35   NA991.D82

ISBN 0-7153-8440-6

Typeset by Typesetters (Birmingham) Ltd
and printed in Great Britain
by Redwood Burn Limited, Trowbridge, Wilts
for David & Charles (Publishers) Limited
Brunel House   Newton Abbot   Devon

Published in the United States of America
by David & Charles Inc
North Pomfret   Vermont 05053   USA

Contents

Our architectural heritage is something of which we have custody, not final ownership. We have a duty to our successors to respect their inheritance. *Jeanne Sheehy, Architectural Conservation: An Irish Viewpoint.*

Let us have sense. Let us preserve the best of our Georgian environments. Let us have comprehensive planning and the capability of concentrating the best we have left in the few areas we can preserve. Finally, let us be remembered as a people who valued their finest possessions rather than as having destroyed them in ignorance. *J. Neil Downes, Irish Independent.*

Preface

The genesis of this book can be traced back more than a decade. As a social geographer, I have visited Ireland every summer during the past twelve years for a variety of research purposes. By necessity, much of my labour has been conducted in Dublin where government offices are concentrated. Innumerable pedestrian forays into the older districts of the capital gradually bred an intimate acquaintance with the Georgian heart of the city. Some projects directly exposed me to Georgian architecture; when researching the peat fuel industry, my work took me to Bord na Mona offices. Visual exposure to these stately structures cultivated a genuine appreciation of their aesthetic qualities and historic character.

With each subsequent trip to Dublin I could not help but witness the insidious forces which seemed to conspire against the vulnerable Georgian streetscapes. Every year there was grim new testimony to neglect, decay and destruction. Once-intact Georgian vistas of unsurpassed beauty were savaged by demolition and unsympathetic architectural infill. Inexplicably, there existed no effective opposition to this wilful and wanton assault on Dublin's unique urban core. Indeed, I sensed that Dubliners somehow accepted this alarming degenerative process as a sort of natural occurrence—ostensibly, all in the name of progress and prosperity. Were Dubliners insensitive to this loss or merely impotent to exert any control over the destiny of their elegant city? Was there no philosophy of stewardship on the part of officialdom and citizenry to preserve this imperilled treasure for future generations?

My initial inquiries about the problems and policies surrounding Georgian preservation promptly convinced me that this was a highly vexing and controversial social-economic issue, often misunderstood and distorted. Personal attitudes and public pronouncements seemed fraught with contradiction, misconception and outright fallacy. It was readily apparent that there were few basic canons of preservation policy even among experienced urban planners and architects. That there is no consensus as to what constitutes 'the proper approach' to preservation is

9

partly explained by the many diverse groups which hold vested interests in the Georgian districts—land speculators, urban developers, government agencies, preservationist associations and residents who still inhabit many of the historic houses. Such disparate groups predictably possess conflicting interests, motivations and tactics in coping with preservation matters. Some motives are highly honourable, others transparently selfish and greedy. To be sure, the saga of Georgian Dublin's destruction and preservation has its lively cast of heroes and villains. But it would be a facile, myopic notion to interpret this complex struggle solely in convenient terms of 'dedicated champions of preservation' versus 'barbaric profit-oriented land developers'.

While much destruction has incontestably resulted from deliberate unabashed rape of the cityscape, a wealth of Georgiana has conspicuously been despoiled and lost from simple benign neglect on the part of owners and occupiers, both public and private. The fragile state of Georgian Dublin today cannot be attributed to the actions of any single group. A myriad of forces has for generations militated against the welfare and survival of the Georgian city. And if certain interests seem to have contributed more visibly than others in recent years to the abuse and obliteration of the Georgian terraces, it must be recognized that Dubliners, for the most part, have passively permitted this débâcle to brazenly occur within full view; within this context they surely must share some culpability. To analyse the preservation dilemma in terms of simplistic dichotomies serves only to generate more distrust and misunderstanding. It discourages enlightened dialogue and co-operation which are so desperately needed.

The preservation problem has reached a critical stage in its evolution. Decisions made during the 'eighties will doubtless determine to a significant extent the future of Georgian Dublin. No factor will have a more profound impact on preservation policy and programmes than public attitudes and action. In the truest sense, the fate of the Georgian city rests precariously in the hands of Dubliners themselves. It seems reasonable to believe that if they deem this architectural legacy worth saving, it will be protected and passed down to future generations. If not, it seems destined to be cannibalized by intrusive forces which have already gnawed away mercilessly at its antique fabric.

It is my intention to examine the origin, evolution and threatened demise of Georgian Dublin in the fervent hope that my treatment of this sensitive topic can, in a modest manner, contribute to heightened public awareness of, and appreciation for, this invaluable Georgian heritage.

Introduction

Dublin is a heartbreak. For all its past inequalities, it had a certain nobility of mien, a dignified bearing, and now is reduced architecturally almost to the provincial squalor of one of England's scrap-heap towns. And all done by ourselves.[1]

The sad truth is that one can no longer be proud to call oneself a Dubliner. The condition of the city, which has succumbed to the terrible increase of urban blight, is a cause for shame and outrage.[2]

For all her blight and her recent architectural misfits, she (Dublin) is still a very beautiful city, at once the most personal and the most surprising metropolis in Europe.[3]

Dublin enjoys a long-standing and justified reputation as one of the world's finest surviving eighteenth century cities.[4]

As evidenced from these contrasting perceptions and protestations, Dublin is a city of decidedly mixed repute; certainly not so jaded and scabrous as her detractors might allege, yet somewhat less majestic and untainted than admirers may acclaim. Few cities have been so variously vilified and revered, by native and foreigner alike. In a real sense, Dublin possesses a schismatic personality owing to its turbulent history of invasions and occupations. It has been claimed that 'there is nothing Gaelic about Dublin except its name—the Norsemen founded it, the English made it their capital, the Anglo-Irish gave it the character that it still retains'.[5] Under such convoluted historical circumstances one can scarcely blame the Irish for their often ambivalent attitudes toward the capital city.

Despite its shrouded early origins, sporadic alien influences and contemporary conflicting imagery, Dublin does possess an identifiable character if one is able to examine dispassionately its urban anatomy. Indeed, although its reputation is often that of an invaders' capital, Dublin is, in reality, 'emphatically an Irish city' whose history is discernibly etched in its street plans, system of terraces and squares, building façades and elegant interiors.

The heart of present-day Dublin is still its Georgian core, the crowning architectural achievement of the eighteenth-century Anglo-Irish community that dominated life in the city during its Golden Age. The aesthetic splendour of the Georgian city, so evident to the discriminating observer, is lasting testimony to an age of refinement, formality, taste and wealth. When constructed, the Georgian districts constituted the 'finest urban façade of terrace housing that the art of architecture ever invented'.[6] Thanks to the merciful vicissitudes of history, a remarkable amount of this eighteenth-century architectural treasure remains, essentially intact but often in a decadent state.

That Ireland failed to share significantly in the Industrial Revolution during the nineteenth century explains in large part how so much of the Georgian city survived. Meagre economic development during this period meant that there was no real need or motivation to demolish the older Georgian structures to provide space for new developments. During the twentieth century Dublin fortunately escaped the ravages of two major world wars which virtually annihilated historic districts in so many other Western European cities. During the post-war period Dublin remained in a relative state of economic dormancy, generally considered a 'European backwater' city. Through the troublesome 1950s Ireland's general economic malaise plagued the country and stimulated emigration, but it also ensured the retention of the Georgian streetscapes. Of course, few Dubliners at the time suspected that the economic stagnation could prove in any way beneficial. Only some years later was it realized that the Georgian city had been preserved unwittingly by economic circumstances to survive as a 'vital part of Ireland's national culture'.

Though economic deprivation abetted the retention of Georgian buildings, it also meant that Dubliners had scant financial resources to spend on maintaining and restoring them in a proper manner. As a consequence, the capital boasts of an enviable number of Georgian dwellings but an alarming proportion have been victimized by dereliction and decay. Nonetheless, since the destruction of Dresden in the last days of World War II, Dublin, despite its tattered form, remains the 'only important 18th century capital left in Europe today'. It is precisely within this broader context that one must appraise the real value of historic Dublin. Since Dublin's Georgian streets and squares represent probably the most complete and coherent system of eighteenth-century street architecture left in Europe, this legacy transcends mere national importance and must rightfully be regarded as an integral part of Europe's architectural inheritance.

Despite the providential survival of Dublin's eighteenth- and early nineteenth-century streets and squares, the Georgian districts are seriously imperilled by the incipient forces of modernization and urban redevelopment. In the late 1950s the Irish Government initiated bold new economic schemes to revitalize the national economy and attract foreign investment. While this was a good tonic for the country as a whole, the vastly accelerated pace of development in the capital posed new threats to the older districts, especially the Georgian section which fast became the most valuable urban landscape in the country.

To understand what has occurred in Dublin over the past two decades, it is helpful to realize that only recently has the Irish nation been able emotionally and psychologically to release its oppressive grip on the past and look optimistically toward the future. A nascent quest to 'modernize' pervades all facets of Irish life. Nowhere is this determination more evident or vigorously expressed than in urban redevelopment. Beginning in the 'sixties, Ireland experienced phenomenal economic growth. Thanks to the cautious guidance of the Industrial Development Authority, much of the industrial development has been judiciously disseminated throughout the country using a system of designated regional nodes and industrial estates. Since the avowed objective was to create a more equitable regional balance, Dublin received a restricted share of new industrial activity. However, there was no way to constrain other commercial development which reflected the new prosperity and vibrant financial climate. As the economic, political and social centre of the nation, Dublin found itself in the frenzied midst of major urban upheaval. As demands for urban space intensified and the office building craze accelerated, the conveniently situated Georgian districts became attractive targets for speculators and land developers. With no real preservation tradition on which to rely, and frail legislative protection, the Georgian houses proved easy prey. The resultant, and aptly named, 'orgy of destruction' which Dublin has suffered during the past twenty years has exacted a devastating toll on the city's urban fabric. Individual Georgian houses have been readily extracted from intact street-scapes and casually replaced with unsympathetic, sometimes grotesque, infill; in other instances, such as the episode involving construction of the Electricity Supply Board office block on Fitzwilliam Street, entire sections of structurally sound Georgian houses have been demolished and replaced by sleek, but sterile, new structures.

13

Not all threats to Georgian Dublin assume such conspicuous form as physical demolition; more subtle perils to the integrity of the Georgian city are at work. Of particular note has been the drastic transformation of Georgian houses from their original form and function as private residences to completely new uses, most commonly office buildings and commercial establishments. When such conversion occurs, the buildings may be structurally saved but they often stand as gaunt skeletons, their once-elegant interiors altered beyond recognition, their 'soul' obscured by modern fixtures. Such architectural adulteration means that they cease to exist any longer in the classical Georgian idiom. Another 'innovative' development is the replacement of mannerly and dignified Georgian buildings, often in cavalier fashion, with counterfeit reproductions, or 'replicas'. This facile approach to preservation has gained in popularity and acceptance over the past decade, and these architectural impostors can be easily detected along such Georgian streets as Harcourt and Leeson. As a consequence of these developments, the familiar face of Dublin has changed with bewildering swiftness.

It was not until the 1970s that Dublin's 'urban crisis' was formally recognized. There are doubtless many reasons which explain why Dubliners failed to acknowledge and heed the inherent dangers of an unbridled assault on their historic city until such a belated date. Many of these factors will be examined in this book. But one prominent factor that should be noted from the outset is that the Irish have been strongly conditioned by their past. Centuries of foreign domination, famine, emigration, economic deprivation and political struggle have imbued the population with a certain wary practicality. Within this context, early efforts at Georgian preservation elicited little emotive appeal in Irish society; simply stated, there were more urgent matters of social and economic import to be concerned about. Initially, many Irish viewed the preservation movement with little more than bemused curiosity. Others saw it as merely some quaint antiquarian crusade to embalm moribund architectural relics—hardly a practical expenditure of time and money. To exacerbate matters, there has long been the lingering notion in the minds of many Irish that this architectural heritage is, in fact, not worth salvaging since it is presumably associated with a distasteful epoch of foreign domination, and the buildings themselves of questionable Irish character. Passive attitudes and outright hostility toward the Georgian architecture have always posed one of the most seemingly intractable barriers to the type of preservation movement now commonplace in most other Western European countries.

Despite the rampant onslaught against its historic foundations, Dublin miraculously retains more of its early city patterns than any other eighteenth-century European city. Yet it is paradoxical that while this architecture has been internationally acclaimed for its historic and artistic merits, domestically it has been woefully neglected and sadly abused. Visitors to Dublin commonly lament, often in wonderment, the maltreatment of this fragile heritage. To be sure, Dublin's preservation dilemma is hardly unique; over the past few decades the older quarters of numerous European cities have become veritable battlegrounds between developers and preservationists. But in Dublin the situation seems more grave. The continuing absence of a definitive and *enforceable* policy for urban preservation jeopardizes the entire Georgian system. There can be no doubt that Dublin has reached a critical point in its history, that the city is now in grave danger of losing its identity and unique character because of the increasing demands and pressures of modern development. Especially disquieting is that Ireland remains conspicuously out of step with preservation efforts in most other European countries. In Britain and virtually every other Continental country there exists a positive, dynamic and well-financed scheme to retrieve and preserve the nation's historic architecture. This philosophy applies not only to monumental structures but also to common domestic street architecture. To date, Ireland has adopted no such bold approach to preservation. The present system of simply 'listing' buildings of historic merit and employing zoning controls to restrict certain disruptive forms of commercial intrusion is, at best, only a laudatory first step. Without government support and financial assistance, preservation agencies remain impotent to guarantee the protection of endangered urban architecture.

Preservationists face an exasperating challenge. They must combat the formidable obstacles of inept governance, commercial greed, public apathy and sheer ignorance which militate against the welfare of Georgian Dublin. And the problems they confront are social, economic, political, administrative, legislative, environmental and even historical in nature. Public education remains their best hope for success. Too often Dubliners seem to believe that they must choose between preservation of the existing historic cityscape or the creation of a new, progressive, modern capital. It is utterly fallacious to accept that one can be achieved only at the sacrifice of the other; preservation is not incompatible with modernization. Quite to the contrary. Continuity and change are necessary, predictable, even desirable processes in historic centres—but the past must be harmoniously integrated with the present and future.

Such an approach demands patience, co-operation, sensitivity and imagination—not simplistic heavy-handed techniques of demolition, rebuilding and replication.

Fortunately, there is still time to redress past wrongs and ensure the future of the Georgian heritage. Though preservation as a vital issue has not yet burgeoned sufficiently into the consciousness of the Dublin citizenry, there is encouraging evidence that public enlightenment is taking place and a preservation movement is at last discernible. But ultimately preservation success depends on the creation of a public spirit and will—a firm resolve, vigorously expressed, that the shared architectural heritage shall not be allowed to perish.

Notes

1 'Heartbreak City', *Irish Times*, 17 November 1979, p3
2 McDonald, Frank. 'Dublin—What Went Wrong?', *Irish Times*, 12 November 1979, p10
3 Wright, Lance, and Browne, Kenneth. *A Future for Dublin* (Bedford, England: The Architectural Press, 1974), p296
4 *Dublin Development: Preservation and Change* (Dublin: a Draft Interim Report prepared by Llewelyn-Davies, Weeks, Forestier-Walker and Bor for the Dublin Corporation, January, 1967), p2
5 Beckett, J. C. *The Anglo-Irish Tradition* (Faber & Faber, 1976), p66
6 Downes, J. Neil. 'The Georgian Architecture of Dublin: Where the Real Magic is Found', *Irish Independent*, 22 February 1962, p6

1
Origin and Character of Georgian Dublin

The Irish capital as far as brick and stone are concerned is essentially a city of the past—an eloquent reminder of an old aristocratic society that, with all its faults, not only achieved distinction at home, but upheld the standards of that age and even added to its culture.[1]

The early origins of Dublin (which derives from *Dubh Linn*, the 'dark pool' of the harbour) are obscured by fragmentary historical evidence. It is thought that settlement dates back to the second century when Ptolemy, the Alexandrian geographer, made mention of it on a map as a maritime city. However, there is no surviving physical proof of a site. Six centuries later marauding Scandinavian seafolk, who were greedily plundering and establishing bases along the coasts of northern Europe, took a serious interest in Dublin Bay. The harbour not only provided a sheltered haven for the seafarers but offered a strategic site for trade. In the ninth century the Norsemen, or Vikings, decided to establish a settlement here. It was situated close to where Christchurch Cathedral now stands. The rich abundance of recently excavated archaeological artifacts from the Wood Quay Viking site provides valuable evidence of these early settlers and their life; yet we know little of the morphology of the settlement itself. They fortified the town by walling it and Dublin grew into a thriving trading node between a number of countries. Settlement along the mouth of the Liffey River also afforded the Vikings easy navigable access to the interior where they discovered monasteries to be plucked of their gold and silver treasures. They found Ireland a readily exploitable land. The island's multifarious tribes, with their allegiance to different kings, were so busily engaged in warring with each other that they mounted no unified defence against the invaders. Nonetheless, to strengthen their hold on the country the Norsemen shrewdly developed alliances by marrying into powerful Irish clans. Establishing themselves

17

firmly on Irish soil, they gradually introduced the natives to the concepts of towns, trade and high standards of craftsmanship. The Norsemen enjoyed a period of security and prosperity until the Irish managed to rise and defeat them at the village of Clontarf (near Dublin) in 1014 under the leadership of their famed warrior king, Brian Boru. Though their power had been broken, the Norsemen were not expelled from the land and they promptly re-established themselves.

Quite a new chapter in Irish history began in 1170 with the appearance of the Anglo-Normans. They readily seized control of the town and displaced the Norsemen north of the river. Like their predecessors, the new invaders were instinctively lured by the propitious river port and its trade potential. They rewalled the city, built a castle in the early thirteenth century and officially secured Dublin as an English holding. Thus began Ireland's long and painful subjugation to her powerful neighbour to the east. For seven centuries Dublin was to remain a seat and symbol of British hegemony. It eventually became the principal gateway through which a flood of English colonists were disseminated throughout the rest of the island. But the boundaries of Dublin changed little between the thirteenth and seventeenth centuries; it remained very much a medieval city, relatively small and rather dilapidated. Its prestige was somewhat enhanced by the establishment of Trinity College in 1591, but there was precious little else to hint that Dublin was on the brink of major architectural, political and economic growth.

CYNOSURE OF THE ANGLO-IRISH DOMAIN

Modern Dublin can be traced to the seventeenth and eighteenth centuries when large numbers of English Protestant settlers flocked to the city. They became, in a real sense, the 'landlords of Ireland', establishing themselves as a ruling caste, monopolizing power and securing economic and social privileges. As a group they became sufficiently diluted with Irish blood and indigenous customs to gain their own identity as the 'Anglo-Irish'. Their privileged position among the Catholic majority came to be known as the 'Protestant Ascendancy'. Dublin was the cynosure of their domain and nowhere is the spirit of the Anglo-Irish more profoundly displayed than in their architectural achievements— regal town mansions, stately squares and noble terrace houses, all glorious memorials to their prosperity, ambition and social flair. The eighteenth century was truly the Golden Age of Dublin, destined to become by the century's end one of the most glamorous and pulsating urban centres in all Europe.

Eighteenth-century Ireland was marked by relative peace and vast improvements in agriculture, both of which contributed to the prosperity for which Dublin became so well known. The English nobility and landed gentry steadily took up residence in the city, gradually accepting it as their home. With a vigorous provincial Parliament it even developed the status of a true capital. Though adopting Dublin as their new home, the aristocracy found fault with its rather dilapidated physical condition. The existing houses, many built of timber, were falling into decay, and the narrow roadways, often no more than muddy lanes, were unable to accommodate the large coaches and carriages. To the growing number of wealthy and discriminating citizens, such a living environment was intolerable. It was in direct response to their demand for refined dwellings and a more suitable urban milieu that Georgian Dublin received its full impetus. New residential terraces were laid out to cater to their needs. Most were developed as unified projects on the estates of local landowners such as Luke Gardiner, Lord Fitzwilliam, Joshua Dawson and the Molesworth family—familiar names perpetuated in major Dublin streets. Luke Gardiner, a wealthy Dublin banker, was especially instrumental in initiating urban expansion. A man of great enterprise and vision, he acquired a vast tract of land north of the Liffey River in 1714 and systematically charted it for development.

The real beginning of Dublin's great building period can be traced to Henrietta Street where, in 1724, 'larger and more commodious houses with profuse internal decoration began to take the place of smaller and plainer houses hitherto built'. Along Henrietta and neighbouring Dominick streets were erected residential mansions of great scale and fine proportions, embellished with exquisite woodwork and plasterwork. About the same time, Georgian houses began sprouting up south of the river. Molesworth Street, for example, took root in 1725. Over the next quarter century the growing prosperity of Ireland was much reflected in the capital city, and in addition to the nobility and gentry an upper-class of wealthy merchants and professional men expanded in number and influence. Building activity kept pace with their growing demands for dignified private residences; by 1750 an estimated 3,000 new houses had been built. At mid-century Dublin's population reached 120,000, about one-fifth the size of London, making it the second city of the British Dominions. Though the city was expanding at an impressive rate, its growth was disorderly and inequitable. The 'nobler proportions of the

19

new quarter' contrasted sharply with the decrepit old town and its 'squalid wretchedness of the streets'. There was great need for organization and urban planning.

GRAND HOUSES AND GRACIOUS SQUARES

In the 1750s Dublin embarked on a period of phenomenal growth and urban development. Indeed, during the last half of the eighteenth century no capital in Europe grew so furiously or splendidly, or displayed a more brilliant social climate than Dublin. During this fifty year span, the city's renowned wide-street system was created, major Georgian terraces laid out and urban squares formed. In large part, this unparalleled period of progress was due to the Wide Streets Commission. Appointed by an Act of Parliament in 1757, this body, one of Europe's first and certainly most successful town planning authorities, was empowered with the rights of compulsory acquisition in an effort to remedy Dublin's ills and generate orderly growth. Much of Dublin's admirable symmetry and scale, dignified character and widely heralded spaciousness resulted from its benevolent direction and enlightened planning. Though the Commission devised planning schemes well in advance of their time, some of its practices were ruthlessly pragmatic. By demolishing all obstacles in their path to create the famed wide street and urban square pattern, the Commissioners proved to be the 'very embodiment of unsentimental utility'. Nonetheless, their dedicated efforts helped to raise Dublin to its peak of glory and magnificence, a capital of 'first-rate visual importance in the history of European culture'.

Throughout the last half of the eighteenth century, Dublin's prosperity grew. Generous rental fees were pouring from rural Irish estates into the coffers of landowners in Dublin who lavished their wealth most conspicuously on houses and socializing. Nobility, gentry, wealthy merchants and prosperous professionals fiercely rivalled one another in the creation of grand domiciles. As historian Seamus Scully avers, these 'lordly houses would be the dazzling homes of an aristocracy whose extravagance would amount to a species of madness'. Yet their splendour was destined eventually to fade to the 'meanest of Dublin slums—their snobbish owners forgotten, like the starving paupers who would die huddled in the bug-ridden, rat-infested basements of what had once been crammed wine cellars'. The resplendent Georgian houses were more than mere dwellings; they were indispensable status symbols. And the enormous sums of money that Dubliners invested in their embellishment became legendary. The social and economic stature of an individual in Dublin could be flawlessly gauged by his address. The rise and fall of prominent personages along prestigious streets was always the subject of great intrigue and gossip.

In 1753 the building of grand houses commenced in Rutland Square (now Parnell Square), the centre-piece of the earlier half of the Gardiner Estate. It appeared that the north part of the city was destined to be the premier residential area. In reality, Dublin was on the verge of a major territorial shift in fashion. In part, this development can be attributed to the Duke of Leinster who, in 1745, decided to build a mansion with spacious grounds along Kildare Street in the south city. When queried by a friend if he would not find it lonely living so far removed from fashionable northside society, he brazenly prophesied that fashionable society would, in due course, follow him southward. His prediction proved infallible, for in 1762 Merrion Square (on which the Duke's property happened to border) was laid out. It was soon to become the most sought-after address in the city. As described in Lewis' 1787 *Dublin Guide*, the square had a special 'air of magnificence about it' and was inhabited by peers, Parliament members, noblemen and persons of exalted rank. In 1818, authors Warburton, Whitelaw and Walsh recorded in their *History of the City of Dublin* that it had become the 'resort of all that is elegant and fashionable in this vicinity'. The north side of the square was the epitome of exclusivity where the Dublin élite would shamelessly promenade about, flaunting their position and finery. This practice of exhibitionism was especially prevalent on summer evenings and Sunday afternoons when a military band usually accompanied the pageantry and spectacle. According to the *Georgian Society Records* (1912 volume), by the end of the eighteenth century owning a house in Merrion Square was considered 'essential for social success'. In the 1780s neighbouring Fitzwilliam Square was begun. It was more modest in scale than its sister-square but Fitzwilliam Square was imbued with a charming domestic quality and intimate cohesive character that survive to the present day. Though lacking the residential luminaries of Merrion Square, it was home to an impressive array of lesser nabobs. Construction of the last of Dublin's great squares, Mountjoy, was carried out in 1791. Representing the highest standards of the day in domestic architecture, it came to be the most elegant urban space in north Dublin and the only 'square' in the city to legitimately qualify for the title. And of all the Georgian squares, it has met with the cruelest fate.

AN OSTENTATIOUS AND FLAMBOYANT SOCIETY

Throughout the latter half of the century Dublin high society revolved gaily around the gracious squares and their arterial Georgian terraces. James Anthony Froude, writing about *The English in Ireland in the Eighteenth Century*, tells us that the city was widely reputed for its 'balls and parties, races, gambling-tables, eating, drinking, and duel fighting'. Conspicuous consumption and sheer exhibitionism were blatant. The sumptuous indulgence so characteristic of Dubliners during this period was the result not only of the wealth accumulated but also the comparatively low cost of Irish food and labour. In fact, for many Anglo-Irish a major compensation for living in Dublin rather than London was the significantly cheaper prices for food, servants, labour and assorted provisions. The temptation to live extravagantly was indeed great. Commonly, even well-to-do Dubliners beggared themselves by their insatiable acquisitive exploits. There was no want of expensive items on which to spend one's money, for Dublin had developed into a thriving centre of luxury crafts—not only those associated directly with architecture, such as wood carving, plasterwork and ironwork, but also coach-building, furniture, silverware and glass. The display of gold, silver and diamond jewellery was also much in vogue. There was a passion for glamour and show. By any standards, Dublin in the eighteenth century was a tantalizing city, full of fascinating characters, exciting ideas, lively gossip, rakes, bucks, whores and tramps. There was something to amuse or offend almost everyone.

Visitors to Dublin could not help but be impressed with the grandiloquent manner in which the upper classes lived. In William Lecky's *A History of Ireland in the Eighteenth Century* we are told that they marvelled not only at the lordly houses themselves but the 'ostentatious profusion of dishes and multiplication of servants' in Georgian homes. It was not unusual at a single meal to serve beef, mutton, ham, chicken, fish, fruits, vegetables, breads, cheeses and a choice of desserts. Not infrequently, foreigners found the behaviour and habits of Dubliners over-indulgent, vulgar and tawdry, often complaining that they 'drank too much and stayed up too late'. The ubiquitous practice of duelling struck many foreigners as particularly uncivilized, if not downright barbaric. Though duelling, or 'blazing' as it was commonly known, was carried out elsewhere in Europe at the time, it typically became excessive in Dublin, reaching almost epidemic proportions. It was a form of swashbuckling sport; duelling clubs were even founded. Disputes over

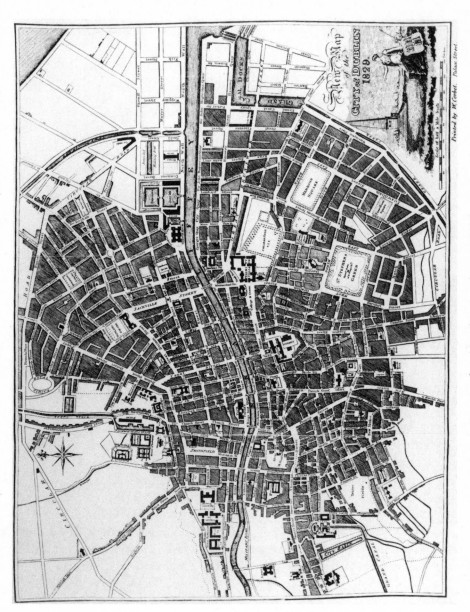

Fig. 1　1829 map of Dublin showing the completed Georgian city

political matters and elections were commonly settled by duelling. However, as Sir Jonah Barrington testifies in his *Personal Sketches of His Own Times*, duels were often prompted by petty provocations as the combatants faced each other in the fields behind Merrion Square and 'gentlemen often got themselves shot before they could tell what they were fighting about'.

Despite the easy spending, high living and excessive duelling, Dublin was, on the whole, a refined and cultured city in which there was genuine appreciation for the finer things in life. The arts, music and drama were liberally patronized and they flourished. Toward the close of the century Georgian Dublin was in full bloom. The architectural system was nearing completion, and Dubliners took immense pride in their fair city which was described in 1826 by John Gamble in his *Sketches of History, Politics, and Manners in Dublin* as 'inexpressibly graceful', bearing a 'strong likeness to London . . . more beautiful, in truth'. Dubliners were not only proud, they were vain. As Gamble relates, 'vanity . . . seems the prominent feature of every inhabitant of Dublin . . . he is vain of himself, vain of his city, of its beauty, of the splendour of its private buildings, and of its vast superiority over London'. Some Dubliners were even moved to brag that they spoke better English than was to be found in London (in rebuttal, Londoners chided that one could hardly improve on the original!). Dublin may not have been a monumental city in the mould of London, Paris or Rome but the difference was merely one of scale, for by the end of the eighteenth century it was incontestably regarded as one of the great political, cultural and architectural capitals of Europe, boasting a 'matchless display of public and private buildings'.

To be sure, Dublin was architecturally resplendent and eminently comfortable—for the privileged. It was, however, also a city of deplorable poverty. Starkly conflicting with the prim rows of red-bricked Georgian houses were the ramshackle huts and muddy lanes of the poor. By the end of the century the city's population had swelled to 182,000, many of whom subsisted in squalid conditions. In *An Essay on the Population of Dublin* (1805), the Rev James Whitelaw noted with alarm the 'wretchedness . . . filth and poverty' that was pervasive and cited the urgent need to 'alleviate the evils of suffering humanity'. Thus, in the years approaching the Union, Dublin was, above all else, a city of notable contrasts.

ANGLO-IRISH IDENTITY

Ireland . . . has no aboriginal inhabitants. All Irishmen, in every part of the country, are descended from invaders, conquerers, and settlers; and no layer of settlement has any exclusive claim to be regarded as the 'Irish people'.[2]

The contributions and flaws of Anglo-Irish society in the eighteenth century will doubtless be debated among social historians *ad infinitum.* This sensitive and controversial period in Irish history is best left to their critical analysis and judgement. However, it would not be possible to comprehend Georgian Dublin, past or present, without some insight into the identity of those who ruled the city and inhabited its stately residences. Prevailing attitudes among contemporary Irish toward the Georgian architectural heritage are understandably rooted deeply in their perceptions of the Anglo-Irish and their role in Irish history and culture. Contradictions and misconceptions still abound.

Simply put, the term 'Anglo-Irish' refers to the English Protestant community that dominated Ireland during the eighteenth century and those who inherited and maintained its tradition in a later age. It is well known that the early Anglo-Irish carved out for themselves a niche of superiority and security. They controlled the Irish Parliament, gained economic advantages, often accumulated great wealth and enjoyed many privileges denied the Catholic population. But contrary to some beliefs, Anglo-Irish society did not consist exclusively of a small, wealthy ruling class. It was comprised of a large Protestant body, representing all ranks of society (though admittedly weighted toward the well-to-do) and perhaps accounted for nearly half of Dublin's population. Despite differing levels of social and economic position within their own ranks, the Protestants did initially share a kind of exclusive egalitarianism. Few objective students of this period could deny that the Anglo-Irish, like other ruling classes of Europe, created and assiduously maintained a highly inequitable social system. My intent is neither to absolve them of blame nor affix further condemnation for their historical deeds, but rather to comment on the authenticity of their Irish identity and their changing image in Irish history as it pertains to their architectural legacy.

As descendants of English settlers, the Anglo-Irish were, in a real sense, victims of conflicting circumstances. While Irish by birth and geography, they were nurtured in an essentially English cultural milieu. But there can be little doubt how most perceived themselves at the time because by the eighteenth century an 'Irishman' meant simply anyone who had taken root in Ireland. Therefore the Protestant population consisted of those who had become Irish *more recently* than other groups, but it was nonetheless legitimately 'an Irish one'.[3] This is not to say that the Anglo-Irish failed to retain pride in their British origins and continuing affiliations, but with each passing generation they increasingly came to think of themselves as predominantly Irish. Although the Anglo-Irish held a privileged socio-economic position within Dublin society throughout the century, a good degree of social assimilation occurred. Protestants and Catholics were surely drawn together in their shared quest for greater autonomy from Britain in governing domestic affairs. The mounting struggle against dominant British rule did much to weaken and dismantle social and religious barriers. Robert McDowell in his treatise *Irish Public Opinion, 1750–1800* concludes that there gradually developed a 'strong sense of national solidarity and warmhearted patriotism' which 'predisposed men to cast aside suspicion and ignore sectarian distinctions'. Some figures who came to be known as Irish patriots for their vigorous support of Ireland's claim to economic independence, such as Henry Grattan and Lord Charlemont, were doubtless motivated in part by their property interests. Nonetheless, they were genuinely sympathetic to, and supportive of, the Irish cause. Beckett contends that Grattan and his Protestant contemporaries 'never doubted that they were Irishmen, without any qualifications'. Many worked in selfless devotion with native Irishmen to gain freedoms and preserve Irish language and traditions. The two groups often merged harmoniously in mind and cause. Thus, the simplistic dichotomy of Protestants and Papists, natives and foreigners, is not wholly fair or accurate. As Sean O'Faolain argues in *The Irish*, it would be an error to regard the Anglo-Irish as simply 'an alien and detached strain in Irish life'.

The appellation 'Anglo-Irish', which is really an historian's term, assumed new meaning with the demise of the eighteenth century. During the reign of the Protestant Ascendancy, Gaelic culture was ignored or repressed by the majority. However, with the decline in British influence the Gaelic forces enjoyed a resurrection and gained popular support. The eventual full Gaelic Revival carefully defined and cultivated a keen sense of national distinctiveness based on rigid cultural identity. Within the increasingly narrow confines of the new nationalism 'Irish' became synonymous with 'Gaelic' and any other claim to 'Irish-ness' had to be qualified. As the Gaelic increasingly became recognized as the only true Irish culture, other cultural traditions were purged, or at least given a label identifying their distinct origin. It was really in response to this emergent, exclusive nationalism that the designation 'Anglo-Irish' came into common usage. If originally the term was devised to distinguish between different *types* of Irishmen, based primarily on *origin*, it eventually came to reflect their perceived status as less pure or authentic; in the eyes of many it assumed distinctly negative connotations. By the more ardent Gaelic nationalists, the Anglo-Irish were viewed with utter disdain, a belligerent caste who had done little but mercilessly exploit the country for their own profit. They were relegated to apostles of a foreign culture, representing conquest and confiscation.

The perpetuation of pejorative stereotypes, by intent or error, has been highly injurious to objective appraisals of the Anglo-Irish and their role in the course of Irish history. However they are seen, as oppressors or patriots, native or colonist, the Anglo-Irish indisputably became an integral part of the country's life and, in Beckett's judgement, there is 'no sound reason for regarding it as less than truly Irish'. In the present age it is more accurate and constructive to accept the title 'Anglo-Irish' as a practical means of distinguishing between the country's *two main* cultural traditions—the Anglo-Irish and the Gaelic Irish. Each has contributed in unique ways to the shaping of modern Ireland. To deny one group its identity as 'truly Irish' is to ignore historical evidence and perpetuate painful divisions of past eras. It also seriously jeopardizes efforts to preserve the most conspicuous legacy of the Anglo-Irish—the wealth of Georgian architecture which now belongs rightfully to all Irishmen and a heritage in which Dubliners especially may take great pride.

Notes

1   Maxwell, Constantia. *Dublin Under the Georges: 1714–1830* (Gill and MacMillan, 1979), p45
2   Beckett, J. C. *The Anglo-Irish Tradition* (Faber and Faber, 1976), p148
3   Kee, Robert. *The Most Distressful Country* (Quartet Books, 1979), p28

2
Architectural Distinctiveness
of the Georgian City

The Georgian buildings of Dublin are a fine native example of
the great Classical style common to Europe at the time. While
directly influenced by the English form of this style, the work in
Ireland has a distinctive merit and character of its own. It is
regrettable that this style of art and architecture is seen,
wrongly, as only an alien import.[1]

The widespread notion that all our architecture was put up by a
foreign ascendancy, is not Irish, and should be swept away . . .
is based on a lot of jingoistic woolly thinking, and is an insult to
generations of talented Irish craftsmen, artists, and architects.[2]

Too often it has been assumed and accepted, quite fallaciously, that the
buildings which comprise Georgian Dublin are simply British architectural types transplanted on Irish soil by the Anglo-Irish. This notion has
long figured prominently in negative attitudes so often espoused toward
the Georgian heritage. The argument that Georgian houses are distasteful
relics of an oppressive epoch, so persuasively waged by those who stand
to profit from their destruction, has undeniably held great emotional
appeal in some circles. The clarion call to erase Georgian terraces from the
Dublin cityscape as a patriotic act of national purification has often been
justified on the grounds, either presumed or contrived, that they are in
no way truly Irish. For specifically this reason, it is important to examine
Georgian Dublin in light of its Irish distinctiveness; only under the harsh
glare of such scrutiny can this persistent and damaging myth be
effectively dispelled.

There has long been in Ireland an attitude regarding architecture that
'if it is artistic it must have been produced by foreigners'. This stigma has
been blindly applied most often to the Georgian structures. In truth,
there is much evidence that Georgian Dublin is, to a significant extent,

the product of Irish architects, craftsmen, artists and materials. But owing to the continuing absence of proper architectural education in Irish society, this information has never been adequately disseminated. This explains in large part why the Georgian heritage has never been fully appreciated by those who inherited it.

The houses we know today by their generic label 'Georgian' were built during the successive reign of monarchs from George I to George IV (1714 to 1830). This period spanned the last great age of architecture, marked by a level of taste and general conformity to accepted canons from which it was simply unthinkable to deviate. Simply put, it was an age of architectural 'good manners'. To be sure, Dublin's Georgian style adhered to Classical principles and respected traditional architectural etiquette, but it developed a distinctively Irish character all its own—immediately recognizable by any expert. Like all divergent art forms, it is basically a combination of elements borrowed from different sources and subsequently revised, refined or expanded.

During the eighteenth century probably half of Dublin's known architects were of British or other foreign origin. And there is no question that non-native architects were largely responsible for constructing the most imposing and prestigious buildings in the city. On the other hand, Dublin's Georgian terrace houses were usually built by what today would be termed speculative builders, most of whom were lost in anonymity. For the most part they were architects and craftsmen from the Dublin area. It is important to recognize that during the eighteenth century the profession of architect was often indistinguishable from that of builder. Thus, many Dublin houses were built by craftsmen-contractors who simply took the liberty of calling themselves architects. Records documenting the work carried out on Dublin residences by these local craftsmen and tradesmen reveal that a high proportion had Irish names. Ordinarily they were not men of great artistic ability. They were, in fact, fortunate that the Georgian style is one of the simplest of the great styles, relying almost exclusively on proportions. But since upper-class Dubliners could afford to loosen their purse strings to generously fund the construction of their houses, builders were encouraged to be creative and original. As John Harvey explains in *Dublin —A Study in Environment*, since Georgian builders were unconstrained by economic limitations, 'planning design, composition, quality of crafts-manship, all the minutiae that goes to make up the soul of a building prospered as they had never in the British Isles prospered since the death of the Middle Ages'. The uniqueness of the Georgian system is the result of their original plan types and ways of handling details that became characteristic only of Dublin. Working together in this climate of freedom and creativity, the city's predominantly Irish architects and craftsmen bred an independent spirit fostering a distinctive school of architecture, and during the late eighteenth century propelled Dublin to heights of refinement unsurpassed in any part of the British Isles.

URBAN PATTERNS AND HOUSE DESIGN

Although eighteenth-century Dublin was in the forefront of town planning in Europe, the Georgian system was not designed as a regimented, homogeneous architectural unit. Quite to the contrary. It is noted for the great variety in streets, squares and houses. There was, of course, a general urban scheme in which squares were laid out as a series of rectangular linked spaces and major streets appropriately patterned around them. But there was no grandiose attempt to fashion a Bath or Nash's London; such an attempt would have contradicted the traditions and principles of building in Dublin where ordinarily houses were constructed in small clusters, a few at a time. The extraordinary consistency of the Georgian cityscape, still readily discernible, was not the result of municipal by-laws, which were then non-existent, but rather of local building techniques and rules of proportion and material usage in the design of street architecture which were commonly accepted throughout Europe at the time. The development of streets and design of houses were subject only to general controls; there was much opportunity for ingenuity and innovation. This resulted in an impressive array of urban architectural types. Dublin's streets and squares are clear testimony to the freedoms accorded their creators. For example, there are long streets like Baggot, Fitzwilliam and Leeson, short links of the Hume Street sort, single-sided streets like Herbert, raised terraces along Herbert Place, reclusive cul-de-sacs such as Wilton Place and Ely Place, curved vistas along Harcourt Street, and residential crescents around Mount Pleasant Square. The squares are no less independent in personality. Each is unique in size, scale, design and landscaping. Some parts of the Georgian city are secluded, domestic and charmingly intimate; others are boldly spacious, bounded by imposing mansions and wide thoroughfares.

Basically, two types of houses were built in the Georgian system. First were the great town houses such as Powerscourt House and Belvedere House, deliberately constructed at great expense to stand as unique and magnificent edifices for residents of wealth and high position. Secondly were the comparatively modest terrace houses, often regarded as the poor relations to the more pretentious Georgian mansions. However, it is the cumulative effect of this domestic street architecture, concentrated in relatively small areas, that imbued Dublin with its essential character and identity. Taken in their totality, these Georgian terrace houses constitute Ireland's most important architectural heritage.

The prevailing architectural ideology, together with the plot size available, strongly favoured use of the terrace as the most efficacious system of residential building. Individual houses were erected on adjoining plots along roads that were narrow compared with plot length. Ordinarily, houses were built in groups of two to five at a time by a consortium of several small tradesmen bound together by rather complex mutual agreements. As a single house or small cluster would be built, gaps were left for filling at a later date. Because of the speculative process, construction was often erratic. Buildings were placed directly on to the street, leaving a maximum amount of space available at the rear for a private garden. This created a generally accepted spatial hierarchy with public streets at the front, separated from private gardens, and access lanes behind the main building. Houses were not individually articulated by spatial techniques; for example, they were not separated or altered along the terrace. Individual units combined naturally to mould the larger cohesive mass. Proportion was the essence of the Georgian idiom and the simple discipline of façades created a generally unified, yet deceptively varied, terrace streetscape. Variations in façade treatments served to distinguish individual houses from the collective grouping.

The materials used in the construction of Georgian houses were largely of native origin. Most houses were built of brick with high-pitched slate roofs behind a parapet. These bricks vary in colour from claret or light red, to brown, yellow, orange and grey. It is sometimes claimed that all the brick was imported from England as ballast in ships. Some brick did arrive in this manner but most seems to have been provided directly from local brickyards. A good number of Georgian houses were faced with granite on the ground floor (as in Merrion Square and Fitzwilliam Place) as a compromise. This granite was quarried in counties Dublin and Wicklow. Timber used for structural purposes and woodwork was almost exclusively imported, but some was probably cut from nearby Wicklow forests.

In terms of size there is no 'typical' Georgian house; some are modest, others palatial. Generally, it may be said that houses north of the river are older and larger. The largest houses, found along Henrietta Street, have above 9,000 square feet of space excluding the basement. They dwarf the far smaller 3,000 square foot variety found along Baggot, Clare and some other more southerly Georgian streets. Between these extremes are the houses around Merrion Square and Fitzwilliam Square which are more representative in size of the overall Georgian city. There is a correlation between street location and house size. Since streets were developed in accordance with a prescribed formula, houses along the same row were kept to a fairly uniform size, allowing for certain variations. Terrace houses were restricted in height to four storeys or less. They were normally two or three windows wide, but could extend to four or even five. Windows were graduated in size according to the importance of each floor. Ground-floor windows were always the largest because they were in the most important quarters such as the drawing-room or dining-room. Upper floors were devoted mostly to bedrooms, dressing chambers and private living space where smaller windows were more appropriate. Spacious windows were practical in Georgian houses because they permitted maximum light penetration along the sometimes dark and gloomy canyon-like terraces.

The prevailing requisites of the age dictated the practicality of providing large basements. By necessity they were used primarily for hoarding basic commodities: water (both for drinking and washing), fuel supplies in the form of bulky coal and turf, candles, soap and other provisions. In more prosperous homes storage space was always reserved for ample supplies of wine and beer for special family and social occasions. Where it was possible to use ice as a preservative, large quantities of such perishable items as meat, fish, poultry, cheese, butter and vegetables were liberally kept on hand. Since even moderate-size houses were commonly staffed with ten or more domestic servants, many doubtless had to take up residence in the dark, dank basements.

Exterior treatment was an important part of the Georgian idiom since it provided individual articulation for each house. During the eighteenth century, Irish wrought-iron and cast-iron craftsmen had strong guilds. They created original ironwork which handsomely embroidered houses and entire streetscapes with railings, gates, window guards, metal arches and lantern posts. This ornamental ironwork, smelted by charcoal before coke was used for this purpose, proved more resistant to rust and

(*opposite*) Thomas Malton's view of Essex Street Bridge and Parliament Street in the 1790s

(*above*) A Malton print of Parnell Square in the 1790s with Charlemont House in the centre background; (*below*) an historic Georgian streetscape: the north side of Merrion Square with its variegated façades (*courtesy of the American Geographical Society*)

corrosion than the latter-day product. The superior quality of this iron explains how it has managed to survive graciously generations of neglect and want of paint.

The Georgian backland environment was also an important component in the architectural system. Backlands consisted of a rear garden and a mews building which served as a carriage house. Backland plots ranged in length from about 50 to 300 feet. They were designed as a spacious adjunct to the main living area, providing the closely knit terrace houses with open air, light and privacy. During the eighteenth century, when flower and vegetable gardening was much in vogue, the backland territory was highly valued and much used. And many houses were built with attractively curved rear walls and fitted with large, arched windows looking out on to the garden space.

THE ART OF SYMMETRY AND VARIETY

Dublin's unique Georgian architecture has been described by architect J. Neil Downes as 'fundamentally a folk art, an unconscious, naïve, relaxed simplicity but using fine art elements—the best of both worlds'.[3] Art appraisal always depends on the discriminating eye. Absolutely fundamental to interpreting Georgian Dublin as an art form are the principles of unity and contrast, symmetry and variety. Considered individually, the eighteenth-century terrace houses are in no way comparable to the great buildings such as Gandon's Custom House or the Four Courts. Architecturally, their importance lies not in their separate identity but in their collectivity, their harmonious unity. Destroy a few houses in a terrace and the artistic cohesion is severely impaired; patch the gap with alien infill and artistic purity is irreparably blemished. Aesthetically, the primary appeal of the Georgian terraces is their visual variety, their colourfully kaleidoscopic imagery. Each terrace is an intricate patchwork of sympathetically contrasting and eminently integrated slices of Georgiana.

The marked symmetry of the terraces, in which houses are generally uniform in scale and proportion, sometimes prompts the allegation that they are visually austere. This is true only if one ignores or fails to decipher the myriad variations in exterior treatment. Upon close scrutiny the terrace houses provide a remarkable study in contrasts. Georgian builders deliberately sought to personalize houses by individually articulating their facial features. Although they had to conform to certain rules of proportion, size limitations and an agreed-upon building line, there was no definitive plan which houses had to follow. It was apparently understood, and probably intended, that initial blueprints were to be treated merely as a point of departure from which the house should organically evolve. Since each house or small group of houses was created by a different team of personalities, the resultant diversity was highly pronounced. The Georgian builder's obvious intolerance of monotony and 'sameness' imbued the streetscapes with an electrifying variegation in brickwork, granite facing, rooftop elevations, window configuration, doorways and ironwork. Each house obtrudes as an independent entity, thereby creating a vertical accent on the horizontal plane. This infused variety led Walter Harris to comment about Dublin's architecture in his 1766 *History and Antiquities of the City of Dublin* that its 'only defect is the want of uniformity in the buildings'. Of course, it is precisely this exhilarating variation and unpredictability that has branded Dublin's native Georgian so architecturally unique and visually exciting. And nowhere is the art of symmetry and variety more in evidence than along the north side of Merrion Square where there is a cornucopia of different brickwork, stone, doors, fanlights and ironwork—truly visual poetry to the cultivated eye. Only the overpowering unity of the age and the relative humility and anonymity of the builders themselves could have masterfully welded such diversity into an overall unity—an architectural phenomenon not likely to be witnessed again.

INDIVIDUALITY AS EXPRESSED IN DOORWAYS

Nothing more dramatically emboldens the streetscape and distinguishes one house from another than the array of richly designed Georgian doorways. There can be no mistaking the highly individualized artistry and taste exuberantly expressed by the striking combinations of door types, fanlights, sidelights, door knobs, knockers and post boxes. Admirers of the Georgian scene are often more attentive to, and some-times transfixed by, these personalized doorways than other architectural features of greater merit. Indeed, the now-famous 'Georgian doors' have become something of a Dublin icon, proudly publicized in tourist literature and attractive wall posters. Visitors typically marvel at the splashes of bright red, blue, green, and yellow colours which always alert, and sometimes perhaps assault, the senses. Whatever the reaction, the doorways are the focal point of most observers.

The remarkable variety of Georgian doorways is the result of inevitably changing architectural styles and personal tastes. During the early Georgian period doorcases were more robust and massive than in later years. They had good proportion but little decoration. Usually the whole doorcase was consumed by the door alone and no fanlight was installed since entrance halls were often wide enough to allow for single window illumination. During the eighteenth century there occurred a gradual shift from robustness to refinement, true not only of doorways but also Irish furniture, glass and silver. Doorways with sidelights made their appearance around mid-century, many copied from those of the great country houses built by Richard Castle and others. It was during the last half of the century that the fanlight became the principal decorative element in the doorway. Doorways containing both sidelights and fanlights were quite popular, allowing for excellent interior lighting of the hallway; usually an arch covered both door and side panels. The houses of the middle classes were more standardized and had less variety than those built for peers, Parliament members and the landed gentry. The fanlight evolved as a work of art in itself, often filled with delicate lead tracery behind which there was an iron grill (said to have been originally installed as protection against thieves). Some fanlights contain a hexagonal glass box designed to hold a lantern, thus adding another dimension to the entrance. Doorways with fanlights only the width of the door itself, and attractively set off by a band of decorative plasterwork, became fashionable during the last quarter of the century. The slender columns of the Ionic order effectively displayed both the lead tracery of fanlights and the decorative plaster embroidery.

As fashion changed during the early nineteenth century, many doorways lost their charm and character, although the basic doorway design with semi-circular fanlight persisted well into the century. While fanlights were often simplified by the use of a single sheet of plate glass, doorways were sometimes embellished by inventive, if not always tasteful, means. For example, during the Edwardian period some doorways (as in the Fitzwilliam Square area) were emblazoned with rather shocking hues of pink and purple and the application of elaborate joinery. Nonetheless, at mid-century the unmistakable vestiges of the Classical Georgian doorway survived in such suburbs as Mount Pleasant Square. Dubliners have retained their fondness for Georgian doorways to the present day—though in superficial form. New homes in and around the city often have their plain faces embellished with a mock-Georgian front entrance, easily created by placing a simple wooden (or sometimes plastic) arch, pediment, or crescent-shaped glass panel over the door.

ELEGANT INTERIORS AND PLASTERWORK

> The independent character of Dublin's street architecture leaves
> its greatest legacy in the variety and richness of the 18th century
> domestic interiors of the city.[4]

Georgian Dublin's mannerly, reticent façades commonly mask splendidly ornate interiors. It is still a delightful revelation for passers-by on a darkened street to peer unsuspectingly into the lighted chambers of a Georgian house and be treated to a scene of wonderfully sculpted grandeur. Such glimpses into the past evoke romantic images of a resplendent society that two centuries ago gathered gaily behind the tall candle-lit windows and fanlighted doorways. Even modest and unassuming houses may reveal richly ornamented interiors. This is a reminder that the eighteenth-century building boom had to cater to a wide spectrum of society. Not only did the gentry and nobility seek to create impressive abodes, but a rapidly expanding class of lesser peers and rising merchants and professionals sought no less eagerly to fashion stylish accommodations, often for reasons of social acceptance and prestige. There was a keen desire not only to 'put on a good show' but to actually outshine neighbours. Such spirited rivalry reflected the secure and supremely confident environment in which Dublin's genteel society thrived.

No element of interior decoration more vividly expresses the wealth, gaiety and vitality of the Georgian period than the exquisite plasterwork which adorns so many of the houses. This, too, has been the subject of much erroneous appraisal. Because Dublin's plasterwork reflected a strong Continental influence and much work on major buildings was carried out by such notable artists as the Francini brothers, it is often mistakenly assumed that all the city's plasterwork may be attributed to the skilled hands of Italians and other non-native artisans. As C. P. Curran notes in his *Dublin Decorative Plasterwork of the Seventeenth and Eighteenth Centuries*, 'spurious folklore attaches foreign names at random' to much of the city's plasterwork and 'such ideas die hard'. In truth, it was largely Irish craftsmen who were responsible for this achievement.

The great period of Rococo plasterwork for which Dublin is so justly famous was introduced in the late 1730s by the two Italian brothers Paul and Philip Francini. However, for two hundred years before their arrival there existed a flourishing guild of plasterers in Dublin with branches in such cities as Cork and Limerick. Before the advent of the Rococo period, Irish craftsmen were rather conservative in their work. They did not recognize the full potential of decorative plaster and were heavily engaged in installing compartment ceilings. But with the infusion of new ideas, Irish craftsmen quickly developed their own delicate style and special techniques. Plaster decoration actually became a Dublin specialty. That Dublin is so astonishingly rich in plasterwork suggests that it became a form of ostentation, even conspicuous waste. Other European cities, of course, exhibit similarly fine examples of this art but in Dublin it is the commonplace proliferation of high quality plasterwork opulently displayed in both abstract and figurative form that clearly distinguishes it from the rest.

Irish plasterers obviously exulted in their freedom of expression, moulding magical displays in dizzying profusion on ceilings, walls and other surfaces. Though inspired originally by the Italian school which stressed modelled figures, fruit and flowers, Irish craftsmen soon devised their own original themes, adding musical instruments, cherubic figures and imaginative plant and animal forms to their repertoire. Some of their explicitly sculpted female forms have been known to embarrass nuns and priests who today inhabit their historic quarters. During the Rococo period the use of moulds was limited and most plasterwork had to be done by hand *in situ*. There was an element of competition as artistic plasterers jealously guarded their 'secret recipes' and techniques. Each added his own inimitable touch to the final masterpiece—the 'final twist of a bird's neck, the choice of flowers in a wreath or garland, a cloak blowing in the wind'. Unfortunately, since plasterwork is such an anonymous art, it is today very difficult, often impossible, to identify the work of particular individuals. Of course, the distinctive plasterwork of such noted men as Robert West is widely recognized and well documented. Most present owners of Georgian houses are quite gracious in admitting curious visitors to examine their elegant plastered interiors, taking great pride in what they have inherited.

Even the furnishings in Georgian homes contributed to the distinctive Irish flavour. Most owners could well afford to order items such as furniture, silver, china, glass and fireplace pieces by catalogue from England, but a good many chose to purchase them in Ireland, giving the decorative setting a decidedly Irish stamp. Irish Chippendale furniture, usually fashioned from dark mahogany imported from the West Indies, was especially popular; pieces littered the salons in most Dublin homes. Like the native plasterwork, Irish furniture boasted of all sorts of quirks and peculiarities found nowhere outside the country and is best known for its ornate carvings of eagle's heads, lion's paws, winged birds, scallop shells and rosettes.

Thus, in literally every stage of its evolution, from architectural conception, use of materials, physical construction techniques, craftsmanship, interior artistry, to the final furnishings, Georgian Dublin was imbued with a distinctive, indigenous imprint making it an authentic part of Ireland's heritage.

Notes

1   *Amenity Study of Dublin and Dun Laoghaire* (Dublin: An Taisce, 1967), p24

2   Sheehy, Jeanne. 'Contribution of History, II', *Architectural Conservation: An Irish Viewpoint* (Dublin: Architectural Association of Ireland, 1974), p35

3   Downes, J. Neil. 'The Georgian Architecture of Dublin—The Best of Both Worlds', *Irish Independent*, 21 February, 1962, p6

4   Rowan, Alistair. 'The Historic City', in *Dublin's Future—The European Challenge* (London: A Conservation Report for An Taisce, The National Trust for Ireland, published by *Country Life* Magazine, 1980), p3

3
Period of Evolution and Decline

METAMORPHOSIS FOLLOWING THE ACT OF UNION

Following the Act of Union in 1801, Dublin experienced profound socio-economic metamorphosis. Few Dubliners could have anticipated or prepared for their new historical fortunes—or misfortunes. In a real sense, the Act of Union committed the city to sleep, plunging it into a prolonged period of social and economic dormancy. The most immediate and conspicuous consequence of political change, directly following the dissolution of the Irish Parliament, was the mass exodus of wealthy and prominent citizens. As Froude explains, it was particularly men of 'intellect and ambition' who promptly departed, simply leaving their homes and estates to be managed by agents. The privileged classes proved highly adaptable to change, easily moving their residences with the tempo of the times—they were not to be relegated to life in any second-rate city. The style of living to which they had so comfortably grown accustomed could be duplicated in lively London or other European cities. With the sudden departure of people of wealth, fashion and power, Dublin's former brilliance was noticeably dimmed. The entire mood of Dublin life was transformed almost as if some malevolent paralysis had gripped the city. Indeed, so swift was the change that Lord Cloncurry, writing in his *Personal Recollections*, notes with dismay that the Dublin to which he returned in 1805 was 'in many respects, so different' from the city he had left in 1797 that he was compelled to digress from his personal narratives just to reflect upon the nature of these changes. Economic changes were particularly startling. No single aspect of life in the city more poignantly reflected the changing status of Dublin than the property market. Property values plummeted to unimaginable levels. Georgian houses which had been purchased for £8,000 in 1791 sold for only £2,500 a mere decade later. And by 1849 the same houses commanded a paltry £500.

41

Of course, not all affluent Dubliners were eager, or even willing, to relinquish their established roots. Many tenaciously clung to their former world, hoping that conditions would stabilize and they could find security in the new social and political order. During this transitional period Dublin increasingly became an Irish Catholic city, a development which bred a certain sense of anxiety and insecurity among Anglo-Irish Protestants witnessing a steady diminution of their own numbers. While a good number of elegant homes remained in the hands of original families too patriotic or too poor to shift to London, most were gradually turned over to the middle and professional classes, many doomed to degenerate into squalid tenements before the century's end. A scant four years after the Union, many of the larger houses around Mountjoy Square and St Stephen's Green were empty and forlorn or had at least been rented out as lodgings. With the displacement of the upper classes, Dublin slowly evolved into a city of doctors, lawyers and tradesmen who had neither the resources nor the interest to live lavishly like their predecessors.

If Dublin was debilitated, at least it did not expire; and all building activity did not grind to a halt. Some important Georgian development proceeded as planned despite the economic lethargy. Fitzwilliam, Merrion and Mountjoy squares were not completed until well into the century. Some new building was actually undertaken and attractive squares laid out in the suburbs, thereby perpetuating the Georgian tradition, albeit on a far more modest and practical scale. Perhaps the most notable, and certainly one of the most beautiful, of the late Georgian developments was Mount Pleasant Square, built around 1830. But as the century progressed, the skills which had created and embellished the stately Georgian houses declined markedly. The erection of great town houses virtually ceased since there was little demand for such luxurious domiciles.

The impact of changing economic and social conditions on Georgian Dublin was distinctly inequitable: the south Georgian city essentially retained its intrinsic character while the less fortunate north gradually faded into but a slight resemblance of its former glory. Even before the Union, the tide of fashion was shifting from the north to the south-east portion of the city, an ominous harbinger of what was to follow during the nineteenth century. Though the north side had developed first as a residential bed of wealth and aristocracy, its premier position proved ephemeral. Its decline may be attributed to several factors. The north setting was rendered less desirable by the construction of a new customs house on the north bank of the Liffey which promoted extension and development of the harbour, leading to industrialization of a large adjoining area. Equally important, the north city's Gardiner Estate was divided up and sold in 1848, paving the way for neglect and deterioration in multiple hands. Conversely, south of the Liffey the Fitzwilliam Estate survived relatively intact into the twentieth century, partly because it remained securely under single ownership and also because it lay advantageously between the commercial centre of the city and the emerging prosperous suburbs to the south-east.

Different groups came to occupy the two Georgian sections. In the 1830s the southern area around St Stephen's Green and Fitzwilliam and Merrion squares accommodated remaining nobility, gentry and the professions. It was also around this time that the legal profession began converging on Fitzwilliam Square. Coincidently, the north city, focusing on Parnell Square and Mountjoy Square, became increasingly inhabited by the lowlier merchant and official classes. With each passing decade the prestige of the north Georgian city was further eroded, the upper- and middle-income groups abandoning the area for the south Georgian districts or heading toward the new suburbs blossoming around the city's edge. This suburban boom which began in the 1830s and accelerated during the subsequent generations established the pattern of city centre-to-suburban migration which still plagues the city of Dublin.

PHYSICAL DETERIORATION

If the nineteenth century was an era of social and economic turmoil for Dublin, it was also a period of physical deterioration. From the outset, structural, topographical and meteorological factors conspired against the welfare of the Georgian city. Many of Dublin's physical ailments can be traced to its rather unpropitious site at the mouth of the Liffey River. Built in part on reclaimed tidal flats, the subsoil proved impervious to good drainage, and the sewers, invaded by the ebb and flow of tides, freely spawned infectious diseases. Since Dublin is nestled in the basin of a river estuary, the air above the city naturally trapped the polluted mist of sulphuric acid formed from the high sulphur content of the soft bituminous coal imported largely from Britain. The city became increasingly contaminated during the nineteenth century. Streets were soiled with catarrhal ejections and the population infected with bronchial disease and spreading tuberculosis. In his *Dublin Historical Record* article which documents the decay of the Georgian city, Donal T. Flood suggests that in their quest to be progressive, Dubliners unwittingly 'fouled their own nest' as their city became one of the most disease-ridden in all Europe.

The prevailing atmosphere of acid-laden smoke and rain not only menaced the population but ravaged their housing environment. The basic layout of the city, seemingly an intelligent one, was compact in nature, nearly circumscribed by the canal system and convenient for pedestrian traffic. Its spatial arrangement and visual quality were unsurpassed. But the orderly, honeycombed pattern of the lofty Georgian terraces, so pleasing to the eye, proved a magnet for catching and retaining polluted smoke and mists which charred façades and corroded the exterior fabric. Since most houses had been constructed with timber supports, they were susceptible to dampness and rot. Exterior slates, roof-fastenings, lead sheathing and guttering all yielded to the acidified rain. Moisture penetrated brickwork, weakening parapets and pock-marking walls. The houses were also attacked from within. Deeply excavated basements, so practical for their utilitarian space, drew ground water and, added to the existing moist, warm air from normal cooking and laundering activities, created an atmosphere of extreme dampness. This dampness penetrated floorboards, roof timbers, and wall foundations, leading to dry rot and eventual woodworm infestation.

Some houses naturally fared better than others. Those benefiting from superior design, materials, brickwork and exterior insulation were more able to resist the harsh corrosive climate. And a good system of ventilation and heating contributed measurably to a structure's life expectancy. Some Georgian terraces benefited simply from their favoured upland location which helped to remove them from the foci of pollution and provided a more salubrious setting. But most owners had to cope with constant problems of maintenance and repair. To combat effectively the process of decay was an expensive task. Generally, only the wealthier residents were able to keep their property in prime form. To secure properly a home against further deterioration often meant re-roofing, better sealing of exteriors, patching brickwork and strengthening mortar joints. While a number of Georgian homes have survived to the present day primarily because they were of superior original construction, the vast majority still exist because of the attention and care given them by former owners and occupants. Houses which were maintained in reasonably good condition until the latter part of the nineteenth century could at least benefit from the advance of new building, repair, restoration and maintenance techniques, thereby extending their life.

But with the exodus of the wealthier classes in the second half of the nineteenth century, the fate of too many Georgian dwellings was to fall into a state of continual decrepitude and often irretrievable deterioration. By this time the middle-class residential population was dissuaded from purchasing these houses because they were far too costly to maintain and demanded expensive domestic labour. The smaller, newer homes under construction around the periphery of the Georgian city were better suited to their more modest spatial requirements and financial resources. This situation essentially left many of the Georgian terraces at the mercy of speculators and lower-income groups who were either unwilling or unable to care for them properly.

POVERTY AND TENEMENTS

As previously mentioned, Dublin was noted for its areas of slums and squalor well before the Act of Union terminated its prosperity. But this condition was greatly amplified during the second half of the nineteenth century. During this period the city experienced the onset of three potent urban processes: the influx of impoverished people from the rural districts, the trend toward tenementation to house them, and the accelerating migration of the prosperous classes from the city centre to the suburbs.

Economic conditions in Dublin during the nineteenth century were bleak compared with those of most British cities. The Industrial Revolution had no appreciable impact on the city. With its antiquated textile industries, a reliance developed chiefly on brewing, distilling and biscuit manufacturing. True, the city did continue to function effectively as an important legal, administrative, educational and religious centre, but its commercial status clearly suffered following the Union. Irish industry simply could not compete economically with the more advanced industrial production in Britain. This created vast unemployment problems among the semi-skilled and unskilled workers in Dublin. This problem was exacerbated by the Great Famine when Dublin became the principal urban catchbasin for the rural masses fleeing hardship elsewhere in the country. By the late 1840s the city had assumed the role of a massive refugee camp. Dublin was ill-equipped in almost every way to cope with this monumental burden. During the period 1841–1900 the population of Ireland as a whole declined but Dublin's increased from 236,000 to 290,000. Only a fraction of the urban populace was gainfully employed because of the economic plight.

A growing proletariat, comprised largely of unskilled migrants from the depressed countryside, converged on the city seeking assistance and shelter. Competition for housing was intense and accommodation limited. The conspicuously spacious Georgian houses, many already abandoned by their original owners earlier in the century, provided a logical solution. Since the middle classes found them financially unaffordable, many Georgian houses predictably fell into the hands of mercenary groups. Once the grand houses had depreciated sufficiently in price, they were grabbed up by slum landlords who found exorbitant profit in catering to the miserable masses continuing to swell the city's population. Under this new breed of *rentier*, houses of nobility were put to drastically new uses. The spacious quarters were converted to tenements, divided up and crammed with poor families. The slum families, many of whom had previously lived in mud huts and weavers' cottages, were eager to accept any type of accommodation. Housing densities reached alarming proportions. A single Georgian house could hold as many as 60 or 70 people. Humanity was packed 'as thick as cockroaches' into the ornate, high-ceilinged rooms once occupied so comfortably by the upper-classes. Lordly houses were fast reduced to verminous wrecks. An incongruous scene was fashioned—poor families huddled together in wretched poverty and sickness in the very chambers where, in an earlier century, pampered young Dubliners in carefree manner had danced the minuet. The poverty became rampant. By 1879 there were nearly 10,000 tenement houses in the city occupied by about 117,000 people, or about 45 per cent of Dublin's population.

The process of tenementation took a heavy toll on the Georgian structures. Invariably, there was not enough space to accommodate adequately those in occupation. As a consequence, interior walls, fixtures and other obstacles were casually removed to create additional living space. One of the first, and most important, interior features to fall victim was the main staircase, which took up an enormous amount of potentially usable space. Whole families were squeezed into the section where the staircase was extracted. Under such conditions of human stress, there was virtually no regard for the artistic merits of the building. Many fixtures which were removed, such as fireplace frames, plaster mouldings and woodwork were sold for a mere pittance or simply discarded as waste material. Practicality ruled the day.

The north Georgian city bore by far the greatest burden of poverty. Here the displacement of the prosperous classes was first and most profoundly felt. Since a good number of Georgian houses had been abandoned in the north city earlier in the century, slum owners and their clients were able to gain an easy grasp here. With the infiltration of the lower classes and the consequent onset of physical deterioration, most of the residual middle-class residents were inclined to depart. Financially secure families attempting to retain their homes were faced with formidable obstacles. Those who bravely and obstinately held their ground while witnessing the worsening decay around them were usually doomed to defeat. The insidious process of residential abandonment and neighbourhood decline (so thoroughly analysed and documented by contemporary urban sociologists) proved a sinister urban phenomenon, expelling even determined families from their Georgian homes in fear that eventually they, too, would be consumed by the infestation of poverty, blight and disease. Faced with the harsh realities of filth and misery at their very doorstep, most relinquished their hold and departed. As the invasion of pauperdom spread unchecked street by street, entire Georgian terraces lapsed into tenements. North Dublin reached its nadir around 1900. People in Mountjoy Square were sleeping six to a bed, the city's death rate was double that of London, and overcrowding, poverty and disease were said to exceed that of any other city in Europe, prompting one newspaper to equate Dublin's slum condition with Dante's Inferno.

Though much of Georgian Dublin was reduced to providing a grubby backcloth for the literary works of some of Ireland's most renowned writers, such as James Joyce and O'Casey, some sections were spared degradation. South Georgian Dublin was not ravaged by tenementation. St Stephen's Green, Merrion Square, Fitzwilliam Square and Fitzwilliam Street survived as 'islands of dignity', relatively unscathed and intact. While most of central Dublin was socially reshaped by the centrifugal movement of the wealthy toward the suburbs, accelerated by the introduction of railways in the middle decades of the century and by other new forms of transport, such as tramways, in the 1880s, the stately Georgian squares managed to retain their attraction as pockets of respectability where society's upper-crust still clustered. But in place of the old nobility were newly prominent types, most notably the professional classes. Many doctors at this time had their homes and practices in Merrion Square; some of these houses still have tunnels connecting house and mews where servants could unobtrusively leave the premises.

TWENTIETH-CENTURY BLIGHT

The fate of the Georgian districts in the twentieth century has been inextricably linked with the welfare of the inner city—which has hardly fared well. Dublin has been steadily drawn from its historic core, resulting in depopulation and stagnation of the urban centre. Efforts in the early twentieth century to remedy the slum problem carried over from the previous century were partially successful. However, in 1914 there were still about 5,000 tenements covering the north side like a malignant fungus. Following Independence the new Irish Government inherited a capital which was described in 1922 in *Dublin of the Future* as a 'city of magnificent possibilities, containing features of the first order but loosely correlated and often marred by the juxtaposition of incongruities and squalor'. Perhaps the most urgent problem facing the fledgling government was the rehousing of more than 60,000 Dubliners, most of whom were living in abominable conditions. The 1925 *Dublin Civic Survey Report* declared that the 'wretched habitations of the masses of the poor cry out for immediate solution', further noting that the 'housing of the working classes for the most part is provided by the use of old Georgian mansions'—prompting the wry observation that Dublin could at least boast of the 'most architectural slums in Europe'.

To alleviate urban blight and poverty, the government initiated a programme of slum clearance and decentralization. Poor inner-urban populations were transplanted to new outer-city housing developments built by municipal authorities. The central city was demographically drained as a sprawling suburban pattern of development took shape around the periphery of Dublin. Not only was the heart of the city plucked of its poor but it was steadily robbed of its remaining middle- and upper-income groups by a highly inequitable trend of urban development which favoured the south-east to the detriment of the rest of the city. As the south-east became the 'fashionable', 'chic', 'smart' location in which to live and work, the inner city was, in effect, condemned to social stagnation and a withering population; the Georgian districts suffered accordingly, especially the derelict north.

In the period between Independence and World War II, the government made some laudable efforts at architecturally reconstructing a few of the city's more notable buildings, such as the Customs House and the General Post Office, which had been badly scarred by the Troubles. However, there was no concerted and coherent policy for urban planning and architectural conservation. Virtually no attention was directed by

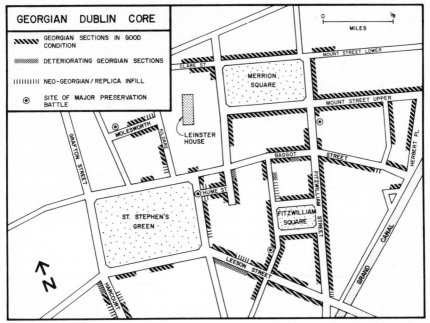

Fig. 2   Map of Georgian Dublin core which identifies streetscape conditions

authorities toward the restoration or preservation of the humble Georgian terrace housing. Furthermore, existing legislation controlling rents meant that landlords had no incentive to conduct basic structural repairs or invest in improvements on their Georgian properties. Yet, the lack of speculative development on any substantial scale during the pre-war years meant that Dublin, though often ragged and in shambles, retained much of its original architectural character. This is confirmed in the *Handbook for Delegates*, distributed to members of the Royal Institute of British Architects at their 1931 conference in Dublin, which states that the Georgian districts remained essentially 'unimpaired by plutocrats or speculating builder'.

In striking contrast to the tribulations of the city centre, the suburbs thrived. Statistics graphically depict this imbalance in urban development. While Dublin as a whole has continued to grow in population during this century, the inner city has declined sharply. Between 1936 and 1971 the inner-city population was halved, dropping from 266,511 to 131,501. It would be incorrect to attribute this loss solely to slum clearance because careful scrutiny of these figures reveals that over half of this decline has actually occurred since 1950 when the bulk of tenements had already been eliminated. Hence, the pattern of depopulation plaguing central Dublin is abundantly clear—the

49

government has assisted in the removal of lower-income groups while the well-to-do have fled of their own volition.

As an integral part of the inner city, Georgian Dublin, once socially vibrant, has gradually ceased to function as a viable environment for normal community life. But not all Georgian areas have suffered total residential depopulation. In the north city there are still skeletal residential populations consisting mostly of poor people occupying sub-standard dwellings. A notable exception is the determined middle-class community along North Great George's Street and their rather heroic story will be unfolded in a later chapter. Many houses in the north district have had the good fortune to have been purchased and occupied by assorted religious and education groups, usually guaranteeing some resident population and good maintenance. Even around Merrion Square and Fitzwilliam Square a small number of red-bricked houses still remain largely in residential use. However, as they have been increasingly deprived of their resident population, most Georgian streets have become ripe for acquisition by developers anxious to reshape their character and function, and the overwhelming trend in both Georgian areas has been toward conversion to offices, shops and other commercial enterprises. Developers are not interested in redeveloping these historic districts for new residential use when the commercial potential is clearly more lucrative. In fact, during this century the Dublin Corporation has been virtually the only house-building agency in the city centre and almost no new residential development for private ownership has taken place here for the last hundred years. Owing largely to the depressed state of the national economy, the government's tradition of benign neglect toward the urban core carried over into the post-1945 years as Dublin stumbled through the 1950s a somnolent city in a financially troubled country.

(above) North Great George's Street with Belvedere House at the upper end (courtesy of the American Geographical Society); (below) an example of the remarkable architectural diversity of Georgian façades around Merrion Square. Variety is expressed in differing building materials, doorway treatment, fanlight design and ironwork

Intricately designed Georgian fanlights with delicate lead tracery. Some *(below)* were provided with a hexagonal glass box to hold a lantern

4

The Assault of Modern Development on the Historic Georgian Core

> The destruction of Dublin appears to be guided at times by mysterious forces, perhaps some marauding band of anarchic leprechauns whose deeds are greeted by the natives in puckish fashion.[1]

> The avalanche [of modern development] is upon us with a vengeance . . . all hell . . . seems to have been let loose upon our unfortunate city, which is beginning to look as though blind impersonal forces had laid hold upon it and were tearing it apart.[2]

The decade of the 'sixties abruptly awakened Dublin from its fitful slumber. The economic boom which affected the entire nation was most visible in the capital. Modernization meant that dreary, old-fashioned Dublin needed a healthy face-lift—sparkling new glass and steel buildings to match those in other European cities. Few could deny that the city legitimately needed economic rejuvenation, modern structures and an injection of progressive spirit. It is equally true that today, in retrospect, most Dubliners would probably concede that the approach adopted for this modernization and redevelopment has been little short of disastrous.

IMPACT OF THE OFFICE BOOM

The phenomenal surge of building activity in Dublin is directly linked to the increase in white-collar employment and the consequent demand for office space. Between 1946 and 1972 Dublin's office population doubled from 45,000 to about 90,000. Despite government efforts to disseminate office employment more widely throughout the country, central Dublin today claims about half of all the office jobs in Ireland. Office-type employment has grown at a faster rate than any other occupational category in the city, creating intense pressure for office space within the central area. While such development has unquestionably been necessary, the scale, location and extent of office building has caused irrevocable damage in parts of the city. Office development is a normal and expected facet of modern urban development; if properly controlled it has the potential to restore and enhance urban centres. But in Dublin, office development has assumed a form which Wright and Browne in their study *A Future for Dublin* determine is essentially 'against the interests of the citizens'. They note that too many new buildings are either improperly located, 'inevitably out of scale' with their surroundings, or 'clothed in an architecture' that clashes with adjacent structures. As a result, office development has functioned as a disintegrating force in parts of the inner city, distorting rather than enhancing the urban fabric. No part of the city has been more consumed by the office movement than the Georgian districts.

The attractiveness of the Georgian districts for office use is part of an overall shift in the geographic location of Dublin's office zone. In 1940 the centre of gravity for the aggregate total of all office establishments was located around College Green and the immediately adjacent streets. It was the focal point for most financial categories, commercial establishments and a number of professional groups. But many embassies and numerous medical groups were already firmly rooted in the Fitzwilliam Square area which was recognized even then for its select and pleasant, yet central, location. Due to various economic pressures, the geographic pattern of central office establishments has changed radically over the past four decades. There has been a distinct shift toward the south-east section of Dublin, consistent with the general investment and development pattern. In the 1960s a number of doctors began moving their offices from the Fitzwilliam Square location to south of the Grand Canal where they occupied new, modern medical quarters. Apart from the obvious advantages of gaining modernized facilities, many doctors were eager to escape the parking problem which plagues the Georgian streets. During the 'sixties the problem of trying to find parking space deteriorated from a mild annoyance to a major aggravation. It was not only a matter of limited parking space but also the restricted periods allowed by the meters which created inconvenience for doctors' patients. There is still a solid core of doctors in Fitzwilliam Square. However, in recent years the section has gained popularity with other professional groups, most visibly lawyers, accountants and architects. By 1970 the centre for all office establishments had migrated south-eastwards around the Merrion Square node. Hence, Georgian Dublin found itself precariously located in the very centre of the primary redevelopment zone.

Dublin was one of the last cities in Europe to experience, or suffer, the office revolution, and it arrived with devastating thoroughness. The driving ambition to build and modernize blurred the good judgement and vision of city authorities, urban planners and land developers—for the city's long-awaited new era of progress also proved to be a period of rampant destruction. The most disruptive impact has been on the city centre. Office development here could only be accomplished in two ways: by clearing existing structures for construction space, or by converting old buildings to new uses. Both schemes, of course, posed immediate threats to the Georgian terraces. Demand for new offices exceeded the space available, generating keen competition to build properties and escalating land values. Pressures to either demolish or convert fine eighteenth- and early nineteenth-century houses to achieve a higher density of floor space became extreme. Apart from their ideal location near to shops, restaurants and public transport, Georgian houses had other advantages. Their historic character and architectural distinctiveness provided a highly prestigious setting, especially for professional occupants. Additionally, their large rear gardens allowed for backland development. As a consequence, office development spread like a cancerous growth through the Georgian streets of the south city. Georgian houses became expendable in the name of progress. Similar historic buildings in England or elsewhere would surely have been protected and covered with notices 'advertising their history and times for opening', but in Dublin the Georgian heritage remained vulnerable, ripe for economic exploitation.

THE DEVELOPER AS DESPOILER

During the past two decades of frenzied urban development, Dublin's Georgian houses have been treated much like 'aristocrats in the midst of a revolution'.[3]

It is important to emphasize that many developers, speculators and property owners during this turbulent period exercised sound judgement and employed responsible, even commendable, approaches in renewing and rebuilding the faded urban fabric. The many well-restored and preserved Georgian buildings currently occupied by different governmental and private groups unmistakably attest to their sensitivity and respect for the architectural heritage. On the other hand, there can be no denying that many developers and land speculators launched a ruthless, barbaric assault on the historic Georgian core. Swathes of 'inconvenient' Georgian houses were obliterated with impunity to create open space for new office buildings. Paradoxically, while developers instinctively sought these prestigious squares and terraces, they proved all too willing and eager to then casually destroy the architecture which gave the area its unique quality and character—all to achieve a higher density of site use and realize a greater profit. Apart from the argument that new buildings allowed for more efficient urban land use, other justification was provided for the ruination of fine old buildings. Some developers were quick to use the old rationale that the Georgian houses were simply offensive symbols of past colonial oppression, best eradicated from Dublin's cityscape. As a 'patriotic' gesture they offered to accomplish this task. Their real motives, of course, were blatantly evident—they perceived the Georgian streets as mere wastelands to be cleared and reconstructed in a modern mould while making a handsome profit.

It would not be an exaggeration to state that the redevelopment of Dublin has been essentially left to the whims and dictates of private developers and speculators. For the past twenty years, amid an unconstrained environment for development, they have been allowed to use the inner city, in the words of one irate writer to the *Irish Times*, as a 'gambling ground for their own ambitions of wealth and power'. During this free-wheeling period of urban growth, the government assumed a modest role in redevelopment. Indeed, while the Civil Service and other public bodies take up almost three-quarters of Dublin's total office space, the vast bulk of this accommodation is rented from private development companies.

By the late 'sixties the appellation 'developer' had become synonymous with 'despoiler' in the public psyche. The tide of destruction that scarred the central city evoked accusations of 'rape', 'pillage' and 'prostitution' of the urban environment. The developers' appetite for reconstruction and profit seemed rapacious as they increasingly cast hungry eyes toward the Georgian terraces. Motivated by hard economics which demanded maximum floor space for minimal investment, no Georgian house, regardless of its historic or artistic merit, was sacrosanct. As a consequence, 'dazed citizens' watched with wonder while Dublin was debauched and disfigured by what *Irish Times* environmental journalist Frank McDonald labels the 'architecture of avarice'. Within full daily view of Dubliners their city was steadily being robbed of a great architectural inheritance with scarcely so much as a plaintive whimper of protest or opposition. Ironically, visitors to Dublin seemed to express more alarm and outrage than did the Irish.

No single factor can account for the manner in which Dublin so readily succumbed to the plunder of modern development. It must be attributed to a combination of prevailing legal, economic and social conditions which unwittingly conspired to create an incredibly permissive development climate. Most notable are weak (or non-existent) legislation, public apathy and the sheer temptation of vast profits to be reaped. Also, the government's unwillingness, or inability, to assume a prominent role in the redevelopment process itself, thereby giving free rein to private developers, surely contributed to the unrestrained atmosphere.

Though the 'sixties seemed to be a period of virtually lawless urban expansion, legislation did exist which was supposed to prohibit such abuse. However, the legislative and administrative system of controls failed to function effectively. The 1963 Local Government Act (or Planning Bill) stood as the principal legislative document. But the Bill was too timidly drafted, and upon close inspection proved to be what Kevin B. Nowlan, Professor of History and head of the Dublin Civic Group, considers an 'inadequate and tangled' measure. It required no special planning permission to demolish a building since this was considered an exempt development. This glaring flaw paved the way for the demolition of some superb Georgian houses along St Stephen's Green, Harcourt Street and Lower Leeson Street, among others. Legislative controls were simply not effectively enforced. And even when the force of law was applied against violators, the penalties imposed were almost trivial. Furthermore, at this time there was no tradition of urban planning, no comprehensive city plan for Dublin, no official city architects and few experienced urban planners.

One can scarcely imagine a city more unsuspecting and vulnerable to the onslaught of urban redevelopment than Dublin. Citizens and government officials seemed equally ill-prepared for the era of the developer. Inexplicably, the populace seemed oblivious to the lessons to be learned from the development destruction in so many other European cities. As Nowlan testifies, public opinion at this early stage was 'confused and ill-informed' on the subject of urban planning and conservation. There existed a naïvety, or perhaps some inherent sense of trust, that all would go well with the city's redevelopment. Instead, there occurred an unbridled assault on the ageing cityscape. Apart from inadequate legislative protection and a generally passive citizenry, another possible explanation for the laxity of zoning enforcement and developmental controls is that some prominent national politicians were, during this period, heavily involved in land speculation. Though this allegation has been commonly expressed, it is virtually impossible to document with authority. Nevertheless, the sometimes astronomical increases in land values in parts of the inner city do seem to have been manipulated by factors other than simple laws of supply and demand. The suspicion lingers that property values have been artificially inflated to gain immense profits.

In 1969 a new Housing Act was adopted which seemingly provided greater protection by requiring that permission be obtained before a structure could be demolished or converted to a new use. However, this document failed to have a significant impact on the abuses of development because its regulations on physical alteration do not apply to buildings already in commercial use, its demolition restrictions can be circumvented by developers and its codes are not faithfully enforced.

THE E.S.B. EPISODE

The unhappy and inevitable confrontation between developers and preservationists sprouted with the advent of the office revolution and continues in agitated form to the present day. But it was really in 1963 that, as Desmond Guinness, head of the Irish Georgian Society, put it, the 'rot set in'. No single episode during the decade of the 'sixties more profoundly epitomizes the development/preservation struggle than the Electricity Supply Board's scheme, first announced in 1961, to demolish their Georgian offices along Fitzwilliam Street and replace them with a new office block. This declaration was greeted by preservationists and a good many other Dubliners as abhorrent and unacceptable. It immediately triggered protests that such an action would completely ruin the character of the area. The ESB proposal ignited a flurry of opposition, led most forcefully by the Irish Georgian Society. The ensuing battle became something of a public spectacle, vigorously debated among authorities and widely covered by the media; it was a classic test case.

This now-notorious case was based in large part on the strongly conflicting and, thus, to the public, often confusing, expert testimony of noted authorities representing the two sides. Sir John Summerson was promptly recruited from England and pronounced the ESB's Georgian buildings 'architectural rubbish . . . just one damned house after another', recommending their removal (examination of his report suggests that he essentially appraised these Dublin structures in terms of Britain's classical Georgian style, ignoring or missing the distinctiveness of the Irish architectural idiom). Conversely, Sir Albert Richardson argued eloquently but in vain for preservation. It is quite true that the ESB offices were housed in the poorest block in the section. Their visual quality appeared inferior largely because their vertical accent or rhythm was less pronounced than on other houses. However, the basic proportions of the individual houses were undeniably as fine as those in adjacent blocks. As a unified streetscape entity, this terrace housing along Merrion Square East, Fitzwilliam Street and Fitzwilliam Place constituted the longest unbroken line of Georgian houses in Europe. Despite its less artistic ESB component, it produced, as a whole, a brilliant vista of original Georgiana. Although the interiors had been rendered of negligible architectural value because of the extensive alterations already carried out by the ESB when they were converted to office use, the buildings were well worth saving. They could have been spared, put on the market, and, as Guinness suggested, sold to 'people who would appreciate them'.

Despite spirited opposition to the plan, the Dublin Corporation ruled in favour of the ESB. In 1963 a total of sixteen structurally sound and complete Georgian houses were destroyed to make space for a sleek new office complex, and in the process the symmetrical Georgian vista was irreparably mutilated. Interestingly, the modern office block which was implanted on the site was the winner of an architectural competition, declared designed to complement the existing streetscape. Unfortunately, this ostensible quality often escapes the eye of passers-by, many of whom clearly view the patch of new offices as a garish intruder on an otherwise dignified streetscape. Although the ESB action resulted in the desecration of the Georgian vista, the Fitzwilliam Street débâcle in many respects marked the real beginning of public awareness regarding urban preservation. It also contributed to the emergence of a Georgian preservation movement in Dublin. Subsequent preservation battles waged during the later 'sixties and 'seventies added their particular impetus to the movement and several will be discussed in a later chapter.

DEMOLITION STRATEGY AND TACTICS

The developers and their fiendish gremlins, the demolitionists
. . . go to work with ball and chain on old Dublin.[4]

For developers the ESB episode set a convenient precedent for the demolition of Georgian housing. Even during the early days of the office boom they realized that the interior design and arrangement of rooms in many old Georgian houses were an obstacle to their plans for conversion to office space. Thus, their demolition became economically preferable to costly conversion and adaptation. By the early 1970s new developments in the office building industry further threatened the Georgian architecture with what commercial interests term the 'end of its economic life'. First, office enterprises were expanding in size, owing chiefly to larger staffs and bulky pieces of specialized office equipment. Secondly, the need for more efficient space utilization, lower maintenance costs and better energy efficiency favoured modern structures. Although Georgian houses could be readily converted to moderate-sized prestige offices, they were not conducive to physical transformation to huge, streamlined offices. Coincidently, the vastly increased demand and competition for land area for office use created an economic situation in which the value of cleared sites within the central urban area, particularly in Georgian districts, was often greater than that of the building which originally existed on the site. These harsh economics doomed many fine Georgian houses.

The unscrupulous developer relies on a veritable arsenal of weapons and tactics to achieve his goals. The most direct and efficient technique for clearing space for redevelopment is outright demolition of a property. When it comes to Georgian houses this requires some scheming. As previously stated, it is now necessary to obtain official planning permission to destroy or substantially change a building. And under the regulations of the 1976 Dublin Development Plan (later to be analysed) most Georgian houses are 'listed' for preservation. But laws and regulations seldom deter greedy developers if there is good profit to be made. They exhibit remarkable ingenuity and cunning in their exploits to circumvent the law. For example, if denied approval to demolish they can resort to deliberate neglect or vandalism of their own property, thereby hastening the process of decay. Such acts of destruction may be accomplished in subtle or bold form. Sometimes they 'inadvertently' manage to leave doors, windows and other apertures open, thus inviting

One of the many Georgian brass door-knocker designs which embellish entrances

Around the major Georgian Squares one can still find original ironwork artistry in the railings, gates, balconies and lampposts

(opposite and above) The famous 'Georgian Doors of Dublin' which give the city
a special historic and artistic character

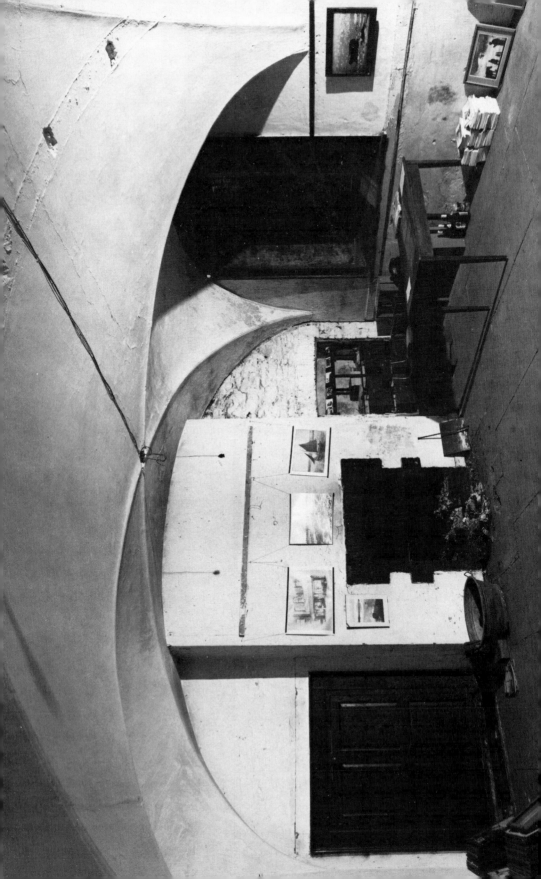

the physical elements and parasitic intruders to ravage the structure at will. If they are impatient they may surreptitiously remove roofing, structural supports and other materials, thereby guaranteeing rapid deterioration of the premises. Once the building is sufficiently dilapidated and dangerous it may be declared a public hazard and it then becomes the responsibility of the property owner or the Dublin Corporation to demolish it as an act of public safety. Initially, such dastardly tactics were only suspected but in recent years they have been well documented and proven in court cases.

Sometimes the process of 'planned dereliction' is less detectable. Many Georgian buildings which fall into the hands of ambitious developers are in admittedly poor condition, often the result of previous absentee ownership and intensive use (such as multi-family flats) which generally leads to a lack of repair and maintenance. Yet, rather than invest in their rehabilitation, developers often contribute to their demise by totally ignoring their upkeep for prolonged periods. This, in effect, condemns the property to a form of structural euthanasia. Of course, during this moribund period property values are conveniently escalating. But if the developer is out for fast profit his best strategy is that of swift kill. As earlier experience in London has amply demonstrated, developers can facilitate their operations if they simply decide to demolish first and answer questions afterwards. If Dubliners failed to learn anything from the British urban experience, at least the developers paid careful heed. Demolition by bulldozing or other large mechanized machines is the most expedient technique, since a building can be completely razed in a matter of hours or a few days at most—insufficient time for effective preservationist protest to be mounted. It also reduces the possibility of legal technicalities being discovered in the course of demolition that might delay the destructive process. When swift demolition is not feasible, developers may employ a shrewd clandestine approach. They can disassemble the building from within, working secretly behind closed doors and shutters, or during weekends, so as to avoid detection until it is too late for opposition. When the building is sufficiently weakened it can be dealt one sudden death blow by the bulldozer. These techniques have been effectively used by developers time and again along Molesworth, Harcourt, Leeson and other streets to bring down Georgian

(*opposite*) Cavernous Georgian basements have always been valued for their expansive utility space. This particular example is at Henrietta Street (*courtesy of the Irish Architectural Archive*)

houses before the public and preservationist groups have time to react. Dubliners are sometimes astonished on Monday mornings to witness the dramatic streetscape change which has occurred during the previous forty-eight hours.

DEMISE OF THE 'LIVING CITY'

Apart from the destruction of historic buildings, preservationists and many others have become increasingly concerned about urban redevelopment divesting Dublin of its residential population. In a real sense, the 'living city' is dying. Old inner-urban communities with rich traditions have been rooted out by planners and developers. The central city has gradually been transformed into a vast 'Mausoleum to Mammon' as streets are swept clean of occupants and their houses demolished or converted to office use. After houses are cleared in one fell swoop of the bulldozer, long-time neighbourhood residents are callously transplanted to socially sterile housing estates. Some citizens' groups have valiantly fought this system of coercive depopulation, but to little avail. In the quest for functionalism and modernization, human needs have simply been ignored. Deirdre Kelly, preservationist, activist and head of the Dublin Living City Group, laments that the city is fast becoming 'dreary, dead Dublin'. The Group conducts periodic studies to document the central city's dwindling population and there is irrefutable evidence to support her claim. Most disturbing is the continual decline in the number of children in the heart of Dublin. According to the most recent survey, there are only thirty-six children left in the entire Georgian complex bounded by Baggot Street, St Stephen's Green, Adelaide Road and Fitzwilliam Street—an area that twenty years ago was 'teeming with life'. The absence of children along the venerable Georgian streets elicits melancholy among many Dubliners who can, with great relish, fondly recall their own youth along the well-worn pavements. It seems an urban tragedy of the highest order. As a proud Dubliner, born and reared, Father Paul Freeney surely expressed the sentiments of many citizens when he verbally lashed out with eloquence and passion against the wilful philistinism of developers:

Development! Ye Gods! The word is supposed to mean growth, improvement. Is it an improvement to devastate our city centre and fill it with glass and concrete monstrosities? Is it an improvement to root out a community which has grown over hundreds of years and substitute the anonymous and characterless blocks that masquerade as modern architecture? Every single office block in Dublin is designed with one object in view—to make every square inch pay. Dublin is not involved. The people of Dublin are not involved. They can go to hell. The maximum return on financial investment, that is the sole criterion. . . .

So I'm angry at the devastation of my native city. I'm angry at the featureless monstrosities that are arising from the well-loved streets, and I'm angry for the city-dwellers who are forced to live in anonymous suburban dormitories. Dublin is no longer a living city. It is the prey of speculators and so-called developers and no one will stop them, because those with a vested interest in this destruction have too much financial power and, sadly, too much political power as often as not. I could weep.[5]

Notes

1. O'Hanlon, Thomas J. *The Irish* (Harper and Row, 1975), p30.
2. Craig, Maurice. 'Attitudes in Context', *Architectural Conservation: An Irish Viewpoint* (Dublin: Architectural Association of Ireland, 1974), p14
3. McGovern, Sean. '18th Century and the Present', *Irish Times*, 22 October 1976, p10
4. 'When All is Ruin Once Again', *Irish Times*, 30 January 1975
5. Freeney, Father Paul. 'Development How Are Ye!', *Dublin—A Living City?* (Dublin Living City Group), p2

5
Foundations of a
Preservation Movement

Dublin has something of a 'split personality which is well revealed when some Georgian Square is threatened with demolition, and the Dubliner's instinct to defend a thing of beauty is tempered by a feeling that he should not grieve at the disappearance of reminders of England's past ascendancy.'[1]

Modern Dublin sometimes seems blind to its [architectural] heritage.[2]

In order to want to preserve something, people need to be convinced of its value.[3]

Historic buildings cannot be treated as merely mute relics because they speak eloquently and truthfully of an earlier epoch. They obtrude as highly visible and tangible symbols of past times and past conditions. For good or ill, the Anglo-Irish legacy is incarnate in Georgian Dublin. It is neither practical nor realistic to discuss preservation attitudes without keeping this verity constantly in mind—for emotional factors always play a major part in restoration and preservation. Decades of preservation experience in western countries has proved that cultural prejudices commonly determine what is to be preserved, what is deliberately destroyed and what is allowed to perish. Historic buildings which evoke a sense of pride are usually safeguarded against abuse and demolition. Those symbolizing shame or negative historical memories may be neglected or expunged from sight.

CULTURAL IDENTITY AND NATIONAL PRIDE

A nation's pride is marked by that which it preserves.[4]

Efforts in the United States and Europe to restore and preserve historic architecture have been strongly motivated by national pride. However, in

Ireland the traditional lack of pride in the Georgian heritage has posed a major obstacle to the emergence of a forceful preservation movement. This absence of 'felt pride' in the Georgian city may be explained in several ways. Firstly, there has been a dismal lack of proper education in acquainting the Irish with their physical heritage in general. An Foras Forbartha (The National Planning Institute) notes in its 1969 report, *The Protection of the National Heritage*, that the wealth of Ireland's historic inheritance, though commonly recognized and appreciated by outsiders, is 'curiously little-known to the Irish people'. An ill-informed populace can hardly be expected to appreciate, cherish and preserve national treasures if it has not been made cognizant of their value. Therefore, many Dubliners have forsaken the Georgian terraces out of an understandable lack of learned appreciation for their merits, with no thought of malice toward origins; the eighteenth-century squares and terraces are often simply 'taken for granted' or else completely 'forgotten about'. Many citizens also incorrectly believe that there is 'so much' Georgian architecture remaining that there is no urgency to preserve it. This sadly mistaken notion has been most deleterious to the cause of preservation.

Secondly, it has been hypothesized that the Irish possess an inherent 'anti-urban bias' that generates prejudice against cities and impedes the creation of a strong civic spirit needed to support the cause of preservation. In an article in *Architectural Conservation: An Irish Viewpoint*, Niall Montgomery suggests that to the average Irishman, with a rural background, perhaps all large town and cities are perceived as symbols of English hegemony. Whether or not most modern Irish actually hold such associations seems highly questionable. However, their attitudes toward the capital do often seem tainted by a certain prejudice. As previously explained, the Georgian city long stood for an alien tradition, for money and privilege, for an urban cosmopolitan culture—not the culture of the *plain people*. Donald Connery in his book, *The Irish*, contends that since Georgian Dublin is still commonly viewed as the work of the old aristocratic Anglo-Irish society, many Irish do not accept the capital as 'really their city'. He is probably quite correct.

In most countries the factor of cultural memory is one of the most potent and persuasive tools used by preservationists to mobilize support for saving historic buildings. This concept is based on the theory that any nation (or healthy society) must probe and accept its historical origins before it can forge a true national identity. Within this context, a good part of Ireland's ambivalence toward the Georgian city can probably be attributed to the nation's own lack of a definitive cultural identity or national character. It has been postulated that modern Ireland is 'virtually bereft of a national cultural identity'.[5] That the Irish have never properly come to terms with their Anglo-Irish component has created a clouded cultural memory, making it difficult to foster pride in the architecture of the period. When, as has so long been the case in Ireland, inherited architecture evokes unpleasant cultural memories and reinforces biases against its historical origins, it functions negatively and hinders, rather than supports, preservation efforts.

Exuberant Irish nationalism during the decades following Independence served to discredit contributions of the Anglo-Irish, and this inevitably cast a shadow over their most conspicuous legacy, the Georgian streetscapes. John Harvey claims that in the 1920s and '30s Ireland was so 'disgusted with the Georgian remains of the Ascendancy that it was determined to sweep them away to build a peasant-Gaelic capital in their place; to root out forever . . . every memory of a culture which it has taken three-quarters of a millennium to build'. Harsh words, but based in much truth. Of course this was never done, but the sentiment has long been latent in the Irish psyche. In the early 1960s an Irish Minister of State was recorded as having remarked to a visitor, regarding the demolition of some Georgian buildings: 'I was glad to see them go—they stand for everything I hate.' A decade later, one nationalistic zealot was inspired to proclaim in a letter to the editor of the *Irish Times* that the 'Georgian buildings are an offence to all true-blue Irishmen, they are a hangover from a repressive past . . . and they must go'. Such impassioned evocations doubtless reflected the thinking of a good many Irish. As J. C. Beckett reasons, the eighteenth century is still often viewed as a 'kind of hiatus in the life of the nation, a valley of humiliation'. Consequently, many Irish, perhaps most, have traditionally not believed that the national culture has anything to do with the preservation of the Georgian districts.

Fortunately, old notions and comfortable biases are subject to change over time and in the light of new circumstances. Social scientists have observed that during the past two decades Ireland has experienced an 'identity crisis' in which the country has struggled to identify and define its national character and contemporary personality. An important part of this identity quest has been the process of trying to sort out historical enigmas, both intellectually and emotionally. This has demanded new and objective soul-searching and an apparent willingness to explore and accept variant strains of Irish nationality. As a consequence, enlightened public attitudes have formed as the result of what sociologists term 'cultural drifts'—or changes in values, ideologies and social perceptions. The decade of the 'sixties, in particular, witnessed a general socio-psychological transformation in Irish attitudes and outlook as the nation snapped out of its mental torpor. There occurred a new vitality and determination to mould a modern, progressive Ireland. Psychological and emotional links with the past were not severed, but they were re-examined and viewed with greater objectivity. It was generally a period of national maturation and critical self-examination. Crisply put, the Irish gradually adopted an attitude of 'realism in the place of emotionalism'. Consequently, narrowly defined and exclusive Gaelic interpretations were no longer embraced without scrutiny and flexibility. Pejorative protestations against the Anglo-Irish and Georgian architecture were heard far less commonly than in the past. Gradually, the barricade mentality that hindered Irish society and government in the post-Independence years was dismantled. Vigorous new economic and social programmes increased Irish exposure to the outside world. Membership of the European Economic Community generated new political and economic relations with neighbouring countries, thereby nurturing a healthier world-view and a more self-confident national image. In looking more optimistically toward the future, Ireland seemed to become more comfortable with its past. This cultivated a social climate conducive to new appraisals of the Georgian architecture and paved the way for preservation efforts.

PRESERVATION BATTLES AND PUBLIC ENLIGHTENMENT

The more that is lost in terms of the architecture, the more conscious the citizens of Dublin are becoming of their heritage.[6]

It is a sad fact of life that we must often face the loss of something dear before we learn to appreciate its real value. This truism is increasingly relevant to Dubliners and their inherited eighteenth-century houses. When the developer boldly intruded upon the scene, he confronted an essentially inert public opinion. The prevailing attitude was to permit the developers free rein, that 'perhaps it will turn out all right'. There was no lucid vision in planning circles or among the public of what form Dublin's future should assume. Only in the mid-'sixties, after the office revolution had already gained a destructive grip on the city, did architectural preservation become perceived as an important issue.

Dubliners were finally alerted, in rather dramatic fashion, to the perils of unbridled urban redevelopment by the preservation battles fought during the 'sixties and 'seventies. Several of these now-famous encounters have become major chapters in preservationist annals. Their importance is manifold. They focused sharp attention and controversy on Georgian architecure for prolonged periods. Since these battles were basically philosophical and ideological clashes between developers and preservationists, they were waged amid furious challenges, debate and media coverage. They often jolted the conscience of Dubliners. Invariably, they were accompanied by a spate of intelligent and enlightening newspaper articles by architects, historians, urban planners and other professionals. These literate treatments by noted authorities provided a valuable perspective on the Georgian system. Rather than being stigmatized as an offensive British relic, Georgian architecture was freshly appraised in terms of its distinctive artistic merits. In 1962, to coincide with the debate over the ESB buildings, the *Irish Independent* ran a lengthy and highly illuminating series of articles on the eighteenth-century architecture by architect J. Neil Downes. The Georgian idiom and Irish craftsmanship were deciphered in great detail for public consumption. Since in Ireland there has always been a certain lack of understanding and appreciation for ordinary buildings, this process of debate and analysis effectively helped to educate the Dublin citizenry. Many Dubliners became aware for the first time of the Georgian city's intrinsic artistic merits and irretrievable character.

The historical/aesthetic duality inherent in the Georgian legacy had never been adequately confronted before. Though it may initially have caused a collision in values, Dubliners were gradually persuaded to view the Georgian terraces less in terms of historical symbolism and more as an existing work of art. They were also cogently reminded by historians that Georgian Dublin is not only the finest architectural heritage the country possesses but the *only one* (Ireland's monastic Romanesque is so fragmentary and slight in quantity that it can hardly qualify as an indigenous architectural 'heritage'—it really best belongs to the realm of archaeology). In *Dublin—A City in Crisis*, published by the Royal Institute of the Architects of Ireland, it is candidly pointed out that while it may be resented that Dublin's glory as a city indisputably dates from a colonial epoch, it must be recognized and accepted by modern Irish that

(*opposite*) Exquisite plasterwork adorns most Georgian interiors: a pedimented doorway in Henrietta Street (*courtesy of the Irish Architectural Archive*)

'what went before [architecturally] has vanished, what followed was mediocre'.

Owing to these revelations, many Dubliners began developing new perspectives on the historic districts. By the late 1960s there had occurred an appreciable growth of public interest in historic buildings. In the 'seventies Dubliners developed an even greater awareness of their built environment. Even Irish officialdom slowly began shedding its attitude of benign neglect toward the historic surroundings. It became acceptable for public figures to go on record as favouring preservation. Public pronouncements and government policy statements increasingly reflected a new interest in the problems of preserving the Georgian areas. This belated awareness of historic architecture led to the formation of the Irish Victorian Society in the late 1970s and cultivated fertile ground for the recent 'Save Wood Quay' movement.

An unmistakable indicator of changing attitudes toward Georgian architecture has been the acceptance of, and increasing demand for, the 'neo-Georgian' housing estates in Dublin's suburbs. As Dubliners have finally come to value the Georgian idiom for its grace, elegance and generally 'civilized' appearance, it has become chic and fashionable in contemporary Dublin to own a so-called 'Georgian' home. Ironically, the neo-Georgian craze has made Georgiana almost synonymous with 'cultured' Irish society—with apparently no thought attached to historical associations.

NOTABLE PRESERVATION BATTLES

During the 'sixties and 'seventies several notable preservation battles were waged in the Georgian quarters along Fitzwilliam, Hume, Pembroke and Molesworth streets. These struggles evolved into lively media events, drawing attention to threatened buildings and generating public interest in Dublin's Georgian districts. They ordinarily began as planning controversies but often developed into bitter battles between opposing forces—developers and planners on one side and preservationists and their supporters on the other. Derogatory name-calling and allegations were flung about with wild abandon as each group sought to impugn the character of the 'enemy'. Preservationists usually depicted

(*opposite*) The intricate detail of the plasterwork art, also in Henrietta Street (*courtesy of the Irish Architectural Archive*)

developers as greedy vandals eager to destroy the environment for a 'few (usually dirty) pounds'; developers dismissed preservationists as 'tiresome busybodies' impeding the course of urban progress for a whim or out of vanity. However, the conflict eventually moved from platitudinous speeches to public demonstrations—even physical confrontation.

The ESB fiasco along Fitzwilliam Street signalled the real beginning of the developer/preservationist antagonism and served as a catalyst in organizing preservation efforts in the city. At the outset, preservation battles were little more than impassioned ideological clashes. However, over time they grew into major confrontations. Preservationists became engaged in zealous missions to save buildings from destruction. Street demonstrations and forcible occupation of imperilled structures became their most effective tactics. Preservation contingents were usually comprised of local residents, members of the Irish Georgian Society and other sympathetic citizens. Even in the early years, student participation played a prominent role in the struggles. University students, especially those in architectural colleges, resorted to activist strategies. It is important to note that in the early 1960s, when the ESB issue exploded into public view, architectural students actually 'took the side of the vandals' and picketed the meeting organized to save the structures. They marched about with banners proclaiming 'Dublin must not be a museum'. In striking contrast to those early days, students have now dramatically shifted their philosophy, surging to the forefront of the fight to save the city's Georgian heritage. Today most students share a healthy idealism which motivates them to protect rather than destroy the historic heritage. Their bold efforts in risking both legal and physical penalties by occupying endangered buildings along Hume, Pembroke and Molesworth streets have been credited with literally saving a number of fine eighteenth-century buildings.

In 1969 the media-dubbed 'battle of Hume Street' began and developed as the prototype for subsequent skirmishes. The confrontation was triggered by a plan to erect two large modern office buildings at the corners of Hume Street on the east side of St Stephen's Green. This meant the destruction of several good, Classical eighteenth-century buildings and the ruination of an important approach to a major Georgian enclave. The proposal immediately provoked a strong reaction from preservationists who marshalled support from a number of other opposition groups. The battle turned out to be a protracted one which indisputably helped to mobilize public opinion in favour of preservation. It also contributed to the formation of the Dublin Civic Group, one of

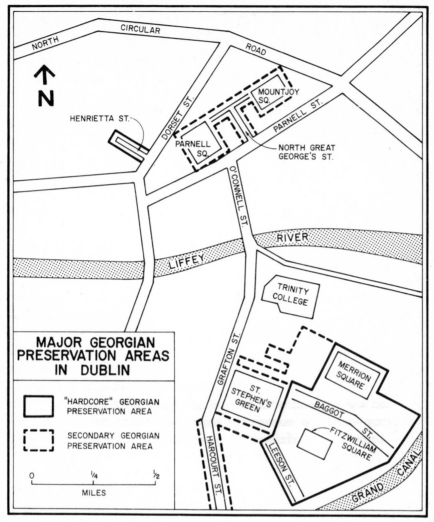

Fig. 3　Map showing the major Georgian preservation areas in Dublin

the most effective preservation groups in the city today. Hume Street importantly marked the first time that preservationists really took to the streets in open defiance; again, student activism played a vital role. The occupation of several Georgian houses by architectural students gained strong public approval, testimony to the already changing attitudes toward preservation. Their sit-in of the buildings lasted for several months, drawing continued media coverage, exerting pressure on the developers and holding the public's rapt curiosity. There were some minor physical skirmishes between preservationists and the developer's work crews as each side attempted to intimidate the other. Although the buildings were eventually demolished, preservationists claimed an important victory because the Hume Street case was resolved only after developers relented and agreed to rebuild in the Georgian style rather than erecting incompatible structures on the site. Some years after the Hume Street saga, the President of Ireland publicly credited the students' activism with saving the architectural character of this important Georgian section. In the mid-1970s a similar preservation conflict erupted along Pembroke Street where several Bord na Mona (The Turf Board) offices were threatened with destruction and replacement with modern buildings. Although these Georgian structures were included on List 1 of the government's plan for preservation, they had been approved circuitously for demolition by a special ministerial order. They were finally saved only by vigorous public reaction and another courageous act of student occupation.

A more recent, and highly inflamed, preservation battle took place in 1978 on Molesworth Street, site of some of the finest remaining eighteenth-century Georgian houses. The threatened buildings had actually been the subject of appeals for a period of ten years but were finally approved for demolition. The battle typically began with the revelation that developers planned to tear down some Georgian and Victorian properties to create space for new office development. Opposition was again led by the Irish Georgian Society and the Dublin Civic Group—as well as 'most of the thinking public'. At first, preservationists directed angry effusions against the venality of the property owners and developers. The second stage involved street protests and the eventual occupation of the premises by architectural students. A vicious struggle ensued as developers and preservationists engaged in a war of wits and tactics to outmanoeuvre the other and gain advantage. Buildings were promptly draped with students' placards demanding a halt to demolition. The students waged determined opposition against what was designated in the press as the 'desecration of Molesworth Street'. Typical of most student occupations, there was a hard core of dedicated participants and a fringe group of supporters, many of whom were eventually persuaded to relinquish the fight out of sheer boredom or legal threats. In the Molesworth Street episode the students' numerical support was eroded by strict enforcement of the Forcible Entry and Occupation Act which intimidated many participants and dissuaded them from challenging the legal system. But the determined students refused to be subdued.

Meanwhile owners and developers used a counter-strategy, claiming that the student occupation of the work site would put labourers out of work and impose an economic hardship on their families. Workers were coaxed into parading the streets, flaunting their own banners. This chaotic interaction created a frenzied public spectacle that drew great attention. Eventually the scene took on the aura of a para-military battle field. Workers on the site erected a 10ft-high hoarding tipped with strands of barbed wire, while supportive students heaved blankets and supplies over the barriers to their comrades in occupation. While in occupation, students attempted to seal openings against rain damage, busily drew up documents detailing the damage to be caused by demolition and solicited favourable media coverage. As tempers flared on both sides some students alleged physical assault by the workers, claiming that they used 'half-starved Alsatian dogs' to drive them out. They also accused the demolition crew of threatening to bring the buildings down around them. Finally, the students were cleverly duped into vacating the property by the developer's promise to negotiate with them late one evening. However, once they had abandoned the site the buildings were feverishly demolished in only a few hours of darkness before they could be re-occupied. Despite their abortive but tenacious efforts, the Molesworth Street preservationists again exposed the developer's ruthless assault on the fragile Georgian cityscape and gained important public support.

Notes

1 Wallace, Martin. *The Irish: How They Live and Work* (David & Charles, 1972), p63
2 LeHane, Brendan. *Dublin* (Time-Life International, 1978), p8
3 Sheehy, Jeanne. 'Contribution of History II', *Architectural Conservation: an Irish Viewpoint* (Architectural Association of Ireland, 1974), p35
4 Winks, Robin. 'Conservation in America: National Character as Revealed by Preservation', in Jane Fawcett (Editor) *The Future of the Past* (Thames & Hudson, 1976), p142
5 Fennell, Desmond. 'The Irish Cultural Prospect', *Social Studies*, 1 no 6 (1979), p28
6 Guinness, Desmond. *Georgian Dublin* (B. T. Batsford, 1979), p28

6
Irish Preservation Groups: Ideology and Action

Walking the streets of an historic district becomes a significant experience for thousands of people. The past way of life beckons to us with its harmony of scale, its variety of style, its closely built urban streets, its rich antiquity. People do not necessarily long to live in the past; they need rather a mixture of past and present . . . an escape from the less attractive aspects of our present cityscape.[1]

Heightened preservation consciousness in Dublin over the past two decades has spawned the formation of a number of preservation groups. This type of collective action to protect the city's historic architecture is a relatively new development. In Ireland there has been no real tradition of citizen-generated preservation, though some earlier efforts did devote attention to Georgian buildings of special importance. In 1908 a number of 'cultivated people' in Dublin, alarmed that so many of the fine eighteenth-century houses were decaying or disappearing, formed the Georgian Society. Their task was essentially limited to surveying and recording Georgian houses of particular merit rather than initiating and sponsoring actual restoration efforts. There has also been in Dublin a practice of preserving and caring for those individual Georgian houses formerly occupied by famous residents, most often literary and political figures. These historical sites are now usually marked with plaques. But these buildings have been esteemed for their associations rather than for their architectural qualities.

The founding of preservation groups has closely coincided with the blossoming of residents' and tenants' associations throughout the city. Both have basically been born of the same fermentation process. It has long been abundantly clear in Dublin that 'individual citizens have no voice in the planning process'.[2] Dubliners' discontent with the bureaucratic labyrinth can be traced back many decades. But with the onset of major urban upheaval in the early 'sixties their plight became more desperate. Too often they have been treated as petty pawns at the mercy of powerful administrators, planning authorities and urban developers. Mounting disenchantment with government insensitivity and outright blundering, combined with the deliberate abuses perpetuated by some developers, generated political consciousness and social activism among threatened citizens. For security and bargaining power they began forming into community groups and residential associations. By resorting to verbal and physical protests they gained strength in negotiating with authorities, particularly the much-maligned Dublin Corporation, often criticized for its allegedly draconian policies in urban redevelopment. Residents' associations were organized along street, neighbourhood and community levels. Although this type of resident activist participation has long been commonplace in many British and American cities, it was a novel development on the Irish scene. But by the 1970s Dublin's residents' associations had indisputably become a 'powerful and effective force in the city's life'.[3]

As in neighbouring Britain, preservation efforts in Dublin began in modest fashion with simple protests in the form of letters to the local and national press, followed by the formation of volunteer groups. Preservation groups formed along the same basic lines as residents' associations, except that members lived in areas of historic architectural importance. Since preservation is an endeavour supported largely by amateurs, it has logically been at the street and neighbourhood levels that most of Dublin's preservation battles have been waged and won. The greatest strength of the preservation crusade rests with the residents of the Georgian streets who are dedicated to saving their own 'homeland'. Personal involvement and co-operation are indispensable. Georgian-based preservationists are confronted with an especially challenging task because developers are naturally attracted to their exploitable districts. Therefore, they have to be more wary, watchful and aggressively defensive against any territorial incursions. Their fight to protect the Georgian terraces has been what Desmond Guinness calls a persistent 'struggle against ignorance and greed'. Developers and government agencies always hold the advantage since they take the initiative, possess financial resources and wield extensive statutory powers. Conversely, preservationists must assume a defensive posture—raising questions and objections, demonstrating against policies, publicly protesting about destructive actions and appealing for public and media support. The plaintive pleas of individuals carry little weight in such situations;

collective action is demanded. Thus, it is a standard verity in preservation circles that 'strong, continuous, well-organized local action' is always the key to successful preservation efforts—and Dublin is no exception.

ANATOMY OF THE PRESERVATION MOVEMENT

It is difficult to determine at what stage the concerted efforts of various preservation groups constitute a bona fide preservation 'movement'. In sociological terms, a social movement is simply a purposeful and collective attempt of a number of people to change or remedy a situation they perceive as unjust or that violates their rights as citizens. Dublin's preservation efforts sprouted from precisely this sort of embryonic process. As Maurice Craig affirms, there gradually emerged in Dublin a small but articulate and vocal group of individuals whose 'critical sense and experience of enjoyment' told them that the Georgian buildings represented a work of considerable art and who resented 'being robbed of a work of art just because it belongs to someone else'. It has been around this core of conscientious Dubliners that a preservation movement has slowly evolved. Social movements are not subject to simple quantification; some number a modest few, others embrace the masses. They are normally judged not by their sheer numbers but by the impact of their ideology and actions on the host society. Typical of the genre, Dublin's emergent preservation movement is numerically modest but its influence is definitely being felt.

Dublin preservationists, though often operating in different spheres, share a common consciousness and philosophy that the continuing abuse and loss of Dublin's eighteenth-century architecture is a social injustice of the highest order—that the rights of both present and future generations are being violated since they are being deprived of an historic and artistic inheritance. This sentiment is rooted firmly in the conviction that the Georgian buildings are a *common* inheritance to be cherished and safeguarded as a collective societal custody. The concept of 'individual' or 'final' ownership is regarded as myopic and invalid, even morally wrong, for Georgian Dublin was bequeathed to all Irishmen and thus the responsibility for its welfare rests with greater society, not special interest groups or temporary residents. This ideology, a basic tenet of most European preservation movements, stresses collective rather than individual rights. Irish preservationists preach the philosophy of stewardship in the hope that gradually the Georgian heritage will come to be viewed as a national treasure and trust instead of merely personal possessions of individuals and companies with the good fortune to occupy them for a brief period of their history.

Preservationists are united by both philosophical and pragmatic ideals. Yet it would be an error to mould all Dublin preservationists into one neat stereotyped image. Dubliners initially tended to perceive them as middle-class 'do-gooders' or wealthy antiquarians embarked on a mission to revive moribund historic relics for their own self-gratification. This popular myth, though considerably weakened, unfortunately still persists. In truth, Irish preservationists represent a healthy socio-economic cross-section of society, embracing individuals of vastly differing ages, income levels and social positions. Preservationists may be struggling university students, businessmen, housewives, professionals or wealthy, prominent citizens. If there is a common trait that tends to provide cohesion, it is probably that most are well educated. Their sensitivity to the historic architecture seems to have been gained primarily through the process of education, either formal or informal. Only in this respect can they be regarded as an élite group.

Preservationists faithfully endorse the dictum that 'architectural decay and human decay go hand in hand—preservation renews the human spirit'. Thus, preservation is not based solely on kindly sentiment or even aesthetics but also on the practical principles of simple urban 'good housekeeping'. Structurally sound historic buildings, though seemingly obsolete, can be rehabilitated and recycled, thereby contributing anew to urban ecology. The cumulative preservation of these individual buildings leads to overall urban conservation. Preservationists also remind authorities that the built environment contributes in a meaningful way to public well-being. A society can hardly be emotionally and psychologically healthy if it is surrounded by architectural rot. Even isolated pockets of stagnation and rubble tend to be socially debilitating. Deterioration of the physical environment not only has a depressive effect on the citizenry but conveys a negative impression to outsiders. One can only imagine the initial impressions of tourists and other visitors to Dublin when they arrive from the airport via the Mountjoy Square route in the north city. Many must be astonished at the sadly dilapidated state of once-elegant Georgian houses crumbling along the south side of the square. It is surely not the image that Dubliners and government would like to project of their fair city.

Another legitimate argument for preservation, especially relevant in Dublin, is that of urban environmental scale and ambience. City folk (even those who commute from the suburbs) conduct much of their daily

83

lives in a kind of restricted geographical space defined by certain street widths, building heights, intervals between structures and open spaces. They become psychologically acclimatised to a particular spatial setting. Over time, if this built environment changes too drastically, it can render a disorienting effect on citizens; they can come to feel alienated from their long-familiar 'natural' urban milieu. Commonly, sweeping changes in the traditional architectural style and scale can result in a vastly altered mood of city life that may not fit the social/psychological needs of the society. The preservation of old, authentic buildings in modernized and futurized cities tends to reinforce social stability, offering people a sort of 'psychic self-defence against mass-produced automobiles and skyscrapers'.[4] The familiar face of aged buildings is often more important than many citizens realize—until they are summarily stripped from sight and the void is numbing.

Dublin is particularly susceptible to unsettling architectural transfiguration because one of its most salient characteristics has always been the compatible scale of buildings to people. The city's mannerly three- and four-storey streetscapes do not intimidate the pedestrian population. There is a certain harmony in which man seems to blend naturally and comfortably with the venerable bricked setting. As Sean O'Faolain poignantly describes it:

> The lovely, small brickwork [of the Georgian houses] has been chromatized and mellowed by centuries of wind and weather into a shifting array that glows now like a ruby port, now like a saffron sherry, now like a primrose muscatel . . . the houses seem to shimmer as if they were made not of bricks but leaves . . . in this mood of nature, houses, people, and streets join together in movement.[5]

This inherent compatibility in Dublin's Georgian world is often recognized and envied by visitors, many of whom are accustomed to the impersonal existence engendered by ultra-modern skyscraper cities. Even many Dubliners are instinctively habituated to seeking the quietude and dignity of the Georgian streets and squares as an escape from the dominating forces which infest the city's more developed, 'progressive' thoroughfares. Of course, the sense of solitude would be immeasurably enhanced if the chaotic traffic congestion could be alleviated. The intrusion of high-rise, modernistic buildings in parts of central Dublin upsets the man/building harmony to which Dubliners have grown so accustomed; this disruptive development is particularly striking when it occurs in a traditional Georgian setting.

GROUP OBJECTIVES AND STRATEGIES

In Dublin the most successful preservation actions have been conducted along those streets where there is still a significant residential population to defend the architectural integrity of the neighbourhood. Many of the Georgian streets have been so socially and physically fragmented that there is only a skeletal residential populace left to guard what remains. But a good number of the more important Georgian areas are protected by vigorous resident preservationists who openly agitate, confront developers and government agencies, and resort to every legal tactic at their disposal to protect their eighteenth-century environment. Some of the more viable, and visible, residents' associations actively engaged in preserving their Georgian environment are to be found along the following streets: North Great George's Street, Fitzwilliam Square, Harcourt Street, Mount Pleasant Square, Upper Leeson Street, Lower Leeson Street and Eccles Street.

These groups function in basically two ways. First, they seek to halt the destruction of surviving historic architecture and prevent any intrusive development which might disfigure the existing streetscape or prove incompatible with the Georgian setting. Secondly, they commonly work to physically restore exteriors and interiors in order to preserve the original eighteenth-century craftsmanship. The most successful preservation associations are those that have adopted sophisticated pressure-group tactics and developed a good organizational structure. Meek and disorganized residents' groups seldom wield much clout in dealing with experienced authorities. The ability of preservationists to relate and communicate effectively on a broad public scale is vital to the movement. Having witnessed the development debauchery of the past two decades, Dublin preservationists have learned well that only public opinion can prevent the destruction of historic buildings. Therefore they have adopted strategies for openly pressuring authorities and gaining favourable press coverage. They now routinely lobby political officials and planning agencies, offering constructive criticism and firm opposition to threatening schemes. Residents coping collectively with their local preservation problems can effectively combat proposed plans that imperil their home environment. An incident of a few years past illustrates their success. Mount Pleasant Square, built at the end of the Georgian period (c1830) is one of the few predominantly residential Georgian communities remaining in Dublin. The area consists of graceful two-storey, well-preserved Georgian terrace houses surrounding an attractive park. In the mid-'seventies developers eyed the park for development into a large car park. Although the houses fringing the park were included on the government's List 1 for preservation, meaning that the entire environment should be protected, the Dublin Corporation surprisingly ruled in favour of the proposed plan. Construction of a car park in the very midst of the Georgian neighbourhood would not only have clashed rudely with the existing architectural idiom but would have generated vehicular activity detrimental to the tranquil residential mood of the square. Appalled at the prospects, the Mount Pleasant Square Residents' Association took their case directly to the Minister of the Environment who was finally persuaded to rule against the Corporation's decision. Only such direct action and strong personal involvement could have won the day and thwarted such offensive development. It was a sure sign of the changing times.

A new strategy (conducted with great success by preservationists in other countries for years) is to attack boldly in the media the 'faceless men behind the desecration' of historic Dublin. Owners of historic properties to be destroyed and the heads of development companies eager to carry out the demolition often seek anonymity to avoid criticism for their roles in the destructive process. Now, careful research by preservationists exposes these individuals and often reveals the huge profits they stand to gain from tearing down a Georgian structure and rebuilding on the site. This highly personalized approach has proven effective in Dublin. Adverse publicity generated by preservation groups can tarnish the valuable image of respectibility so coveted by businessmen and their companies. Some developers now admit to being 'scared by protests and preservationists'. Others have become more aware of the preservation issue without such intimidating tactics. As a result, there are now positive signs of a more enlightened approach on the part of some development companies. By the mid-'seventies there was an encouraging trend among developers to negotiate with, rather than confront, preservationists. This generated some healthy dialogue between the two sides and alleviated tensions. Some developers even began seeking consultation with preservation groups prior to requesting planning permission for their schemes. Conservation-mindedness of this kind resulted in the preservation of such fine Georgian houses as Number 6 Leinster Street and the former St Vincent's Hospital complex on St Stephen's Green. Unfortunately, not all Dublin developers are so enlightened.

THE SAGA OF NORTH GREAT GEORGE'S STREET

> If you can anthropomorphize a street, then North Great
> George's Street is the Marlene Dietrich of Dublin City. No
> matter how many owners have passed through, no matter what
> a wreck she became, those bones are still lovely and, yes, she is
> going to make another comeback.[6]

To comprehend better the preservation movement, it is helpful to focus on a specific struggle. The most illustrative current case-study is found along North Great George's Street where there is a thriving community of Georgian restorationists. Here there is also an epic battle shaping up between preservationists and city planners. The battle is of particular importance because it involves the future of not only one of Dublin's nobler Georgian streetscapes but one of the finest streets of its kind in all Europe. North Great George's Street dates from the 1770s and is an essential surviving element in the north city's Gardiner Estate. Since the houses were built during the last quarter of the eighteenth century, they represent some of the finest work in Irish architecture. Some of the greatest artists and craftsmen of Irish decorative plaster and stucco work, such as Charles Thorp, Michael Stapleton and Francis Ryan, applied their talents to these tall, stately brick houses.

The street's architectural heritage is matched by its lively social legacy. It has experienced a colourful and checkered history. In the words of Maurice Craig, 'when the street was young and pink-bricked in the 1790s, her fanlights and steps gleamed and the brightest stars of the pre-Union golden firmament shone in her intelligent windows'. Some of Dublin's most distinguished citizens have resided within these walls: Sir Samuel Ferguson, noted author of *The Lark in the Clear Air*, whose home was commonly visited by famous literary colleagues of the period; Isaac Butt, leader of the Irish Party prior to Parnell; Sir John Pentland Mahaffy, a former provost of Trinity College; and Sir Arthur Clarke, the distinguished physician. One building housed the renowned Daughters of Erin, a revolutionary group founded by Maude Gonne McBride. Another notable Dublin figure, Arthur Guinness, was for a time employed as a butler in house number forty-three, once owned by the Archbishop of Cashel. Local legend has it that Guinness's first pint of the famous brew was made in the cellar of the house. Perhaps most relevant to the Irish today are the many literary connections with novelist James Joyce. The street's historical pageantry has imbued it with a special mood that one can still sense. To anyone discriminating enough to properly interpret the antiquated, though partially enfeebled, streetscape there is to be found an authentic glimpse into Dublin's lively past.

Following the Act of Union, a great proportion of the houses were occupied by the legal profession throughout most of the nineteenth century. Around the turn of the century the houses began to fall victim to poverty and tenementation. They ceased to be stately family residences and were transformed into grubby shelters for the huddling masses. Interiors were altered drastically as rooms were divided, partitions installed and fixtures stripped for the sake of space and utility. The constant changing of ownership and occupation contributed to neglect and decay. That so many of the houses have survived to the present time is testimony to their unusually strong construction. During the first half of the twentieth century the street seemed often on the brink of extinction as numerous surrounding Georgian rows met their demise at the hands of demolitionists. But along North Great George's Street there were elderly residents and assorted other stalwarts who tenaciously clung to their enclaved living quarters, despite often depressing and dilapidated conditions. For many it was the only home they knew and they were frightened at the prospect of being expelled and transplanted elsewhere. This solid nucleus of residents deterred demolition and managed to save the street for restorationists who later filtered into the neighbourhood with fresh ideas and abundant energies. Also, it proved beneficial that the street stood in the midst of a badly blighted zone which held little appeal for developers. Hence, the street survived into mid-century 'almost alone and by chance' amid the menacing surrounding dereliction.

In the 1960s urban redevelopment struck its first cruel blow at the historic street. The Dublin Corporation evacuated and demolished four houses along the lower west side. The razed site was converted into a car park. This casual destruction of Georgian houses alerted residents and preservationists to the potential perils of modern planning. Other houses along the bottom of the street were also decrepit and conspicuously vulnerable to a similar fate. Then, in the mid-'sixties, a small miracle took place. A few Dubliners, discriminating and eccentric enough to recognize the beleaguered houses for their historic importance and aesthetic charms, began quietly moving in along the street. Initially they engaged in practical rescue operations to save their own moribund dwellings. There was little organization and co-operation among individual owners and no comprehensive view toward a unified preservation plan for the street.

During the 'seventies, residents of the street became increasingly concerned about the welfare of their neighbourhood as a number of deteriorating houses fell ominously into the hands of the Dublin Corporation and were officially condemned. Coincidently, city planners were beginning to consider the merits of attempting to regenerate residential living in the city centre. Residents of North Great George's Street realized that if 'life moves back into the central city' their strategically situated area could be targeted by planners and developers for a high-density residential building complex. They feared that their street could meet the same tragic fate as its symmetrically balanced sister, Dominick Street, to the west which in the early 1950s was demolished almost in its entirety to make space for a modern housing block. Growing apprehension encouraged communication and co-operation among residents. Shared ideals and objectives gradually created a sense of solidarity and purpose. Meetings were arranged, ideas exchanged and proposals considered. Leaders emerged to represent the community in its struggle. This evolutionary process led to the formation of the North Great George's Street Preservation Society in 1979. The basic premise for creating the society was that a comprehensive scheme for the entire street is more judicious than a well-intentioned but piecemeal approach by individual preservationists working separately.

The Society, which has now grown to about twenty members, is not a typical Dublin residents' group. Its largely middle-class composition distinguishes it from most inner-city populations attempting to protect their neighbourhood from intrusive forces. (Indeed, that so many residents' associations are comprised chiefly of lower-income, poorly educated citizens explains in part how they have been so easily manipulated by authorities and developers.) Since members of the Society possess ample financial resources, education, keen social and political consciousness and professional skills, they are armed with considerable power in challenging authorities and assuming the daunting task of renovating two-hundred-year-old houses. There is a healthy social and occupational mix, including several businessmen, five architects, two accountants, a university professor, a china restorer and a Montessori school teacher. Owing to this 'colonization' by restorationists, there is now a visible social and architectural renaissance under way. Sixteen of the street's forty-three surviving houses are either restored or undergoing restoration. The creeping senility which was claiming the street in the 'sixties has been arrested and the depressive gloom of the neighbourhood exorcised. As the houses have been renovated and returned to residential use, the street has blossomed with life and activity. Patrick 'Lucky' Duffy, an 'old-timer' who has spent more than fifty of his seventy-two years along the street, may refer to the newcomers as 'blow-ins' but he praises their ambition and credits them with literally saving the street for future generations. Despite some initial misgivings, Duffy and other long-time residents now understand that the restorationists are not an élitist group 'hankering after the rebirth of the aristocratic society of the 18th century'[7] but rather hard-working, self-sacrificing Dubliners who care deeply about the old houses they have 'adopted'.

The North Great George's Street Preservation Society has evolved into the most organized and articulate group of its kind in the city. There is a keen sense of social cohesion and 'community'. Regular meetings are held on a rotating basis at members' homes to discuss strategy for protecting the streetscape. It is clearly the decaying lower portion that is most vulnerable to planners' designs. The upper portion of the street, focusing on the Jesuit-owned Belvedere House and six homes owned by the Loretto Order of Nuns, is fairly secure. Society members have learned from experience that preservation groups always wield the greatest bargaining power if, instead of merely opposing a proposed city government plan, they can present their own intelligent counter-proposal. Ideally, preservationists should take the offensive whenever possible. This demands innovation and imagination. For example, in 1979 the Society sought to bring together the Dublin Corporation and Trinity College as improbable allies in a preservation project. Trinity was asked to assist financially in restoring several Corporation-owned derelict buildings on the lower portion of the street to be used as a student hostel. Though the university declined the opportunity, the Corporation showed an unexpectedly open-minded attitude.

The Society is now confronted with a new Dublin Corporation plan that would seriously sully the architectural integrity of the street. It calls for the demolition of five more Georgian buildings at the lower end to clear space for a Corporation housing scheme. As envisaged, a four-storey terrace with a total of twenty-one living units would be built. Especially alarming to Society members is that this housing complex would be constructed with an imitation pastiche *Victorian* façade. Predictably, the Society vehemently opposes the plan on several grounds. First, the insertion of a bogus Victorian structure would adulterate the character of the still-harmonious eighteenth-century setting. Worse, it would give the street a ludicrously schizophrenic personality that would not only offend informed observers but utterly confuse neophytes. Secondly, such

(above) The assault of office development along Harcourt Street; *(below)* sixteen structurally sound eighteenth-century houses were demolished to create space for the modern Electricity Supply Board office at right, thus annihilating the Fitzwilliam Street Georgian vista *(both, courtesy of American Geographical Society)*

(above) Decay and demolition are a common sight along many Georgian streets; a structurally sound eighteenth-century structure being torn down along Harcourt Street for new office space; (below) a surviving Georgian house between two sadly deteriorating properties along the south side of Mountjoy Square

a development would result in high density occupation with no provision for a recreation area for children. This could well encourage increased vandalism in the area. Thirdly, the whole of North Great George's Street is listed in the City Development Plan as an area of noted architectural merit and scheduled for protection. By carrying out such a plan the Corporation would be violating its own recommendations and policies. Such action could be put to a court test.

To counter the Corporation's plan, the Society launched a publication entitled *The Restoration of North Great George's Street.* This well-written and professionally illustrated booklet not only rebuts the Corporation's interest in pulling down more Georgian houses but outlines the Society's architectural conceptions for the future of the street. That the Society's membership includes several architects was a distinct blessing in the preparation of the publication. In essence, the Society rejects outright the destruction of any surviving Georgian houses along the street. It considers even the dilapidated houses to be retrievable and suggests that the Corporation sell them for a modest amount to the Heritage Trust which could then find some viable means for having them rehabilitated. Furthermore, it is recommended that a new housing development visually compatible in scale and appearance with the existing vista be constructed on the present car park site. To avoid the pitfalls of cheap counterfeit reproduction, the Society believes that there should be no attempt at Georgian copying. Rather they favour new buildings with granite bases and continuous iron railings to at least match the existing eighteenth-century motif. The new structures should be set back from the general building line and fronted with a small play area and several parking spaces. There would also be some landscaped plots with trees, consistent with an early photograph of the street. An especially important feature of the Society's scheme would be a Georgian-style gate erected at the end of the block on the corner of Parnell Street. At present the street is plagued with an epidemic of 'rat-running' by frenzied motorists seeking alternative routes to the traffic-congested main streets. The Georgian gate would transform the stately streetscape into a quiet cul-de-sac befitting its historical status.

Although North Great George's Street has experienced a remarkable revival over the past fifteen years, its future is still in some jeopardy. There is no guarantee that the Corporation will heed the Society's suggestions and spare the houses at the lower end of the street. Also, many of the houses along the street remain in dire need of rescue and restoration. To encourage an influx of new restorationists, especially families, the Society makes every effort to display its successes. Restored houses, particularly the 'showpiece' homes, are put on public display at every opportunity. The Society is also vigorously promoting the idea that since the street abounds in rich literary and historical associations and is centrally located in the heart of Dublin just off O'Connell Street it has the potential to become an important tourist asset for the city. House number thirty-five, which has some interesting Joycean connections, is an integral part of the tourist plan. The house, with its splendidly proportioned exterior and beautifully ornamented interior, was originally on the Corporation's 'hit list' but was mercifully spared as the result of pressure. David Norris, head of the street's preservation society and a professor of literature at Trinity College, with an expertise in the writings of Joyce, is engaged in an effort to restore the property and convert it into a Joyce Centre. This would be most appropriate since the centenary of the distinguished novelist's birth falls in 1982. It is thought that such a tribute might provide a positive rejoinder to Joyce's acrimonious contention that the brown brick houses so vividly recalled from his boyhood in Dublin were the 'incarnation of spiritual and cultural paralysis'.

The strong sense of confidence in an enduring community is a crucial factor in the street's long-term salvation. At present, the reliance upon one another for emotional and psychological security is still rather tenuous, especially in the case of families. The departure of several prominent restorationists could cause others to become dispirited, thereby weakening morale and solidarity. If the restorationist community fell below the 'minimum threshold' (which is impossible to predict) there could occur a fatal downward spiral. However, this is not likely. In fact, there is evidence that the community, rather than losing members, will probably expand in coming years. In 1981 the street seemed on the brink of actually becoming fashionable again, as a number of well-to-do Dubliners were seriously considering the prospect of taking up residence. To bolster further residents' spirits, the Society was given a preservation grant by the European Economic Community and £2,500 from An Taisce. These generous endowments unmistakably attest to the importance of restoration and to the trust and confidence placed in the Society. The continuing saga of the rehabilitation of North Great George's Street is surely one of the happiest and most inspirational on the entire preservation scene.

INFLUENTIAL PRESERVATION ASSOCIATIONS

Apart from 'local action' type preservation groups, there are several associations which exercise considerable influence on Dublin's preservation scene. The most notable of these private bodies are the Irish Georgian Society, An Taisce (The National Trust for Ireland), Dublin Civic Group and the Dublin Living City Group. Each group is involved in some facet of urban conservation and preservation, wielding influence in various forums. Collectively, they contribute importantly by vigilantly monitoring urban developments and promulgating opinions on all aspects of urban preservation. However, they enjoy no official status in matters relating to actual control of Dublin's growth and redevelopment. Nonetheless, they have acquired recognition and respect in government planning circles largely because their membership includes noted university professors, architects, urban planners and other professionals and qualified authorities. As a result, they have been tacitly granted an unofficial, yet increasingly significant, role in many matters of preservation policy. Since they are bound to neither government nor business sector, they can forcefully represent the best interests of the citizens.

The Irish Georgian Society
Of all the preservation groups in Ireland, the Irish Georgian Society clearly holds the premier position. Its respected reputation stems from admirable achievements in the general field of architectural restoration. However, its fame may also be traced to the tireless activities of its founder and head, Desmond Guinness, the indisputable 'champion' of preservation in Ireland. Founded in 1958, the Society seeks to 'stimulate an interest in Irish art and architecture of the Georgian period'. Its headquarters are at Castletown, one of the finest Palladian houses in Ireland, 12 miles west of Dublin. The Society acts as the paternal agency in the preservation movement and provides conspicuous leadership at every level. It conducts seminars on Irish art and architecture, raises funds for specific preservation projects, issues a newsletter citing buildings in danger of demolition, publishes its authoritative *Quarterly Bulletin* (carrying articles on Irish architecture, gardens, plasterwork and the decorative arts in general), awards monetary grants to private preservationists and freely dispenses valuable advice on restoration.

Historically, the Society has concentrated its major efforts and financial resources on the more important Georgian town mansions and country

houses which were on the verge of irretrievable deterioration. In recent
years more attention has been given to the relatively humble Georgian
terraces of Dublin. During the city's major preservation battles the
Society moved to the forefront, even participating in public protests.
This supportive action has provided invaluable inspiration and impetus
for lesser preservation groups and has served as an important centripetal
force in the evolution of the preservation movement. Despite its
ambitious fund-raising efforts, the Society hardly possesses the financial
resources to single-handedly save the Georgian architecture. The Society
depends for funding upon its broad-based membership; it boasts of over
3,000 members scattered throughout more than twenty countries. This
distinctly international composition clearly attests to the world-wide
interest in Dublin's Georgian inheritance. About 60 per cent of the
Society's membership is comprised of foreigners, many predictably of
Irish extraction. Nearly half the members reside in the United States
where there are twenty-two chapters in such cities as New York,
Boston, Chicago, San Francisco, New Orleans and Dallas. Guinness's
energies ordinarily take him on the circuit of the United States twice a
year on fund-raising jaunts. Usually he resides with friends to conserve
funds for preservation needs. Throughout Britain there are another 500
members; but members may also be found in such unlikely countries as

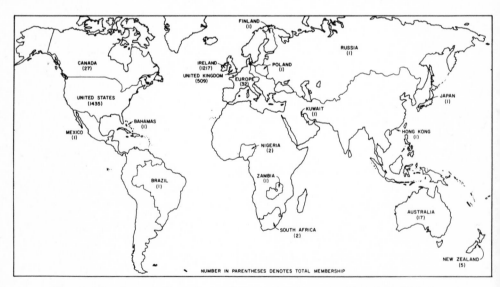

Fig. 4   Map showing the widespread international membership of the Irish Georgian
Society

Russia, Kuwait, Zambia and Brazil. Though the Society raises nearly £25,000 per year in membership dues and contributions (nearly three-quarters of which comes from abroad), it is a paltry amount in terms of what is really needed to revive and protect the Georgian architecture. For this reason, the Society must selectively choose its preservation projects. And not all efforts meet with success. For example, in the early 1970s the Society initiated the 'Save Mountjoy Square' campaign by purchasing twenty-two Georgian buildings with the intention of re-selling them to individuals capable of restoring and maintaining them. It was hoped that most would be put into predominantly residential use. However, the plan failed owing to the blighted nature of the environment which acted as a deterrent to new residents, and the properties advanced into further decay.

An Taisce

An Taisce is another important organization in the preservation move-ment. Founded in 1948 it works diligently for the protection of Ireland's architectural heritage, mostly by examining and commenting on planning applications. It is an entirely voluntary organization, operating as a highly effective pressure group, forwarding the ideals of urban conservation in all forms and actively opposing the destruction of historic buildings. As a private organization An Taisce is proud of its independent status. It does not depend on the state for its major source of income, seeking support instead from the general public and financial backing from industry, the professions and various institutions. Owing to its autonomy, it operates with objectivity and a critical view, without interference from outside official agencies. This independent spirit has gained An Taisce great credibility.

In its early years An Taisce exerted little influence. But with the development controversies of the 'sixties it matured and expanded its role and functions. It gradually emerged as the 'vanguard in promoting an appreciation of vernacular architecture' in the capital. This is especially important because of Ireland's traditional lack of appreciation for common or undistinguished buildings. An Taisce has successfully drawn attention to the historic and aesthetic qualities of Dublin's so-called 'everyday buildings', including many of the simpler Georgian terrace houses which in the past have not been considered worthy of preservation. In this context, An Taisce has helped to educate the public.

In the mid-'sixties, amid the furious redevelopment in Dublin, it was realized that there was an urgent need for a coherent, sane conservation plan that would designate areas of special architectural merit and actually list some individual buildings. This pioneer project was undertaken by An Taisce and resulted in its highly acclaimed 1967 publication *Amenity Study of Dublin and Dun Laoghaire.* This definitive document proved imperative reading for urban planners and city authorities and its findings and recommendations strongly influenced subsequent thinking on preservation in Dublin. In fact, the basic tenets of the report were incorporated almost in their entirety into the Dublin Development Plan of 1976. Today, An Taisce occupies a pivotal position in matters relating to the preservation of historic architecture, not only in Dublin but elsewhere in the country. In 1979 members of the local An Taisce branch in Waterford used protest demonstrations and a petition drive to save the historic Holy Ghost Hospital. An Taisce's Archive, situated appropriately in Merrion Square, is developing a valuable collection of photographs and other archival materials relating to Georgian Dublin. Their reading room is open to the public and provides easy access to important historical data.

A lesser-known but most tenacious organization is the **Dublin Civic Group**, born of the preservation-development squabbles of the middle 'sixties. This body has gained immensely in stature over recent years and provides a valuable function by examining all planning applications that come before the Dublin Corporation and, where necessary, filing objections to preserve streetscapes and interiors. The **Dublin Living City Group** is small but deeply committed. Its goals are to press for a balanced development of Dublin, to insist on the protection and main-tenance of residential streets, to protect residents from the pressures to migrate to suburban developments and to ensure the continuity of urban communities; in short, to retain a truly living city. To accomplish this, members organize discussion groups, conduct research, issue reports, lobby officials and publish *City Views*, a thoughtful and provocative monthly newspaper. The Dublin Living City Group is perhaps the most vocal and militant of the city's preservation bodies, exhorting other groups to join together in battle against the powers that destroy the city.

There is regular communication among all of Dublin's preservation groups and particularly close co-operation between several. They are mutually supportive and often co-ordinate their efforts and resources in attacking a common problem. There is sufficient integration and co-operation among the city's preservation groups to justifiably label their collective efforts a legitimate preservation movement. In unison they have immeasurably advanced public awareness of Dublin's eighteenth-century historic architecture. They have, in fact, contributed to the citizenry's consciousness of the general historic environment. This was evidenced by the Wood Quay demonstrations of September 1978 in which an estimated 15,000 Dubliners took to the streets to protest against the planned building of offices on the archaeological site. It signified an unprecedented public outcry against planning decisions which threatened the city's historical relics and was clearly perceived as a direct 'challenge to the politicians'.

Thus far the preservation movement in Dublin has been moderately successful. There is no doubt that preservation groups have now established enough credibility and political leverage to at least be recognized as a force on the urban scene. But compared with preservation movements in most other western countries, the Irish movement must be regarded as still in its infancy. Its full potential as a social, economic and political instrument to counter government authorities and developers has scarcely been recognized—by either side. One of the major failings of Dublin preservationists is that they have not yet realized how powerful and effective they might be if only their energies were fully mobilized and properly channelled. Their fragmentation and absence of central leadership still retards the potential power they might wield. Though preservationists freely concede this shortcoming, there seems to be no concerted effort to remedy the situation. This problem is bluntly addressed in an editorial in *City Views:*

> There seems to be very little cooperation between inner-city groups. It's time they got together to make a last stand, and this they must win. If they don't unite, their present isolated battles will be in vain. It must be a case of 'United We Stand' because it's very obvious that divided we're falling.[8]

Notes

1 Ziegler, Arthur P. Jr. *Historic Preservation in Inner City Areas* (Pittsburgh, Pennsylvania: The Allegheny Press, 1971), p16

2 McDonald, Frank. 'Dublin—What Went Wrong?', *Irish Times*, 19 November 1979, p14

3 Wright, Lance, and Browne, Kenneth. *A Future for Dublin* (The Architectural Press, 1974), p285

4 'The Restoration of Things Past', *Newsweek*, 23 March 1981, p86

5 O'Faolain, Sean. 'Fair Dublin', *Holiday*, April 1963, p76

6 Craig, Maurice. 'An Irishman's Diary', *Irish Times*, 16 January 1980

7 McDonald, Frank. 'Battle to Save One of City's Finest Streets', *Irish Times*, 13 December 1980, p7

8 'Dublin City's Falling Down', *City Views*, No. 12, 1980, p1

7

Preservation Policy and the Role of Government

It is a continuing scandal that this city, once gracious and full of character, is being reduced to a brick desert of anonymous and soulless office blocks . . . surely the time has come not just to shout stop but to urge our 'planners' to produce a plan which would be a blueprint for preservation.[1]

[Dublin] badly needs a rational system of local government and a reincarnation of the spirit which once made it a Georgian jewel.[2]

Governmental urban planning in Dublin over the past two decades has been a nightmarish affair. The question of mismanagement has been almost constantly before the public eye. Public authorities and government agencies seem forever castigated for their alleged incompetence and insensitivity. Journalistic proclamations that the 'cancer of urban blight . . . has assumed epidemic proportions', and even that the 'City Fathers are now prepared to concede that Dublin is rotting to the core', elicit strong sentiment. Such scathing indictments of the government are sometimes justified, other times undeserved. They do, however, attest dramatically to the troubled state of present-day Dublin. It is readily apparent that some horrendous planning decisions have been perpetrated against the city. These calamities can scarcely be denied or ignored because they obtrude throughout the city as ugly behemoths on the architectural stage for all to witness. Many seem to defy basic logic and sound judgement. It would, of course, take a masterful detective to track down the culprits actually responsible for some of Dublin's more notorious eyesores. Hence, it is always convenient and fashionable to lay blame on the beleaguered Dublin Corporation—the omnipresent public target. It has been charged that the Corporation is 'bankrupt of ideas', that it has no real overall grand design for the future of the city. Others have lauded the Corporation for

100

Striking contrast between the deteriorating, tenemented lower section of
North Great George's Street and the fully restored private residences at the
upper end

Two historic Georgian rows which could have been saved and restored but now are virtually beyond redemption: the south side of Mountjoy Square *(above)* was once one of Dublin's most fashionable addresses *(courtesy of American Geographical Society)*. Fownes Street *(below)* is a classic example of early Georgian architecture

Two scenes which portray dramatic streetscape change: Georgian property on left in Mountjoy Square *(above)* has been restored for office use while the adjacent house remains derelict *(courtesy of American Geographical Society)*. Along Harcourt Street *(below)* three processes can be seen: building on left is a Georgian replica, centre structure is being demolished and the house on the right has been well restored

Stark contrast between a deteriorated Georgian façade along Henrietta Street in North Dublin *(above)* and the immaculately restored property fronts in fashionable Merrion Square *(below)*

its achievements in urban redevelopment. 'Progress' is very much in the mind of the beholder!

The principal failure of the Government Planning Authority in Dublin seems to be its belated effort to devise far-sighted conservation and preservation policies. If such policies had been formulated and enforced in the 1960s, the city would doubtless have been spared much of its sad litany of disfiguration and destruction. But this was an age of relative innocence in which many Dubliners would probably have regarded conservation and historic preservation as frivolities or luxuries rather than essential urban safeguards. Things have changed. The city is now in a state of great flux and the hazards of modernization are all too apparent to most Dubliners. Management of the capital has become a complex and cumbersome task. The population has escalated sharply between 1960 and 1980 and has now reached the million mark. During this frenetic period of urban redevelopment, planners and city authorities tended to concentrate on coping with the present rather than thoughtfully contemplating the future. The result has been a plethora of myopic decisions and plans. Coincidently, mounting urban pressures bred an expanded and convoluted administrative/legislative system—but not necessarily a more efficient and effective one. Indeed, as most Dubliners will attest, one of the city's most conspicuous problems is its 'tangled maze of bureaucratic undergrowth which passes for local government'. Dublin is being strangled by a myriad of government agencies which not only compete but often conflict with each other. There is an apparent absence of any central decision-making power. Effective policies and enlightened programmes seldom emerge from such an entangled bureaucratic web.

PRESERVATION IN THE EUROPEAN CONTEXT

Every country in Europe has, to one extent or another, recognized an obligation to past and future generations to carefully nurture their cultural heritage . . . many have given architecture, sometimes of the simplest domestic kind, the same attention as painting and sculpture . . . almost all have learned to value what is passed down to them by history for its basic and artistic quality irrespective of its social or political origins.[3]

There appears to be [in Europe] a definite parallel between success in [architectural] conservation and the extent to which there is some form of official acknowledgement and support for the property owner.[4]

To gain a fair and proper perspective on Irish architectural preservation and the role played by the government, it is helpful to first examine policies and programmes in other European countries. It may be stated unequivocally at the outset that Ireland is conspicuously out of step with other European preservation movements. Several factors help to explain, but do not necessarily justify, Ireland's lagging position. First, many European countries suffered the devastation of historic cities during two world wars. This made them acutely aware of lost architecture and the necessity for restoring and preserving that which survived. During both post-war periods these countries gained valuable experience in restoration techniques. Physical restoration of historic buildings became an integral part of Europe's overall urban reconstruction. For most war-torn countries, the primary objective was understandably to salvage those historic or artistic structures of special importance. Initial efforts were therefore directed at rebuilding monumental government buildings and other prestigious architectural landmarks. However, Europeans have not neglected their lesser architectural inheritance. In fact, in most countries there has been a growing affection for simple vernacular architecture that possesses no special distinction but reflects the culture of the people. Since Europeans have lost so much of their visible past, they are sensitive to the need to preserve for their descendants even the common architectural idioms which have been spared.

Most of Europe also had to contend with the onslaught of the developer at an earlier date than did Ireland, and often on a larger scale. It is estimated that in the period 1968–78 alone, European cities suffered more urban damage from demolition than was sustained during World War II. For nearly three decades now the historic quarters of many Western European cities have been the embittered battlegrounds between urban developers and ardent preservationists. Thus the concept of preservation is well understood by most Europeans although there are variant philosophies regarding its proper implementation. It is inexplicable that the Irish seemed to learn so little from the preservation struggles so furiously waged in neighbouring countries and failed to appreciate the dangers of modern urban redevelopment when it finally confronted them in the early 'sixties.

Another factor retarding Ireland's preservation initiative, at both the public and private level, is the aforementioned lack of felt-pride in the Georgian legacy. On the other hand, in most European countries intense national pride in the historic architecture has been the major stimulus in preservation activity by government and citizens' groups. France has been the model of conscientious preservation in the European community. This is doubtless explained in part by the country's well-defined national character and keen sense of historic and cultural pride in its long and gloriously perceived past, as proudly reflected in the wealth of architectural heritage. The British, Dutch, Germans and Danes have been similarly motivated to protect their visible past. In most European countries preservation is a joint effort by state and private agencies. But ordinarily the national government assumes the role of leadership and financial benefactor. Citizens endorse the cause of preservation and contribute to its achievement but the government clearly plays the principal part. Each country, of course, has developed its own approach to preservation. The British experience contrasts somewhat with the standard Continental model. Whereas most Europeans rely heavily not only on governmental control and finance but also on bureaucratic expertise, the British still depend on considerable assistance from dedicated amateurs, independent scholars and professionals. In this sense, the fledgling Irish preservation movement is more closely aligned with the British, since so many Irish academics and professionals are leaders in the field. However, the British enjoy substantial financial support and encouragement from their government.

It is interesting to note that in the United States preservation evolved in quite a different manner. The American movement has essentially been a grass-roots effort. For most Americans preservation is a 'thoroughly romantic movement' based strongly on patriotic affection for past glories and symbols which have some meaning for certain populations. Virtually every town and community has its endearing historical relics and buildings, even if they are sometimes a bit contrived or inflated in importance (Europeans often find great amusement in the American conception of what constitutes an historic relic or antique). Thus, American youths are inculcated (if not inundated) with local, state and national history, thereby implanting a strong sense of identity with tangible reminders of past events and historic sites. As a consequence, preservation in the United States has really sprung up spontaneously as basically an amateur activity, usually dependent on private funding. Since local and sectional initiatives have provided the groundwork for preservation, the state and federal governments have assumed a relatively modest role. Private and volunteer groups manage the preservation burden with ease. The wealth of many American communities has afforded them this luxury. In the case of large-scale preservation of historic inner-city districts, government grants can usually be obtained.

107

France was the first European country to engage in serious preservation efforts and today her legislation on the subject is generally considered to be the most extensive. The first list of historic French buildings to be protected was drawn up in 1840. Successive French governments upheld and expanded interest in preservation. But in most European countries architectural preservation did not become a serious concern until the wake of World War I. World War II made Europeans even more aware of the fragility of their historic built environment. By the 1960s the practice of classifying and listing buildings as public assets to be protected had become part of the bureaucratic paraphernalia of most European nations. In some countries, such as Great Britain, preservation planning actually developed into a sophisticated specialty in urban renewal.

The official listing of historic buildings is a laborious and expensive task, usually conducted by the government; but it is an essential basis for any restoration and preservation effort. Some countries compile more elaborate and detailed lists than others. In Denmark preservation lists are revised every five years; in other countries such lists are only infrequently up-dated. Only by listing can the architectural stock be properly inventoried, managed and protected. Preservation is not limited to individual, unrelated structures. In a number of countries, most notably Britain, France, Denmark and the Netherlands, the idea of entire 'conservation/preservation areas' has gained importance. These areas may be composed of small urban neighbourhoods or include whole historic sections of the city. The British have given such preferential treatment to York, Bath and Chester. Similarly, in a number of Continental countries expansive urban districts have been declared historically sacrosanct by planning authorities and given full protection against the threats of modern redevelopment. In France, when such an area is identified for preservation, a moratorium is announced and no alterations of any type are permitted until a detailed plan has been prepared. Determinations are then made by government experts about restoration procedures and the location, type and scale of any new development to be allowed in the area. Once the preservation plan is approved, it is faithfully enforced and the architectural integrity of the district is ensured by law.

Experience in Europe has shown that legislation is a 'dead letter' if it does not force owners to maintain their historic property in good condition. This means that the government must be committed to contributing financially to restoration and maintenance. Hence, the role, or *duty*, of local and national governments in assisting financially private

108

property owners is always vital to success. European governments recognize that if they list a building as worthy of preservation they have a clear responsibility to contribute to its welfare, that it would be unfair and unreasonable to expect private citizens to shoulder the full financial burden of restoration and upkeep. This working philosophy is based on the belief that the owner, by preserving his historic structure, is rendering a valuable service to the community in which he lives. This concept is fundamental to understanding the rationale for European governments funding private preservation efforts; it also distinctly sets Ireland ideologically apart from its neighbours.

Most European countries use financial incentives as a sort of pump-priming in the preservation process. In other words, the government initially provides a financial stimulus for restoration/preservation work. Ordinarily, this financial incentive takes the form of outright grants and relief in local, national or property taxes. This may be supplemented by a system of low-interest government loans and the provision of free consulting or supervision services on all aspects of preservation. The actual system of financial aid varies from one country to another. In Britain an individual may obtain one-fourth of the required money from a state grant and another quarter in the form of a municipal grant. Hence, he is required to provide only half the necessary funding. In Belgium, owing to a generous programme of state and local grants, the property owner may have to contribute only about 15 per cent of the full cost of his property's restoration. Likewise, in both East and West Germany preservation is heartily encouraged by offering owners of historic properties enticing exemptions in their income and property tax. Since 1962 French citizens have been eligible for loans of up to 60 per cent of the cost of restoration, and special grants covering another 20 per cent. If they are unable to provide the remaining one-fifth, the property is compulsorily acquired by a special committee consisting of representatives of the local authority, preservation societies, chambers of commerce and banks who make up the balance of the project. Upon completion of the work the owner has the option to re-acquire his property by simply contributing his 20 per cent of the total cost. If he chooses to decline this opportunity, the building may then be sold to another owner. The Netherlands boasts of one of the most imaginative preservation programmes. Here the government not only contributes substantially to preservation costs but offers without charge a wide variety of architectural, research and supervisory services to preservationists. Furthermore, the Dutch have pioneered in Europe a system for locating and stockpiling historic building materials and fixtures such as bricks, timber and ironwork to be used in the faithful restoration of the country's old buildings.

The dominant role of government in European architectural preservation illuminates the vexing problem of private property rights versus society's rights. Does an individual owner possess the right to neglect, alter or destroy his property at will if it has historic or artistic value? Or is he legally and morally responsible for preserving it, to the best of his ability, as a social inheritance? Prevailing European philosophy stresses the rights of society, the collective interest, over the rights of individual owners. In Denmark, the state is empowered to purchase, restore and re-sell threatened properties of historic merit if they cannot be saved by private enterprise. France has perhaps the most trenchant policy. The French Government is ultimately responsible for ensuring the retention and protection of the country's historic architecture. If an individual fails to act responsibly in maintaining his valued property, the government can act to protect it in the interest of the French people. In fact, during the period of actual restoration, the government can evacuate rent-paying tenants. Upon completion of the restoration work, if the tenants cannot afford to pay the increased rental fee, authorities are obliged to find alternative accommodation for them. Although this approach may be regarded as somewhat ruthless, it has been found to be a viable one in a democratic country where the government must negotiate with a host of owners and occupiers along streets designated for preservation. The principle of society's rights taking precedence over those of individuals has proven to be a harsh but realistic necessity in preservation matters. It has been suggested that the French approach to preservation might prove to be the only functional one for Dublin, in which some Georgian streets are occupied by a complexity of residents and tenants who sometimes impede restoration and preservation efforts.[5]

THE IRISH PRESERVATION SYSTEM

To meet the cost of restoration, adaptation, and maintenance of buildings of architectural or historic interest, adequate financial assistance should be made available to local authorities and financial support and fiscal relief should likewise be made available to private owners.

(Statement from the 1975 *Declaration of Amsterdam*, signed by the Ministers of the Council of Europe, including Ireland, at the Congress of Amsterdam.)

> The Planning Authority is aware of the great quality and value of Dublin's architectural heritage and in particular of those buildings, streets, and squares which constitute a unique example of eighteenth century street architecure. It is also conscious of its responsibilities to secure the preservation of this heritage which constitutes an essential element in the character and historical development of the city.[6]

When the Local Government Act of 1963 was passed, there was no tradition for and little experience of physical urban planning in Ireland; the concepts of architectural conservation and preservation were even less familiar. Although this Act called forthrightly for the 'preservation of buildings of artistic, architectural or historic interest', it was little more than a rhetorical declaration because it was not buttressed by any programme of action. It is true that in accordance with the National Monuments Acts of 1930 and 1954 some preservation has occurred. But the National Monuments codes really pertain to archaeological sites and medieval buildings; virtually no structures dating from 1700 have been designated by the government for preservation. Thus, preservation may have been 'on the books' for some time, but during the post-war period when Dublin was experiencing housing shortages, an office-building revolution and vehicular traffic chaos, it was conveniently ignored.

The Irish Government finally addressed the question of urban conservation and preservation in its long-awaited 1976 Dublin Development Plan. This document was presumably to cure many of the city's most persistent ills. It neatly divided Dublin into a series of land-use zones to be covered by specific regulations and controls; at long last it promised a sane approach to urban redevelopment. Its most important dictates focus on conservation and preservation. A distinction needs to be made between these two semantic entities. Simply put, conservation is about *places* or *areas*, whereas preservation refers to specific *buildings* or *groups of buildings*. Conservation implies action taken to identify amenities and architecture within a spatial zone to be retained, developed and properly maintained. Within such conservation areas are certain elements that should actually be preserved. Preservation most commonly means that a structure is retained in its original form (and, ideally, function), often through restoration, and safeguarded against alteration or deterioration. Therefore, features of the cityscape to be preserved for future generations are often found within general conservation districts.

The Dublin Development Plan states the need to protect and preserve buildings of special historic merit which contribute to the unique

111

character of the city. It also importantly recognizes that the 'relationship of Dublin's street façades to the human scale' is widely regarded as a major attraction and must be retained. It was with these ideas in mind that the Planning Authority designated conservation areas. Generally, these areas consist of mainly residential neighbourhoods having an attractive (but not necessarily historic) quality of architectural style, design or scale, and which are often associated with Dublin's open spaces and other valued amenities. These conservation zones are clearly demarcated on a large, multi-coloured land-use map produced by the Dublin Corporation. In conservation tracts the 'overall quality' of the urban environment is the major concern, meaning that special care is given to even relatively undistinguished architectural components that blend harmoniously with the greater mass. The objective is to keep the existing social/economic/physical milieu. Therefore, proposals for development or redevelopment are scrutinized for their potential disruptive impact. Zoning controls are meant to prohibit the intrusion of developments which might prove incompatible with the present environment in terms of building design, height, scale, function or intensity of site use. The basic character of the area is not to be substantially disturbed. Even developments threatening to increase traffic or generate excessive advertising are ostensibly outlawed. Under the planning code, proposals for development must be advertised in the public press or by notice affixed to the premises. These advertisements must precede lodgement of proposals with the Planning Authority. This is an important safeguard because it alerts interested parties, such as An Taisce, the Irish Georgian Society and residents' associations to the intentions of developers and allows them the opportunity to present their views prior to final decision-making. It does not, however, mean that their objections or advice will be heeded.

PRESERVATION DISTRICTS: A GEOGRAPHICAL PERSPECTIVE

The architectural heart of Dublin's conservation areas are the Georgian preservation districts. To protect these historic buildings, the Irish devised a system of listing which is seemingly comparable to that used in most other European countries. There are three lists simply labelled 1, 2, and 3. List 1 includes those buildings or groups of buildings to be strictly preserved; theoretically, they are sacrosanct. Buildings placed on List 2 are not ensured outright preservation but their ultimate welfare and survival are supported by a code for architectural protection; they cannot

(above) A Georgian 'survivor' along Pembroke Street whose future is in jeopardy; *(below)* in south Dublin Georgian properties have been transformed into exclusive shops such as antique dealers and wine merchants

One of the most
architecturally incompatible
sights in Dublin is that of the
modernistic bank building
along Dame Street towering
over the humble early
eighteenth-century houses of
Fownes Street. This is a clear
case of bad urban planning
which resulted in the
violation of an historic setting

A pastiche Georgian
reproduction built at the
corner of Hume Street and
St Stephen's Green.
Controversy over this project
led to the 'Battle of Hume
Street', a confrontation
between developers and
preservationists

be materially altered or demolished without permission from the Planning Authority. List 3 includes those important state-owned structures of special architectural or historical importance. Since they are usually under the aegis of the government, their future is reasonably secure. Most Georgian buildings are contained in either List 1 or 2, although the rationale for their placement in one category rather than the other is often highly questionable.

When a significant number of buildings listed for preservation are concentrated in a particular vicinity, they constitute what may be termed a 'preservation district'. The most important preservation district in Dublin is that which the Planning Authority simply refers to as the 'hardcore Georgian' section. It is formed by the coalescence of basically intact eighteenth-century streetscapes in the Merrion Square, Fitzwilliam Square, Fitzwilliam Street, Upper Mount Street and Leeson Street complex (see map on p49). Most of the buildings encompassed within this hardcore zone are of the List 1 type. The only hardcore Georgian unit not included in this vicinity is Henrietta Street, north of the Liffey River. A secondary Georgian preservation district centres on North Dublin in the environs of Mountjoy Square, North Great George's Street and Parnell Square; but it also includes some streets south of the Liffey such as Harcourt, Kildare, Molesworth and Mount Pleasant Square. Most of these lesser-perceived Georgian houses are classified in List 2, but a number of especially fine dwellings along Parnell Square are on the premier list. These two Georgian areas are not only geographically distinct but they have evolved economically and socially in a separate manner. For this reason, the Planning Authority realistically views them as disparate entities in terms of development regulations. A current geographical assessment of these two eighteenth-century sections illuminates their unique characters.

THE NORTH/SOUTH GEORGIAN DICHOTOMY

Surviving Georgian Dublin is best interpreted within the context of its five major squares: Mountjoy, Parnell, Merrion, Fitzwilliam and St Stephen's. The first two are north of the Liffey, the other three south. Each constitutes a distinctive architectural/cultural enclave within the larger cityscape. St Stephen's Green, the largest and earliest of the squares and reputedly one of the greatest in Europe, has regrettably lost much of its eighteenth-century personality. The bold intrusion of modern offices along its north and south sides has irretrievably altered its once-elegant

115

character. The west side of St Stephen's has become particularly offensive to traditionalists because of the sordid infestation of gaudy shops and cinemas catering to a youthful clientele. Hence, the square, or 'green' as it is really known, has become an outlier component, detached from 'pure' Georgiana. But a number of its remaining Georgian buildings are included on preservation lists.

Quintessential Georgian Dublin is indisputably still to be found in the Merrion-Fitzwilliam squares area, the most prestigious locus in the entire eighteenth-century architectural system. These two famous squares, combined with Fitzwilliam Street and Upper Mount Street, create probably the finest townscape of its kind in Europe. This is precisely why the ESB's mutilation of the streetscape so incensed preservationists. Merrion and Fitzwilliam squares offer the best single reference point, both in terms of their geographical position and architectural idiom, for interpreting the unified Georgian scene. As documented earlier, both were laid out during the last half of the eighteenth century and were not completed until the second decade of the following century. One of the reasons why these squares remain so charming and captivating is that they are architecturally intact and retain much of their domestic quality, evoking romantic images of their original role as elegant domiciles for family living. Fitzwilliam is the only Georgian square whose park area is still reserved for residents; hence, it can still claim a certain aristocratic exclusivity of which its relations can no longer boast.

Apart from these two renowned squares, there are numerous import-ant arterial Georgian streets. For example, along Hume Street and Ely Place are some of the finest large Georgian houses dating from about 1775. Both streets were architecturally 'chaste' until about a decade ago when the tentacles of modern development snatched a few buildings from their midst and despoiled their purity. Quite a different Georgian flavour is to be discovered along Herbert Place, Wilton Place and Wilton Terrace where smaller houses built toward the end of the Georgian period overlook the canal. In its totality, this hardcore Georgian part of the city is internationally celebrated for its spatial qualities, unity of grace and proportions, and exterior and interior detail.

The Dublin Development Plan is designed to accord this Georgian core maximum security against contaminating intrusive development. Land-use zoning ordinances are supposed to restrict the types of development allowed here. Ordinarily it is now only permissible for these Georgian buildings to be put to a few limited uses, such as residential, embassy or cultural organizations. Some other types of development are 'open for consideration'; these include such uses as offices, educational, institutions, private clubs, medical services, consulting firms and guest houses. But although these functions may be considered, they are not normally permitted any more. Certain developments are strictly prohibited— hotels, shops, restaurants, night clubs, health centres, industry, warehouses and car service stations. Despite these constraints, the architectural and functional integrity of some Georgian streetscapes is blemished by the appearance of quaint shops and exclusive restaurants and clubs. These 'intruders' established roots before restrictive regulations were drafted. Since the 1969 Housing Act, which was designed to protect the remaining eighteenth-century stock of private houses from mass conversion to office space, Georgian houses have not been permitted to change functions without the approval of the Planning Authority. However, this Act did not apply to those buildings already in some form of commercial utilization. This explains the present-day incompatibility of site use along such Georgian stretches as Leeson and Harcourt streets.

The north Georgian city is today glaringly different from its more fortunate counterpart south of the river. It is an area of economic hardship, physical deterioration and social stress—badly blighted in patches, long ignored by planners and assiduously avoided by south-siders. The north side has degenerated into what *Evening Press* journalist Aodhan Madden calls a 'slummy jungle fit for vandals, graffittists, and other wayward children of the new urban frontier'. It is a land of grim and sorry sights where spectral figures peer from the bowels of decrepit Georgian hallways, front doors ajar. Parnell Square and Mountjoy Square form the Georgian nucleus; Gardiner Row, Gardiner Place and Denmark Street provide the basic axis linking the two squares. Despite its general ambience of dereliction and decay, the area still remains a 'locality of extraordinary subtlety and consistency both in layout arid detailed design'. Unfortunately, the maze of derelict sites, empty windows, broken fanlights, crumbling brickwork and unpainted and rotting woodwork obscure the many fine features that still remain. Such stark sights also detract from the potential for restoration. These Georgian streets are highly unpredictable, reflecting the convoluted history of the vicinity. Some houses have been magnificently restored while those directly adjacent may be rubble heaps. Parnell Square typifies the schizophrenic personality of the environment. When this square was completed, it boasted a total of forty-eight elegant private residences and contained a strong element of uniformity and proportion. Today the square is in sad disarray. The east side has fared worst, deteriorating into a row of neglected and dilapidated buildings with interspersed survivors. By contrast the west side is relatively intact and preserved, having the good fortune of being occupied by assorted organizations attentive to building maintenance.

The anatomy of Georgiana reaches its most alarming state of decrepitude in Mountjoy Square; here the contrasts are extreme. There is surely no more depressing sight in Georgian Dublin than along the south side of the historic square where most of the houses have rotted beyond redemption. Despite the skeletal remains, it is still possible to imagine the original scene of grandeur. The west side of the square is more intact than the south but is nonetheless impregnated with gaps and tawdry shops. The north and east sides are still respectable, mostly in office use.

The Planning Authority recognizes the desperate plight of the north Georgian city, noting that it is a special area where 'preservation and restoration must be considered together'. Land-use regulations are more liberal and flexible to encourage redevelopment. According to the new Development Plan, the objective is to 'protect, improve, or renew' the existing character and design of the surroundings. This is a considerable challenge since in some places the physical fabric appears beyond retrieval. For this reason, preferential treatment is a necessity for reviving the area. The Planning Authority permits Georgian structures here to be used for certain functions that are denied in the Merrion/Fitzwilliam area. These include hotels, guest houses, various offices, nursing homes and health centres. Authorities are also favourably disposed toward allowing restaurants, night clubs, sports clubs and wholesale shops. A good example of the resultant commercial flavour can be witnessed along Denmark Street and Gardiner's Place where there are lively combinations of shops, hotels and guest houses. This diversity of functions is a notable departure from the relatively staid setting along the south city's Georgian streets. Only such offensive developments as industry, warehouses, motor car sales and cash-and-carry establishments are prohibited outright.

Further testimony to the separate treatment accorded the two Georgian districts are the contrasting rates of acceptable office utilization. Ideally, the government desires a healthy multiple-role function for both preservation areas. This means that there should be a favourable balance between residential and office/commercial/institutional use. Preservationists strongly endorse the concept that the Georgian streets, to retain some semblance of original identity, must keep some residential population. To encourage residential occupation in the office-entrenched south Georgian areas, a degree of alteration or redevelopment for living accommodation is permitted either in the main building or in the backland where it is unobtrusive. Also, for Georgian structures undergoing functional conversion, the Planning Authority now limits the office content to 40 per cent of the total floor space. Conversely, in the deprived north Georgian city, buildings may be put into 100 per cent office use if this is deemed the only method for restoring the faded streetscape. Despite the more liberal statutes covering this area, there are still strict controls on design, scale and elevation of any new buildings; they must harmonize with the eighteenth-century setting.

Some of the detached fragments of Georgiana not securely integrated into the two principal preservation districts warrant special mention. Henrietta Street, built in the early eighteenth century, is the only 'alienated' hardcore Georgian street. It was once the grandest, most prestigious street in all Dublin—home to a glittering array of Dublin's élite. Long ago Henrietta Street succumbed to tenementation and decay, but like a proud, tattered aristocrat it is today struggling toward rejuvenation. One house is in the process of slow restoration and several others have been bought by an architect who plans to revive them. Fownes Street is another special case; situated just off Dame Street, it contains probably the best row of early Georgian houses left in Dublin. Yet, because of their poor structural condition, they are not on any preservation list and their future is much in jeopardy. Already they have been dwarfed by the futuristic bank building insensitively constructed by their side. To exacerbate matters, Fownes Street now finds itself precariously in the path of the city's proposed new rapid transit centre. Demolition seems imminent unless the street can be saved by public protest or some miraculous financial endowment—both of which are hardly likely. Harcourt Street is another imperilled component of the overall Georgian system. Dating from the 1770s it has its own character, enhanced by a rather refreshing, sweeping curve; no other street in the city is quite like it. Although part of the secondary preservation area, it is a distinctly detached limb; thus, it is far more vulnerable to desecration than neighbouring streets aligned with the Merrion Square-Fitzwilliam Square node. Demolition and modern development are gnawing away at both sides of the street. Citizens passing by daily seem utterly oblivious to this loss. Furthermore, the streetscape has been scarred in recent years by the insertion of neo-Georgian reproductions. These 'pretenders' have already devalued the architectural authenticity of the street.

119

Collectively, surviving Georgian Dublin constitutes only about 5 per cent of Dublin's core area (roughly a radius ranging one mile in distance from the College Green centre) and less than 1 per cent of the entire urban area. Officially, the government lists only 339 buildings and groups of buildings for preservation. However, listed buildings are not identified in the Dublin Development Plan by their specific architectural type; thus it is not possible to know with certainty whether they are of the Georgian, Victorian or some other period. When queried about the number of remaining Georgian structures in the capital, most official sources either plead ignorance or typically reply 'perhaps several thousand'. Detailed examination of the 1976 Development Plan preservation lists, on a street-by-street basis, at least provides a general index to existing Georgian architecture. Georgian buildings on List 1, mostly included in the hardcore district, number about 680. Approximately 750 other Georgian structures are on List 2, the majority found north of the Liffey. Therefore, it appears that there are perhaps 1,400 individual Georgian properties covered by the government preservation programme.

MAJOR DEFECTS IN PRESERVATION POLICY

If only the Government would realize that the effective protection of the material remains of the past is the true mark of a civilized country then there might be some hope of new legislation.[7]

In theory, the Irish Government's approach to urban architectural preservation may appear compatible with other European policies. The adoption of the Dublin Development Plan by the corporation certainly suggested that at least a 'little progress' was being made in the field of historic preservation. However, careful scrutiny of the preservation policy reveals that while Ireland may well be pursuing a course somewhat akin to that followed in other western European countries, it is in what Kevin Nowlan considers 'muted, inadequate, and unimaginative' form. As explained by a Dublin architect employed at a very high level of city government, the Dublin Corporation, armed with its new Development Plan and ostensibly possessing the authority to approve or refuse planning applications, 'theoretically should be able to control the future of Georgian Dublin'. But in truth it is 'inhibited by a number of democratic constraints' which hinder the implementation of the development plan; for example, the inability to prevent demolition pure and simple. Crisply stated, the Corporation can draw up the rules and regulations but appears to lack the real power and genuine determination to enforce them faithfully. For this reason preservation is still more of an idealized concept than an applied plan of action. In reality, the Irish preservation system is riddled with flaws and deficiencies. The most serious problems are:

1　An inadequate procedure for listing buildings to be preserved and the consequent neglect of interiors
2　The absence of grants and other financial aid to encourage and support preservation efforts
3　Lack of enforcement of existing regulations

Inadequacies in the Listing System

There is no weaker link in the Irish preservation scheme than the listing process itself. A comprehensive, accurate and detailed index of historic buildings is the fundamental basis of any urban preservation programme. But the Corporation's procedure for listing buildings for preservation is highly inadequate. Deficiencies are both qualitative and quantitative. Alistair Rowan, writing in *Dublin's Future: The European Challenge*, alleges that in terms of serious protection of historic structures the Irish Government's 'official neglect is patent and quantifiable'. He points out that in terms of both scale and aesthetic value Dublin is quite comparable to the Georgian New Town of Edinburgh. The Scottish Development Department has methodically inventoried its stock of historic buildings with impeccable care. By contrast, Dublin's listing procedure is incomplete and amateurish.

The crux of the problem is the manner in which the buildings are inspected and rated. In most European countries such inspection is a painstaking process. Scrupulous attention is given to both exterior and interior treatments. This demands the use of professionals with the expertise to detect and document craftsmanship as expressed in design, brickwork and plasterwork. Those European countries with the most successful preservation record also have the superior listing systems. The French, for example, boast of an extraordinarily intricate and accurate system of listing, and the results speak for themselves.

A conscientious approach to listing is particularly important in Dublin because often the most praiseworthy features of Georgian architecture are quite subtle; they often defy cursory appraisal and must be ferreted out by

121

patient inspection and a trained eye. Looks can be quite deceptive. One must always probe beyond the obvious to discover the real soul of Georgiana. Simple-appearing façades commonly harbour architectural nuances of importance, but these may be discernible only to experts. Hence, superficial examination can lead to inadequate and faulty documentation. This appears to be the situation in Dublin where appraisal of Georgian buildings for listing is a relatively casual process. The listing system is particularly bedevilled by the façade approach. In other words, the structural condition of exteriors determines in large measure how a building will be listed, or completely omitted from protection. To judge historic architecture in such a cavalier, superficial manner is woefully inadequate; it necessarily leads to serious errors and distortions. As scholars and preservationists like Rowan hasten to admonish, by using such a flimsy procedure the 'very existence of quality is ignored by officialdom'.

In the judgement of most preservationists, the government's claim of support for preservation reaches its zenith of hypocrisy in the unabashed neglect of interiors. It is often in the interiors of Georgian houses that their most intrinsic artistic character is to be found. It is viewed as quite unconscionable to ignore this vital element. It is also in striking contrast to preservation efforts in most other European countries where interiors are usually given equal, if not greater, attention than exteriors. Since interiors were completely unprotected under the 1963 Planning Act, many were destroyed with impunity. The 1976 Local Government Act finally gave some attention to interiors, calling for the 'preservation of plasterwork, staircases, woodwork, or other fixures or features of artistic, historic, or architectural interest'. This provided local planning authorities with the right to list and protect interiors; theoretically, some advance was made. In practice, however, the Corporation has failed to list *any* of the city's interiors for preservation and thus they are still, in truth, completely without legislative protection. Because authorities do not exercise their powers of control over Dublin's richly ornamented Georgian interiors, owners and occupants are at liberty to modify, alter or mangle them at will. Staircases and walls may be removed and elevator shafts installed for the sake of utilitarian space. Plasterwork is often stripped or defaced. An entire exquisitely plastered ceiling might be extracted so that a more efficient system of office illumination can be installed. The vulnerability of these eighteenth-century treasures is one of the most contentious issues in the preservation struggle.

In defence of its position the Dublin Corporation contends that it would prove an insuperable problem to try and enforce legislation covering the preservation of the city's interiors—that it would require an almost continuous surveillance system. It cites existing staff shortages and high personnel costs that would impede such a 'policing' action. But preservationists find fault with this argument. They concede that a constant monitoring system would not be feasible in terms of economics or manpower. However, a procedure for periodically checking protected interiors, on a purely random basis, could easily be devised and implemented. By vigorously enforcing present regulations and relying on the threat of legal action, authorities could dissuade owners from improperly tampering with their historic holding. If occasional violators were detected and prosecuted, it would doubtless serve to alert and alarm other unscrupulous types who might entertain similar, destructive notions. After all, in an orderly society it is the simple threat of being apprehended that serves as an effective deterrent to legal violations. This same fundamental principle might be applied successfully to the protection of the Georgian heritage. No such imaginative plan has been developed by Dublin authorities.

As a consequence of façade appraisal and neglect of interiors, there are serious inconsistencies in the government's preservation lists. Owing to their visibly unkempt exteriors, some of the city's finest Georgian houses have been placed on List 2; their richly endowed interiors simply go undetected and unregistered. Alarmingly, not a single dwelling along North Great George's Street enjoys the protection of a List 1 rating— although several of these houses are magnificently restored both within and without. Classification on the second list places them at certain risk. Meanwhile, some less meritorious Georgian architecture has been given List 1 status merely because it has the good fortune to be externally intact and adjacent to higher quality structures. This unscientific approach to indexing historic buildings calls into serious question the validity of the present listing system. Careless misplacement of Georgian houses on the wrong list can prove a disastrous mistake because the Corporation has exhibited a 'certain softness' in protecting structures on the secondary list. In fact, as one critic observed, placing a building in the second category is tantamount to issuing a 'licence to kill it . . . an open invitation to have it demolished'. Experience has shown, especially in north Dublin, that List 2 buildings are very vulnerable to destruction. It is small comfort to preservationists to learn that a Georgian house has been placed on the Corporation's second list; they must continue to keep a vigilant eye on its welfare.

123

The Financial Factor

An equally serious defect in the government's preservation plan is the absence of financial assistance. It has become a verity in Western European preservation circles that 'putting buildings on lists won't preserve them . . . there is also a need for financial help'. The Irish Government obviously does not share the philosophy that the state has the responsibility to contribute to the restoration and maintenance of historic properties. The 1963 Planning Act contained a provision enabling local authorities to assist in the preservation process; thus the mechanism exists for issuing grants and other financial aid. But, to date, not a single grant has been awarded to an individual for this purpose. Yet all evidence shows that such fiscal incentives are absolutely essential. In the mid-'sixties the Dublin Corporation commissioned a private firm to conduct a preservation feasibility study on Dublin. In the resulting 1967 report, entitled *Dublin Development: Preservation and Change*, it was bluntly stated that governmental financial compensation is 'a most critical factor' in any preservation policy. Inexplicably, this document was never circulated for consideration and open discussion and was, in fact, according to an architect long-employed by the Dublin Corporation, rather carefully and quietly secreted away. In light of the greater European experience, it is highly incongruous for a government to presume to put forth a preservation plan without investing a single pound for its implementation.

A commonly offered rationale for this curious contradiction, routinely cited by authorities, is that Ireland is simply 'too poor a country' to subsidize preservation. This claim is convenient, but arguable. It might help to explain, and even partially justify, Ireland's belated appearance on the European preservation scene. Traditionally, Ireland has undeniably had scant financial resources to devote to such efforts when compared with some wealthy neighbours. However, the contention in the 1980s that the country has absolutely *no* finances to spend on urban preservation is patently absurd. After all, even such countries as Poland and Czechoslovakia, as well as other modestly endowed European countries, have managed to allocate sufficient attention and money to restoring and protecting their valued historic architecture. In Warsaw most of the historic core, reduced to rubble during World War II, has been successfully rebuilt. It was important to the people and government to do so.

In modern-day Ireland it seems to be not so much a matter of lacking funds but an entrenched set of national priorities in which urban architectural preservation has been accorded an abysmally low rating.

When the Irish Government sets out to attack a problem it deems important, it can muster impressive energies, imagination and financial support. The success of the Industrial Development Authority in developing Ireland's industrial sector over the short span of two decades is powerful testimony to what miracles can be wrought from sheer determination. The government has also committed itself to the preservation of the Gaelic language and culture through its revival programme for the Gaeltacht (those residual Irish-speaking communities mostly in the far west of Ireland). Similarly, one might consider the recent progress made by Bord Failte in exploiting the lucrative convention trade. Long a neglected aspect of Ireland's tourism programme, the Bord has finally recognized the enormous potential for luring conventions to the country. They proceeded to establish new priorities, devised clever promotional schemes and allocated the necessary funding. They succeeded admirably. Therefore, the government's persistent lament that there is simply no money available for promoting Georgian preservation must be honestly questioned in the light of past endeavours and present priorities.

Frailties of Preservation Enforcement
Preservationists are equally distressed by the government's feeble enforcement of existing preservation statutes. The continuing failure of planning authorities to uphold uniformly their own dictates undermines the entire preservation effort. The attitudes of authorities toward preservation, which range from 'hesitant involvement' to 'sad indifference', is an important part of the problem. Unlike other European countries, in Ireland there is no real preservation spirit in government. There is no genuine committment to the cause, no enthusiasm for the task. In some instances preservation matters are attended to almost grudgingly, as if by coercion of the Dublin Development Plan.

One could compile a litany of violations against preservation regulations because excuses are commonly found for allowing exceptions to existing codes. As Deirdre Kelly boldly puts it, the 'planning laws have loopholes so big that you could walk through them'. Enforcement of preservation regulations seems, at best, a haphazard, arbitrary and capricious affair. And it has already been described in an earlier chapter how conniving developers adeptly circumvent the rules to convert or demolish Georgian houses. The results are all too evident; for example, the approval in 1976 to demolish the perfectly fine Bord na Mona offices

125

despite their supposedly secure position on a preservation list. In 1980 a classical Georgian building at the end of Ely Place was summarily demolished even before preservationists found out about it. The structure was not only listed for preservation but had been cited for its unusual architectural design with regard to window structure; it was a unique link in the Georgian system. Similarly, despite articulate opposition, and in clear violation of existing height restrictions, the Central Bank Building arose ominously along Dame Street, adulterating the very environment of which it was to have become part. Within its menacing shadow stands forlorn Fownes Street, its early eighteenth-century buildings in pathetic decline. The resultant scene is nothing short of sadly ludicrous. In short, new buildings are put up in violation of existing laws while Georgian houses on preservation lists are torn down; even List 1 historic properties have been razed and no penalty incurred.

It would be unfair to lay full blame for planning and preservation abuses on the hapless Dublin Corporation, despite their well-documented history of blunders and indiscretions, because an examination of the record reveals that 'time and again decisions of the Dublin Corporation in defence of conservation interests have been reversed by the Minister'. Much of the responsibility must lie with the far larger and more serious failure of the general governmental system to work in the best long-term preservation interests of the citizenry. This habitual failure to enforce existing preservation laws can be seen in other spheres of Irish life as well. For example, the laxity in protecting and retaining Dublin's rich array of old shopfronts. Owing to the Dublin Corporation's liberal policy regarding major alterations of original shopfronts, many of the old commercial streets are fast losing their charming historic character. According to the Dublin Living City Group 'at the rate the old Dublin shopfronts are disappearing soon they'll all be gone'. There is even scant sanctity for the nation's archaeological sites. It is estimated by An Foras Forbartha that since the middle of the last century most counties have lost between 30–40 per cent, and in some areas as much as 60 per cent, of their archaeological heritage. In Ireland the maximum penalty for destruction of an archaeological site is a paltry £50, a ridiculously insignificant sum for so brutal a crime. In parts of rural Ireland prime agricultural land is now fetching over £4,000 an acre. Farmers and others are enticed into levelling archaeological earthworks on their property to gain great profit for cultivable acreage. There is also provision for a term of imprisonment up to six months for such a destructive act but it has never been invoked by the courts. As a predictable consequence, the destruction of Irish archaeological relics is carried out with almost certain immunity. The written consent by the Commissioners of Public Works to destroy an archaeological site of international importance at Wood Quay actually encourages citizens to ignore preservation legislation, since even the government seems to have no intention of enforcing it. The identical situation applies to the Georgian preservation scene; by conspicuously failing to honour and uphold even those preservation regulations that do exist, the government, in effect, invites developers and others to take bold liberties. Hence, there seems to be a verifiable *pattern* of governmental negligence toward past relics which realistically belong to all the people of Ireland.

A few preservation injunctions are admittedly troublesome for planning authorities. For example, under current policy the exteriors of protected Georgian buildings cannot be significantly changed. However, the question of exactly what constitutes 'significant alteration' of a façade is a delicate one; it is very much a matter of judgement. Here the guidelines clearly need to be more definitive for forceful application. The present lack of exacting restrictions permits owners to modify or mar their façades with great freedom. The Planning Authority does at least guard most listed Georgian properties against hideous structural change. But subtle aberrations on the Georgian fabric are constantly appearing. Cosmetic alterations on Georgian fronts are routinely made which, in their cumulative effect, severely blemish the streetscape. For instance, on a number of Georgian houses plastering has been applied over the original brickwork. In itself this act may seem innocent enough, but it visually destroys the continuity of texture that is so integral a part of the vista. Plastered surfaces are sometimes painted with incompatible colours, clashing with the adjacent natural brick tones. In Mount Pleasant Square one house in the centre of a graceful curved row has been plastered and painted in a garish purple, mutilating the harmonious spectrum of natural brick architecture. The Planning Authority should outlaw such acts since they violate the integrity of the larger architectural environment, cheapening neighbouring properties by their very presence. A similar distraction is the unrestrained application of name plates, signs and other assorted paraphernalia on Georgian faces. These changes, seemingly innocuous enough on their own, conspire to disfigure the existing symmetry and mood of the antique streetscape.

Traffic control along Georgian streets presents another enforcement problem. Simply stated, the bodies of most Georgian buildings are aged and brittle; they are very susceptible to cracking and other structural damage. Vehicular traffic, particularly that generated by large trucks, creates vibrations and pollution damaging to historic structures. For this reason, traffic has been declared a major menace in most Western European preservation districts; laws restrict the traffic flow to safe levels. An Taisce alluded to the fragility of the Georgian houses in its 1967 study and recommended reducing heavy traffic in order to minimize damaging vibrations. But the government still does not enforce such controls. Large vehicles freely rumble along the antiquated terraces emitting tremors potentially very destructive to the fracturable structures. Indeed, the Georgian streets are typically among the most traffic-clogged in all Dublin.

THE ROLE OF BORD FAILTE

A recurrent, and often impassioned, argument of preservationists is that the Irish Government has dismally failed to recognize and properly promote Georgian Dublin as a premier tourist attraction. Bord Failte (the Irish Tourist Board) is most commonly assailed for this omission. In the early 1960s the head of the Irish Georgian Society lamented that 'we are the only country in Europe that has not yet developed its architecture as a tourist asset'. He exhorted Bord Failte to attract the many 'civilized culture seekers' who roam Europe in quest of architectural and historical wonders. Two decades later, Bord Failte has failed to heed this plea. Curiously, throughout all Ireland there is a general disregard for cities as tourist attractions. Tourists, of course, use cities and towns as a base from which to explore nearby attractions. And there are certain mandatory sights within some cities which warrant visitation, such as monuments, museums, historic sites or parks. But most tourist guides on Irish towns are concerned primarily with the local political, literary or historical associations. As Patrick Shaffrey documents in *The Irish Town* it is a 'rare thing indeed' to find any significant reference to architectural and aesthetic qualities.

Bord Failte does not completely ignore the Georgian heritage but the proportion of attention devoted to this element, relative to all others, is minuscule. A cursory glance through the Bord's luxuriant literature reveals an identifiable set of tourist priorities. The Bord's handsomely illustrated 1980 tourist booklet *From Ireland With Love* serves as an illuminating index. This 30-page publication covers the spectrum of Ireland's major attractions. In terms of both photographs and text the emphasis is on landscapes, sporting and recreational pursuits, festivals, literary heritage and shopping jaunts. Architectural sights are not entirely forgotten. Two lavishly illustrated pages are given to Ireland's grand country mansions and castles—but Georgian Dublin is scarcely mentioned. In fact, the reader can find but one scant photograph of Baggot Street and the simple caption that Dublin's 'Georgian architecture gives it a predominantly eighteenth century atmosphere'. Hardly enticing lure for so richly endowed an area. This 'eighteenth century atmosphere' is neither described nor elaborated upon, despite the fact that many tourists could surely be induced to explore it with little effort.

Bord Failte is to be credited for some promotion of the Georgian city. In past years it has included several articles about the Georgian architecture in its magazine *Ireland of the Welcomes.* And its popular 'Doors of Dublin' poster is predominantly displayed throughout the country. Yet, the Bord's approach to the Georgian realm is essentially a superficial one in which the eighteenth-century architecture is mere 'stage scenery' to be dispassionately glimpsed and photographed for the record. There is no evidence of serious concern for what is to be discovered behind these antiquated façades. Given the opportunity, tourists would likely marvel at the delicate plasterwork which adorns Georgian interiors. Access to properly furnished Georgian houses could provide tourists with a unique view of an elegant past era. The North Great George's Street Preservation Society plans to open one of their restored houses for regular public visitation; this will have been accomplished without any encouragement or assistance from Bord Failte.

Bord Failte is surely one of the most professional and successful tourist organizations in Europe. Its organizational structure, management techniques and promotional campaigns are to be lauded. The problem, again, seems simply one of established priorities. Preservationists sometimes contend that the Bord should contribute financially to Georgian restoration and preservation. However, this is not their responsibility; nor are they funded to conduct such work. Their business is the promotion of tourism, not the upkeep of architecture. However, the Bord does have a responsibility to contribute to the cause of Georgian Dublin's welfare in other ways. As one of the country's statutory bodies which is provided with information about planning applications, the Bord is free to voice its opinions and objections. In past years the Bord played a productive 'watchdog' role in such vital matters. However, in more recent times it appears to have largely relinquished this valuable function. The Bord still officially voices support for urban preservation but in practice it has assumed a distinctly passive posture. It has been harshly criticized for allowing fine Georgian houses to disappear from the cityscape 'without so much as a murmur of dismay'. George Bagnall, manager of the Environment Department of Bord Failte, confesses that the Bord now subscribes to the general *laissez faire* philosophy held by so many public bodies; in essence, this is based on the conviction that Georgian preservation should be solely the 'role of private enterprise including individuals and organizations'. Because of its insouciant attitude toward the historic architecture, preservationists hold the Bord partly culpable for the attrition of the Georgian terraces.

Since Dublin could use an injection of additional tourist pounds, it seems like good business sense for the Bord to become more vigorously involved in developing the Georgian areas as a major attraction. But this would have to be accomplished with some sensitivity. There is little doubt that many more tourists could be enticed into sampling the Georgian grandeur. Yet it would be a mistake to popularize this heritage in carnivalesque fashion. At present, most tourists are hurried through the Georgian squares as part of a general city bus tour; there is scarcely opportunity for a hasty photograph. Certainly a more substantive treatment should be encouraged. However, it would not be desirable to draw the masses of tourists into these limited spatial enclaves. The environment, already clogged with vehicular traffic, could not withstand a pedestrian invasion. To maintain the 'prim and proper' dignity of the Georgian setting, the Bord would probably do best to seek deliberately a certain type of discriminating tourist. Bord Failte already caters to particular interests of special groups, such as sportsmen and convention delegates. They might well adapt some of their publicity efforts to the more culturally cultivated clientele. The Georgian architecture should be promoted and proudly displayed like any other national work of art. At present, tourists and even natives have limited access to the Georgian realm. Georgiana can be viewed superficially from the street but this hardly does it justice. There is no substitute for enjoying the splendorous interior features that reflect craftsmanship long forgotten. Discriminating visitors already seek to plumb the deeper charisma found behind reticent Georgian façades. Indeed, many occupants of the Georgian houses, both in private residence and office use, admit that they are often approached, or outright pestered, by inquisitive tourists eager for no more than a fleeting glimpse of their intriguing interiors. There certainly appears to be a ready made market for this untapped tourist attraction. A bit of imagination on the part of Bord Failte could reap wonders.

130

Two examples of infill architecture in Georgian areas: along Molesworth Street *(above)* new brick offices at left are fairly compatible in scale, design and proportion with the existing Georgian houses *(courtesy of American Geographical Society)*; by contrast, along St Stephen's Green *(below)* the modern offices at right visually clash with the two Georgian buildings at left

Some Georgian properties still retain their attractive backland plots with garden and mews building *(above)*, but many rear sections are being cannibalized for car parks and other development *(below)*

A QUESTION OF VIABILITY

Is the Irish Government's approach to preserving Dublin's imperilled Georgian architecture a viable one? In the light of past and present experience the answer must be an unqualified 'no'. Dublin restorationist architect and urban planner Uinseann MacEoin concludes:

> The Government can point to the conservation and restoration of a small number of showpiece buildings, usually ones connected with a patriotic event, but in all other cases it has not shown, or made preparation for, positive conservation. Free rein has been given to free market forces, frequently at great economic and social cost.

In its present form the Corporation's preservation policy, as stated in the Dublin Development Plan, is a lethargic proclamation. The Corporation lamely asserts that it is 'active in the struggle' to preserve the Georgian districts; in truth it is not much of a struggle. As admitted by one of the Corporation's planning assistants, there is 'no finance available to encourage people to preserve buildings and no legislation to ensure that the buildings are maintained'. Corporation staff members readily concede that, in reality, the preservation plan 'does not always function satisfactorily'. This is quite an understatement. The current preservation programme (if the term 'programme' can be validly used) is so frail that it cannot even maintain the status quo; each year more Georgian structures fall further into desuetude and decay or meet their untimely demise at the hands of greedy developers.

Ireland's preservation plan may have been honourably conceived but it has been dismally executed. Any preservation programme based on a deficient listing system, unenforceable (or simply unenforced) planning controls, neglect of interiors and a total absence of financial funding is doomed to failure; indeed, it is a mockery. At best, there exists in Dublin a timid preventive strategy of trying to protect the Georgian stock by half-heartedly implementing a series of inherently weak development controls. By all standards of western preservation theory, this approach is a distinctly *negative* one. Preventive devices are, of course, an important part of all urban preservation schemes; but never are they the *only* component—as in Ireland. Restrictive regulations adopted by the Dublin Planning Authority to discourage or prohibit disruptive development along the Georgian terraces are helpful; hopefully they will prevent radical alteration of the streetscapes. But they do absolutely nothing to actually assist in restoring and preserving the buildings. What Dublin so

133

desperately needs is a *positive* preservation strategy as found in North America and Western Europe. This demands dynamic government leadership backed by a financial commitment to ensure restoration and maintenance of all buildings listed for preservation. The Irish Government sponsors no such ambitious scheme for architectural rejuvenation. The only positive preservation currently conducted in the city is that carried out by the Irish Georgian Society, the North Great George's Street Preservation Society and similar groups.

If Georgian preservation is to become a reality rather than remaining a limp utopian ideal, Irish officialdom must exhibit ingenuity. For example, for the past two decades the government could have been working in fruitful partnership with private developers and investors to create mutually beneficial urban renewal schemes in the Georgian areas. It is precisely this sort of joint strategy between government and the private sector that has worked so effectively elsewhere in western society. Experience in innumerable western cities has shown that blighted sections of the historic core can be miraculously rehabilitated by the insertion of pieces of 'healthy urban tissue into the deserts'. New shops, residential units or office developments, harmoniously integrated, serve as magnets attracting further redevelopment by the private sector. However, it is typically up to government agencies to make something happen. This regenerative process is usually initiated by the provision of grants, loans or tax relief. The north Georgian areas are ripe for such a rebirth. But the continuing unwillingness of the government to provide positive impetus contributes to further decay and reinforces the undesirable status of the poorer Georgian sections in the eyes of potential developers.

Instead of initiating a healthy joint endeavour with private enterprise, the Irish Government has basically left the redevelopment of Dublin almost entirely to the whims of property speculators. The result has been catastrophic as the government's passivity over the past twenty years invited abuse of the Georgian streets. It is quite evident that many developers do not take preservation policy and planning controls seriously. In most other European countries developers would not dare to take such liberties with the nation's architectural heritage. By comparison with the rigidly enforced dictates in neighbouring countries, preservation in Ireland is a sham. The Dublin preservation scene begs for governmental dynamism, leadership, imagination and tangible support. What the government has offered preservationists to date is tokenism, pure and simple.

134

Notes

1 'The Destruction of Dublin', *Irish Times*, 23 January 1981, p13
2 McDonald, Frank. 'Dublin—What Went Wrong?' *Irish Times*, 15 November 1979, p14
3 *Dublin Development: Preservation and Change*, (Dublin: A Draft Interim Report prepared by Llewelyn-Davies, Weeks, Forestier-Walker and Bor for the Dublin Corporation, January, 1967), p7
4 Fox, Kevin. 'European Perspective', *Architectural Conservation: An Irish Viewpoint* (Architectural Association of Ireland, 1974), p69
5 *Dublin Development: Preservation and Change, op cit*, p9
6 *Dublin City Development Plan—1971* (Dublin: Government Stationery Office, 1971), p23
7 Barry, T. B. 'The Destruction of Irish Archaeological Monuments', *Irish Geography*, Vol 12, 1979, p113

8
The Pragmatic Approach to Preservation

For Dubliners, the Georgian districts 'present a focus for identity. Even where they have lost completely their social relevance and are juxtaposed in ruins between buildings modern and insensitive their good manners seem to exist still . . . their retiring, unobtrusive, and well-bred natures indicating a respect for political and social forms no longer fashionable and a faith in the rational nature of man no longer justified.'[1]

THE PRESERVATION CONCEPT

Preservation should not be conceived as a kind of petrification of antiquated relics. Historic buildings need not be 'museumized' in some suspended state of mummification—especially Georgian houses which evoke such a lively past. They deserve to be reanimated and put to some meaningful use. One of the most challenging aspects of the entire urban problem-solving process is the need to find viable contemporary functions for preservable buildings. But sensibly integrating houses of the past into the present and future is no easy task. It demands imagination and ingenuity.

The preservation concept may be inherently idealistic, but it also has its distinctly practical aspects. This dual character is particularly evident in the restoration-preservation process itself. When it comes to deciding what types of physical restoration and preservation techniques should be applied, there is a healthy range of ideas and attitudes. Important questions arise. How best to restore preservable structures? Once saved, to what uses should such buildings be put? Is the functional conversion of historic houses to non-residential use a legitimate form of preservation? What kinds of architectural 'infill' are acceptable in a preservation district? Do neo-Georgian reproductions serve a constructive or destructive role? Exactly what constitutes the proper or most appropriate approach to preservation is a debatable subject among architects, urban planners and preservationists since all share a keen interest in Dublin's redevelopment.

For the sake of simplicity, it may be said that there are two approaches to Georgian preservation in Dublin: the *pragmatic* and the *purist*. The first method accepts the practicality of converting old houses to new economic uses; the second (which will be examined in the following chapter) favours complete authentic restoration and a return to original function. Preservationists recognize the genuine need for both types; thus, they embrace certain precepts from the two approaches in what might best be termed preservation 'realism'. In its 1967 report An Taisce also endorsed both the pragmatic and the purist forms of preservation, so long as the basic architectural character of the greater unit is retained. It is on this most important point that Irish preservationists seem in complete agreement—that in historic quarters the 'genius of locality' resides in the *whole of it*, not only in its finest elements. An Taisce stated unequivocally that the Georgian areas must be considered to have high architectural merit as an *entity*. While the quality of individual buildings may vary, the intrinsic value is to be found in the 'unity of the whole, and it is this unity that should be preserved'. To preserve a few select buildings to be left in unhappy isolation as others around them remain in ruin or dereliction is hardly a sensible solution. For precisely this reason, preservationists are dedicated to protecting the *precinctual character* of Georgian Dublin. This can only be accomplished by restoring and pre-serving entire Georgian streetscapes (or what may be left of the vista), not reviving sequestered fragments in an incoherent manner. Though this is the ideal it is not always attainable.

THE ECONOMICS OF PRESERVATION

If a Georgian house cannot be puristically restored and returned to private occupation, the most acceptable compromise becomes conversion to non-residential uses. This is an economically rational solution because at present the cost of purchasing, restoring and maintaining Georgian properties, without any financial assistance from the state, is prohibitive for most Dubliners. Thus, the only realistic chance of salvation for most Georgian houses rests with their acquisition by private companies, professional firms or government bodies for whom preservation *is* a financially viable proposition. They not only possess the capital with which to purchase a Georgian building, but the cost of restoration and maintenance can be used as a valuable tax credit.

When conversion occurs, the architectural form is saved but the original function, residential use, must be sacrificed. An Taisce recognized this reality fifteen years ago when it noted the 'special attraction and potential' of Georgian houses for office space and actually recommended that this utilization be encouraged in order to maintain stable property values for the historic areas. This conversion philosophy is also wholly consistent with the guiding principles of the 1975 Amsterdam Declaration, favouring the unobtrusive adaptation of historic buildings to new functions which fit the needs of contemporary urban life, providing that such transformation does not impair the architectural or aesthetic character.

In a highly inflationary age the rejuvenation and recycling of old buildings assumes new logic. Indeed, throughout the western realm the concept of restoration and preservation has gained considerable appeal in recent years, based primarily on its fiscal merits. In the United States reviving fine old buildings is no longer a fad but a mission that is sweeping American architecture. In Dublin it used to be more profitable simply to demolish an aged structure and build a new one on the cleared site. However, escalating construction costs, based on both material and labour, have changed this situation. Now, rehabilitation of Georgian houses is normally cheaper than demolition and rebuilding (in some cases this is not true and the margin between the two can be quite slim). Furthermore, owing to their thick-walled construction, many eighteenth-century dwellings are more energy efficient than modern buildings. Since Georgian conversion often involves a degree of restoration, there is yet another positive factor to be weighed; work on old buildings is very labour intensive in Dublin, generating a far higher rate of employment than new construction. It also serves to resurrect and maintain older crafts and trades. In this sense, conversion and restoration are healthy for the larger urban economy.

The market value of Georgian houses is based on several important factors: a shrinking Georgian housing stock, physical condition of surviving properties, size and location, potential for backland development, quality of interior features and perceived prestige. Values are always determined by a combination of these factors, but essentially it is a classic textbook case of the law of supply and demand. Owing to a dwindling supply and insatiable demand, the highest value uses predictably win out. All economic realities favour office/commercial occupation and militate against residential use.

Dublin's stock of eighteenth-century houses has been depleted by about 40 per cent over the past two decades, due chiefly to decay and demolition. This includes an estimated 437 prime List 1-type houses simply eliminated from the scene. The greatest number of casualties have been along the less visible, and thus more vulnerable, secondary Georgian streets adjoining major squares and terraces. Loss of buildings in the hardcore Georgian districts has been around 10 per cent. If current trends continue, another 240 Georgian properties will disappear by the end of the century. Although there are approximately 1,400 Georgian houses on the government's two preservation lists, if one considers the integrity of both exterior and interior there may not be more than 763 truly intact eighteenth-century houses left in all Dublin.

The physical condition of surviving properties determines the potential for conversion and strongly affects their value on the market. Since Georgian structures are between 150 and 250 years old, the processes of deterioration and disintegration have long been at work; yet most have held up remarkably well. Despite some flaws in their original construction, most were strongly built—but they clearly show wear and tear. The most common signs of deterioration are found in roofs, chimney stacks, brick walls, doorways and granite steps. The most persistent problem over the years has been water penetration in roofs, exterior walls and basements. Simple neglect of roofs has caused the most damage. This is especially troublesome because, owing to the unified terrace system, water seepage in one roof often leads to damage in neighbouring buildings. Dampness entering the bases of parapets has led to serious brick decay on the majority of Georgian houses, requiring the renewal of upper parts of main walls. This is quite evident from viewing the contrasting brickwork atop most of Dublin's Georgian buildings. Dry rot is another common ailment, though often exaggerated. Developers have long used the cry of dry rot to conjure up plague-like visions in the minds of planning authorities in the hope that they will panic and issue demolition orders. Actually, most dry rot can be fully corrected. Unfortunately there is no 'medical record' on the anatomy of individual Georgian houses from which to deduce their past ills. But careful inspection shows that most have been denied any programme of regular maintenance and often repairs have been of the patchwork variety. Nonetheless, serious structural decay is far more rare than many people, including some architects, imagine and most Georgian houses are definitely restorable. With the proper doses of money and skill, almost any eighteenth-century building in Dublin can be resuscitated and made to last indefinitely.

As the Georgian houses have continued to decline in number, their value has risen—like that of any vanishing species. In fact, the rocketing value of Georgian properties has been phenomenal. In 1905 a Georgian house in Fitzwilliam Square sold for about £550. With the onset of the office revolution in the early 'sixties prices soared; they rose even more dramatically during the 'seventies as competition for office space intensified. Between 1970 and 1974 the price of a typical Merrion Square property increased from £30,000 to £90,000. On the current market a good Georgian building south of the Liffey commonly fetches between £250,000 and £400,000. Such values effectively eliminate opportunities for individuals to buy the properties as private residences. And the income from letting Georgian property in the south for residential flats is less than half that to be earned from renting it as office space. In many European cities, such as London, there is great demand for expensive or luxury flats in the inner city; no such high-clientele market exists in central Dublin, so there is no incentive to develop high-value Georgian rental units around the squares.

Since market value is also directly related to urban location, the Georgian dwellings in the north 'wasteland' sell for far less. Little more than a decade ago dilapidated but fully restorable houses around Mountjoy Square, Henrietta Street and North Great George's Street could be purchased for as little as £3,000 to £5,000. Today the price is between £20,000 and £40,000—still a bargain when compared to the south side. The importance of location is not limited to the north/south dichotomy; it is also a matter of specific streets and neighbourhoods in Dublin which have become strongly stereotyped as respectable or unrespectable, desirable or undesirable. As a consequence, individual houses in certain sections tend to enjoy or suffer a collective fate. For example, an inferior house nestled fortuitously along a prime Georgian street will always benefit from its immediate proximity to prosperity, commanding a higher price than it justly deserves. Conversely, a quality house along a substandard row is usually viewed as an anomaly, priced far below its true value. Along North Great George's Street a magnificently restored Georgian house will bring no more than about £80,000. But if it had the good fortune to be located in the fashionable south squares it would surely bring at least £300,000. Therefore individual market values are often distorted by the 'associative' factor based on proximity and shared imagery. In one sense, high prices have a positive effect since they encourage proper rehabilitation and maintenance. One would hardly pay a small fortune for a Georgian property and neglect its upkeep. Of

(above) Georgian restorationists must cope with badly corroded exterior brick-work and plasterwork; (below) scraping the paint and grime off a doorway with a blowtorch can take several weeks of labour

An example of the artistic
designs found on coal-hole
covers in the Georgian areas

Two examples of the boot-
scrapers still found beside
many Georgian entrances

(*above*) Along Henrietta Street one can still find fine examples of creative ironwork over 200 years old; (*below*) unfortunately, much ironwork has been neglected and is now in an advanced state of corrosion — yet there is still elegance in the decay

course, this same principle works against the historic architecture in the north; here low property values can tolerate and even breed dereliction and decay. The conspicuously empty gaps left for years along north-side Georgian rows would never be found in the south districts.

CONVERTING OLD HOUSES TO NEW USES

There are three general uses to which Georgian houses can be converted: office, commercial and institutional. There are no statistical records documenting the number of Georgian properties in various uses. The most accurate, albeit tedious, index to building occupation is gained through field inquiry and consultation with urban planners. A visual survey of the streets on a building-by-building basis is the most reliable indicator of property use. Even this is an imperfect system since not all façades tell, or even hint, of their interior use. Those devoid of any external identification stand as enigmatic figures. But most Georgian buildings are conveniently emblazoned with brass post-boxes and name-plates testifying to their occupational use. In terms of total space utilization within Georgian buildings, there is a notable disparity between the north and south city:

	South Dublin		*North Dublin*
	per cent		*per cent*
office	60	office	20
residential	20	residential	18
institutional	15	institutional	22
commercial	5	commercial	40

(These statistics are based on extensive field research, consultation with urban planners and city architects, and information contained in the Dublin Architectural Study Group's 1981 Georgian survey report.)

The south is discernibly more 'high-brow' and there is an ever-increasing demand for prestigious Georgian offices, especially among the growing professional classes. The Georgian-scape is dotted with the name-plates of doctors, lawyers, accountants, engineers, architects, publishers and consultants. Medical and legal professions are especially

(*opposite*) Restorationists face a daunting challenge since many eighteenth-century interiors are in appalling physical condition with crumbling brickwork, gaping holes in floors and ceilings, and dry rot (*courtesy of Irish Architectural Archive*)

enamoured with the eighteenth-century offices which create the aura of exclusivity they commonly seek. Such dignified surroundings instil in their clients a sense of confidence and security (and perhaps provide justification for their high fees). Georgian office space is also ideal for many small to middle-size Irish companies who wish to establish a 'swanky' corporate image. High-ceilinged, elegantly plastered, chandelier-lit Georgian rooms overlooking beautifully landscaped squares are perfect for executive suites, conference rooms, libraries and visitors' quarters. A host of government bodies are also housed in Georgian buildings around the squares and along the major streets. About one in every seven properties is in some type of institutional use. Schools and institutions usually occupy the larger houses. A fair number of buildings have also been converted to foreign embassies. The relatively few commercial enterprises that have gained a grip in their area tend to be fashionable shops such as wine merchants, antique dealers, expensive boutiques and exclusive restaurants. Although about 20 per cent of the Georgian space is still in residential use, there are probably not more than 1,000 people still living in the hardcore Georgian areas, a source of increased concern to those interested in the living city concept. In south Dublin about half the Georgian buildings are devoted exclusively to office use and perhaps 15 per cent in solely residential occupation. About a quarter are in some form of mixed use, mostly office-residential. A number of professionals, business executives and institutional officers choose to live in their work building as a matter of convenience. Ordinarily, this residential content is found on the upper floors or the basement where room size is more suitable and there is greater privacy. Despite the constant demand for office space, there is a brisk turnover of occupiers and Georgian properties are regularly on the market. There are many reasons for such transition. Doctors are increasingly finding it to their advantage to leave the Georgian squares to be nearer to new suburban hospitals and clinics. Government bodies and private companies often simply outgrow their Georgian quarters. Others develop new staffing and equipment needs that are inappropriate for Georgian space. When Georgian properties are put on the market, they usually sell rapidly, since in Dublin there is a growth of small private firms which fit conveniently into several thousand feet of prime urban space.

The north Georgian zone has quite a different occupational content, clearly reflecting its less respectable status. Streets between Parnell Square and Mountjoy Square have a markedly lower socio-economic component, characterized by a scattering of cheap shops, retail outlets, bed-and-breakfast accommodations, moderately priced hotels and small businesses. Office space, which accounts for only about 20 per cent of the total Georgian content, is more functional than prestigious. The better-preserved sides of the two squares are occupied by assorted government agencies, firms' offices and private insititutions or organizations (such as religious orders, labour groups and various clubs). The residential content is chiefly comprised of tenants and lower-income groups. Low market value of these Georgian buildings does not encourage investment in restoration and maintenance.

It is worth noting that the concept of Georgian conversion has recently been applied to one of Dublin's most distinguished edifices, Powerscourt House. Built by Lord Powerscourt in 1774 as his town house, this elegant eighteenth-century mansion possesses superb plasterwork ceilings and walls. In 1980, Power Securities Ltd undertook a £3m project hailed as a 'sensitive adaptive re-use of a listed building'. Both courtyard buildings and main house have been changed into a series of tasteful shops and restaurants quite compatible with the historic character of the setting. It is surely one of the most imaginative developments on the current Dublin scene, and it is hoped that the Powerscourt complex will eventually become one of the city's major shopping and tourist attractions.

Although the conversion of Georgian houses to profitable new uses is a sensible economic solution to the problem of preservation, it is not without its severe penalties. Indeed, the adaptive process has taken a great toll on the architectural integrity of the Georgian system, both within and without. Corporate and professional owners are not usually inclined to alter façades in any appreciable form—though the name-plates and post-boxes so liberally installed do constitute a sort of visual blight. But interiors often suffer a terrible fate. Since they are not officially listed for preservation or inspected by authorities, they are susceptible to abuse and may be changed at mere whim. When a Georgian house undergoes conversion to office or commercial use, functionalism is usually the dominant theme. This commonly means the installation of lifts, bathrooms, staff kitchen units, fire escapes, heating and air conditioning systems, lighting panels and bulky office equipment. Such modern contrivances are admittedly necessary in many cases, but too often the process of transformation is insensitive and tasteless, resulting in profound changes within the body of old buildings. Doorways are expanded, false ceilings erected, fireplaces stripped or blocked up and staircases removed. Many major alterations are of an irreversible nature, meaning that there will never be an opportunity to restore the house to its original state. The adulteration of Georgian interiors is greatly accentuated when several adjoining properties happen to fall into the hands of the same developer. This always strikes fear in the heart of preservationists—with good reason. Past experience shows that there is always a strong temptation to remove joining walls and mould the separate houses into a single 'more efficient' functioning unit. When this is done, it annihilates the original scale and proportion and all sense of building individuality is irretrievably lost.

No less distressing is the cruel treatment accorded the Georgian backlands. The spacious, linear plots behind the main buildings have always been an integral part of the architectural system. They provide open air, sunlight and garden space through which the tight-knit Georgian terraces freely breathe. In the north city over the past half century, large portions of these strips have been sold off as space for small factories, shops and repair centres. Consequently, Georgian houses along such streets as North Great George's retain only 50–75ft of garden space. South of the Liffey most of the backlands, which are typically 200–300ft in length, have been retained, but this is fast changing. With the intensification of office development, rising property values and worsening traffic congestion, these expansive areas of unbuilt urban land have become an extremely valuable asset in terms of overall market value and development potential. Where once existed neat rows of pleasant residential gardens, there is rapidly developing an ugly conglomeration of structural extensions, car parks, storage sites and scrap yards. It is now common practice in the Merrion Square, Fitzwilliam Square and Fitzwilliam Street area freely to add extensions on to the main house to augment utility space. This may take the form of exterior lift shafts, bathrooms, kitchens or entire rooms. Behind every Georgian row there is now some tandem development which severely alters the natural proportions, spatial pattern and visual appearance of the backlands. Some extensions are modest but others jut out crudely like malformed limbs. Though the Planning Authority allows such appendages, it does at least try to limit their size. Under what is known as the 'rights of light' regulation, no gargantuan additions are permitted which would appreciably diminish the amount of light received by neighbouring buildings.

By far the most destructive development has been the widespread cannibalization of backlands for car parks. Competition for parking space has reached Darwinian proportions around the Georgian squares, and property owners have resorted to paving over their entire garden plot to provide guaranteed parking spaces for their staff, clients and visitors. Years ago it was usually only the executives who drove cars to their jobs; now the masses own private vehicles. Since a single Georgian building can employ up to fifty people, parking space is at a premium. Appalling though it may be, there has even been the suggestion that the central area of the Georgian squares be converted into car parks to alleviate the problem.

The mews buildings at the extremity of the backland plots are also seriously threatened. Originally they served as carriage houses but they constitute a distinctive architectural style that deserves to be preserved. Most of the mews buildings in the north Georgian sections have been destroyed but in the south about half still remain. Many have been sold to a different owner and now have their own separate economic identity. The majority have been changed into car repair and service centres, wholesale merchants, appliance and repair shops, and a scattering of small offices and restaurants. Nearly a third of the mews buildings are vacant—a senseless waste in the midst of a city experiencing furious redevelopment. About 25 per cent of the buildings are in residential use. Some of these have been starkly modernized but a surprising number still hold their eighteenth-century charm. Indeed, the mews territory constitutes a curious and fascinating 'underworld' of Dublin. The little lanes are usually bustling with activity and the present-day occupants of the old carriage houses keep up small flower and vegetable gardens and even sometimes raise doves and chickens, giving a rural flavour to the inner-city backlands. Unfortunately, this exotic realm is often missed by pedestrians because the small mews lanes (with such quaint names as 'Lad Lane') are sequestered from major thoroughfares by high stone walls and archways. Thus, for most Dubliners it remains a hidden mini-world.

INFILL ARCHITECTURE IN GEORGIAN AREAS

Dublin . . . is like a man who once had a perfect set of teeth and some have fallen out and been replaced by wooden false teeth.[2]

One of the most delicate problems in the field of urban preservation is that of infill architecture in historic districts. Infill architecture means any new buildings inserted in a built environment. Dublin's infill record is a rather dismal one. Some classic streets have been ruined by acts of infill barbarism. This is quite apparent along O'Connell Street. Originally, the street was predominantly residential with a scattering of small shops to serve the populace. Its once-dignified mien has been replaced by a 'honky-tonk mix' of gaudy recreation centres, fast-food joints, sleezy restaurants, banks, cinemas and department stores. The result is a 'featureless, insipid, even hideous' streetscape.[3] Some streets bordering St Stephen's Green have suffered a similar fate; a few seem to be in a state of constant flux. Around St Stephen's the injudicious juxtaposition of glaring glass and steel cubical structures next to reticent Georgian neighbours elicits disdainful glances. Indeed, these strikingly contemporary office buildings jammed cheek by jowl with the eighteenth-century architecture tend to make both look out of place—the modern brazen and the old shabby. Such infill is simply an affront to good architectural mores. It is also a textbook example of insensitive urban planning. Banks and insurance companies have been the chief despoilers of old Dublin; of all the vandals that have preyed on the historic city, none are guiltier. Their gleaming new offices seem always out of style and scale with the surroundings. The role played by banks and insurance companies in Dublin's redevelopment is both curious and unfortunate, because as prosperous and influential bodies they are in a position to set a positive example. In fact, in many other western countries it is the banks and insurance firms that promote preservation and sponsor urban renewal. In Dublin they too often set a negative precedent.

In Georgian Dublin the need for infill arises when a building has deteriorated beyond redemption or has been demolished, leaving a gap in the terrace. The infill problem is especially acute north of the Liffey and along such south streets as Harcourt and Leeson where dereliction and demolition are at their worst. How best to plug the voids is crucial to the integrity of the surviving streetscape. Sympathetic infill has the capacity to contribute to precinctual preservation. Conversely, inappropriate infill has the potential to corrupt the historic fabric. These important decisions are too often left in the hands of developers motivated by profit rather than aesthetics. Preservationists have to monitor their proposals and protest against their actions when they threaten the existing environment. Since Georgian terraces were designed as a unified architectural entity, the principal concern is for their continuing cohesion. If the continuity is broken by an open space or contradictory building, the symmetry is visually impaired.

Basically, infill can take three forms: reproduction, sympathetic contrast or 'alien' architecture. The first type seeks to recreate a new structure that closely resembles the original. The second involves

150

integrating a new kind of architectural unit into the existing pattern but without perceptibly clashing with older adjacent structures. Alien infill refers to architecture that fails to harmonize with, or completely violates, the surrounding environment. Any good infill requires sensitivity as well as some humility on the part of architects and developers. This is especially true in historic quarters where it is difficult to match the antiquated setting with modern insets. Preservationists may accept or merely tolerate the first two types of infill, but they regard the third as perverse and unconscionable. Of course, exactly what constitutes 'sympathetic' as opposed to 'alien' architecture can be a highly subjective matter. For example, the ESB building is certainly an abrupt visual departure from the adjoining eighteenth-century houses, yet it is relatively harmonious in terms of scale, colour and texture. Some preservationists find it more objectionable than others, but all agree that a more horrifying structure could have sprouted on the site.

Sympathetic infill architecture in the Georgian areas might depart in style and design but it should at least be reasonably compatible with the indigenous scale, texture and colour. This means closely conforming to Georgiana's vertical four-storey scale and its typical horizontal scale (between 25–30ft). These traditional dimensions are not conducive to modern streamlined office units. Therefore, instead of replacing an individual Georgian building with a new one of identical size, the tendency has been to implant a single larger office block where previously several structures stood. This is more economically efficient since it creates greater space for office use; but it also changes the functional scale of the street. The ESB building is a solitary block occupying space formerly held by sixteen individual Georgian houses. This type of massive modern infill does not allow for individual articulation of façades consistent with the eighteenth-century tradition. In terms of colour and texture Georgian Dublin is, of course, the product of its bricked façades. The various hues of mellow brickwork render a warm tonal impression. The granite facing provides variety without distraction. Modern bricks for infill architecture can be used to blend naturally with the old, providing consistency. An effort to maintain at least some semblance of colour and textural harmony is seen along Molesworth Street where new offices have been faced with a shade of brick which, though not perfectly in agreement with the original scene, is at least relatively inoffensive to the eye. Far worse is architectural infill made of reflective glass and steel, as constructed around St Stephen's, which completely violates the original Georgian brick and stone setting.

THE NEO-GEORGIAN REPRODUCTION SOLUTION

> If this policy [Georgian reproduction] persisted it could
> ultimately lead to absurdity and we would be left with a wild-
> west-saloon-front Dublin.[4]

One of the most controversial developments on Dublin's preservation
scene has been the appearance of neo-Georgian, or pseudo-Georgian,
buildings. Preservationists have found it disquieting that this facile reproduction solution has gained such acceptance and popularity over the past
decade. They place much of the blame on the 1963 Planning Act and on
the Dublin planning authorities; both view the city as essentially just a
collection of façades. This superficial attitude has provided a permissive
climate for reproduction.

The two major types of Georgian architectural reproduction are
replication and *pastiche*. There are important differences. Replication is an
attempt to duplicate the original structure by producing a facsimile or a
nearly exact copy. Pastiche is really a form of architectural eclecticism, a
'medley made up of various sources composed in the general style' of the
original. Rather than an honest attempt at imitation, it is a fake creation
of something ostensibly 'Georgian'. As one detractor caustically
proclaimed, pastiche architecture is no more than the 'gratuitous
assembly of dead parts'—charging that the use of pastiche façades is
'positively wrong and destructive to the very values which it lamely tries
to save . . . a simulacrum of everything that the 18th century builders
achieved'.

It is considerably more difficult to judge Georgian replicas because they
vary so greatly in quality and authenticity. Good replicas always
subscribe to fundamental Georgian tenets of design, proportion and
differentiated window size. Some boast of fine detail and exterior
ornamentation. A few replicated façades even bear the old stone tablet
from the original house identifying its eighteenth-century birth date
(though this often befuddles the public). But the nuances of brickwork,
doorway treatment, window configuration, chimney stacks and
ironwork are exceedingly difficult to duplicate with accuracy. There are
few Irish architects sufficiently educated in the intricacies of the classical
eighteenth-century style to produce first-rate copies. As a result, even
honest attempts tend to be 'full of fruitless ambiguity', suffering from a
lack of understanding of the Georgian balance between uniformity and
variation. In an obvious attempt to economize, some builders even resort

152

to using fibreglass door-frames and plastic glass in their reproductions. Since it is so difficult to create a successful Georgian replica, many preservationists actually feel that, rather than inserting a poorly crafted imitation, it is often preferable to have an 'honest' contrasting structure so long as there is a basic compatibility.

The best streets for examining Georgian reproductions are Leeson, Baggot, Harcourt and Hume. But even the finest imitations are usually betrayed by some irregularity, such as a penthouse obtruding atop the skyline or a conspicuous flaw in window or entrance design. Viewed from the proper angle, some mock-Georgian façades reveal a sprawling modern office complex behind. Such examples can be found along Harcourt Street. Not even the most authentic-appearing reproduction can pass the scrutiny of a simple glimpse within. It is this odd incongruity between exterior and interior that most distresses 'conscience-stricken' architects and preservationists. There is rarely any attempt to create an eighteenth-century motif inside a neo-Georgian building. Most display low ceilings, functional partitions, and modern furniture and lighting panels—a typical contemporary office setting devoid of distinction or charm. To have such a drearily ordinary interior masked by a replicated Georgian façade seems at once a contradiction of ideology and form—there is something disturbingly unnatural about it. One almost feels a sense of embarrassment at having made the discovery.

The debate over the virtue and vices of Georgian reproduction is likely to intensify over the next decade since they are fast becoming accepted as a glib solution to what should be a stimulating and challenging problem. To be sure, neo-Georgian has its advantages. It is fairly easy to produce and is infinitely preferable to an utterly alien building that might be inserted in its place. Few would deny that bogus Georgian is at least more tolerable than ultra-modern steel and glass façades. Yet the case against neo-Georgian is argued eloquently and persuasively by Professor Edward McParland of Trinity College.[5] He points out that what reproductions most lack is the essential Georgian element of eccentricity that imbued eighteenth-century architecture with its spirited vitality. Although such originality can hardly be recaptured, it is suggested that replication could at least gain some respectability if there was greater attention to articulation of façade features and some preservation of original room height, proportions and structural systems. But McParland opines that to demand eighteenth-century façades for modern office interiors is to 'call eventually for a city of stage sets'. This concern is echoed by a noted Dublin journalist who expresses the fear that, if present trends are allowed to continue, it is 'almost certain that in ten years time Harcourt Street will consist of nothing but pastiche buildings'. If this indeed occurs, it will be due in large part to what has been termed the 'misguided policy' of Dublin Corporation. The Corporation has a liberal policy toward sham façades which, in the censorious words of one critic, can realistically only please the 'galloping horseman and the economist'.

Perhaps the major objection to Georgian reproductions is simply that they are deceitful, that they 'con the public' and 'dilute the value of the valid survivor from the past'.[6] To some, this is a quasi-moral issue. However, it also has its practical implications. Solecisms in design and technique may be readily discernible to the trained eye but they can easily escape detection by neophytes. Thus, it is an alarming thought that future generations of Dubliners might possibly take these architectural frauds for the originals—as tourists so commonly do already. But there is a more immediate and serious problem with reproduction. At a time when it is crucial to educate the Dublin citizenry in the ways of responsible preservation, the gimmicky falsification approach tends to muddle minds and confuse values. Maurice Craig affirms that damage has already been done by the 'confusion between the desire to conserve the masterpieces of the past and the desire to produce counterfeit copies'. At precisely the moment in Dublin's history when a clear vision is needed for the protection of the Georgian heritage, public perceptions are being blurred as to the real meaning and value of Georgian preservation. Plainly stated, preservation needs to be *truthful* if it is to be comprehended and supported by the public.

Georgian reproduction does have its proper place; the question is one of quality and quantity. An unrestrained temptation to rely on convenient reproductions can be dangerous. An unchecked dissemination of pseudo-Georgian buildings throughout the city would be abominable. Indeed, there have been proposals for the building of entire terraces of replicated Georgian houses in the inner city. The result would be falsified streetscapes sadly devoid of architectural and cultural integrity. There must be strict control in terms of number, quality and location. Such restrictions would have to be imposed by the Dublin Corporation. Ideally, replicas should be used sparingly and only in the most strategic slots. An authentically crafted replica does have the potential to contribute toward the preservation of streetscape symmetry and continuity if plugged into a barren gap. But scrupulous attention should be devoted to eighteenth-century architectural style. To ensure this, guidance and leadership must come from Ireland's architectural colleges.

A fascinating corollary to the inner-city Georgian reproduction trend has been the spate of neo-Georgian housing estates throughout the greater Dublin region. This recent development warrants attention because it is testimony to the increasing acceptance and respectability accorded the Georgian style in contemporary Irish life. The nascent affection of Dubliners for chic pseudo-Georgian living quarters blossomed during the 'seventies as something of a fad; it has now reached almost cult proportions. It is reasoned that the 'cult of neo-Georgian houses . . . has arisen largely from the conservationist agitation over the Georgian heritage'.[7] Whatever its impetus, the idea of 'civilized' residence in a 'Georgian' house seems to have captured the fancy of many middle-income Irish. Neo-Georgian housing estates in such places as Celbridge, Foxrock, Castleknock and Kildare are prospering. In 1980, a new neo-Georgian town-house estate was opened in Grosvenor Park. These new homes and town houses typically sell for between £50,000 and £60,000. Builders unabashedly entice prospective buyers with advertisements claiming that 'our construction methods are 264 years behind the times' and 'we make it our business to build them much the same way as the Georgians built theirs'. Discriminating buyers can live in a new home featuring 'Georgian-style balustraded stairways' and 'Adam style' fireplaces. The neo-Georgian craze has even filtered into the do-it-yourself market. Hardware and other utility stores now stock fake plastic Georgian door-frames, false plaster-like ceiling decorations, and imitation plasterwork mouldings and fireplace fixtures. Georgiana on a modest budget! All this is innocent enough and preservationists seem more amused than offended. Derided one observer, the present rash of 'Georgian' housing estates and villages in the outer suburbs is 'faintly ridiculous but relatively harmless to anyone but a demented purist'.

Notes

1 McGovern, Sean. '18th Century and the Present', *Irish Times*, 22 October 1976, p10
2 'Dublin's Changed—But They're Terrible Changes', *Irish Independent*, 31 August 1980, p5
3 Walker, Robin, and Woulfe, Stephen. 'Street Infill: The Centre', *Dublin—A City in Crisis* (The Royal Institute of Architects of Ireland, 1975), p39
4 Barry, Francis. 'Reproduction: For and Against', in *Dublin—A City in Crisis, op cit,* p54
5 McParland, Edward. 'The Case Against Neo-Georgian', *Irish Times*, 14 August 1974, p10
6 Cuffe, Luan. 'Indicators', *Architectural Conservation: An Irish Viewpoint* (Architectural Association of Ireland, 1974), p6
7 Grogan, Dick. 'Conservation "threat" to Modern Design', *Irish Times*, 18 November 1975

9
The Purist Approach to Restoration and Preservation

Ambling along a Georgian street is rather like entering a magical timewarp—'listen and you'll hear the murmur of ghosts . . . the soft and poignant clamour of the past. And in the air when you're passing by you'll hear the gentle heartbeat of yesterday. You might also hear the ghostly tinkle of a piano from some musical evening long ago when, in a street like this, Dublin was an elegant lady and every evening was enchanted.'[1]

THE PURIST IDEAL

Preservation exalts the human spirit—especially when conducted in its purest form. The purist approach is the most idyllic and challenging. Those who expound its virtues usually do so with great fervour. Based on the ideals of authenticity and traditionalism, it is regarded as the most 'honest' treatment of historic architecture. Architecture lovingly restored in the purist tradition also tends to be the most revered and enduring.

Purist philosophy holds that even if a Georgian building is meticulously restored in the physical sense, its true ethos cannot be recaptured unless it is also returned to its indigenous use, that of a private residence. This functional authenticity is always a vital concern. Therefore, the purist approach demands faithful restoration of both *form* and *function*. The eighteenth-century Georgian scene was one of a healthy mixed society. The social milieu harmonized with the built environment. Daily life patterns revolved naturally around the terraces and squares. The Georgian city was a socially salubrious cell, as it was designed to be. However, its original functionalism has long been lost. The Merrion Square and Fitzwilliam Square area may be admirably preserved physically through the process of office/commercial conversion, but the social character of the streetscapes has been perverted by the incursion of professionals and office workers and the consequent desertion of residents. This displacement has socially impoverished the historic core. The absence of families, children and prams along the Georgian streets is really an unnatural sight. Georgian houses were meant to be lived in, not to serve as work-places for a mere eight hours a day. The multitude of brass name-plates adorning most doors in the squares is an unmistakable symptom of this disease—the transformation of once-ebullient Georgian rows into staid business blocks. Most of Georgian Dublin is now functional only on a nine-to-five basis. In the evenings it suffers near total social abandonment. It exudes little more life than an industrial estate. No longer is it an environment for normal social circulation. This is an unmitigated waste. Preservation purists contemplate the idealistic notion of returning Georgian streets to their native social use (albeit not in any élitist form), but they realize that modern economics and governmental apathy militate against this sort of reversal. Nonetheless, the North Great George's Street community is proving that such ideas are not mere fantasy.

CHALLENGES AND DYNAMICS OF RESTORATION

Restoration is interpretation, not science . . . it's art . . . often an art that requires extraordinary feats of discipline and humility.[2]

The office-conversion approach to preservation is, as previously described, essentially a corporate or government endeavour found in the prosperous south parts of Dublin. Conversely, the purist-restoration process is an intensely individualistic pursuit confined largely to the north side. It is a simple matter of economics. Georgian houses in this distinctly unfashionable part of the city can still be bought in poor but restorable condition for between £20,000 and £40,000; some can be found for even less. This puts Georgian restoration within grasp of middle-class Dubliners, but it poses Homeric challenges. The disreputable image of the notorious north side poses a major obstacle to most prospective restorationists. It takes considerable courage and independence to defy social convention and cross the city's north–south 'apartheid' lines. Virtually all those who have taken the risk and bought Georgian houses north of the Liffey were advised by friends not to do so. If living in a north-side Georgian house does not actually constitute a Bohemian life-style, it is, at the very least, considered unorthodox by Dublin standards.

It takes an uncommon degree of simple faith and vision to engage in what sociologists would term a counter-cultural movement. When most 'smart' Dubliners are flocking to the secure and comfortable suburbs, Georgian restorationists move into a social and economic wasteland fraught with insecurity, uncertainty and sacrifice. For all, it is a major financial, physical and emotional struggle. But Georgian restorationists are motivated by a keen sense of history, realizing that they are a small but important part of the social stream that flows through the enduring Georgian heritage. All are fiercely individualistic with an uncanny ability to cope with hardships that would surely break the spirit of most. They are an extremely dedicated lot, exhibiting a pioneer attitude and frontiersman-like zeal for their mission. They settle along the harsh north Dublin urban wilderness without any support from the government and largely ignored by greater Irish society. It is a lonely expedition into unknown territory. Some succeed, others fail. Owing to the bleak social environment, it is far more rigorous for families with young children; individuals can afford to be tougher and more independent. For most, Georgian restoration is a prolonged, tedious venture. For some, it literally becomes a planned lifetime project—a way of life. It is a matter of financial sacrifice, physical rigour, skill, tenacity, adaptation and emotional durability. The vicissitudes of restoration comprise one of its most gruelling aspects. Restorationists become accustomed to both defeat and triumph; they commonly vacillate between exuberance and despair. The mental battle is as crucial as the physical and financial one. In the final analysis, the element of simple faith that the task can eventually be completed becomes the vital ingredient in success.

One of the first challenges of north Dublin Georgian restoration is coping with, or solving, the tenant situation. Along these poor rows still reside many sitting tenants, some of whom have spent most of their years in a tenemented Georgian house. A Georgian house occupied by such residents can often be purchased at bargain prices (sometimes as low as £15,000) but the buyer inherits a burdensome and frustrating liability because the tenants cannot by law be evicted and they pay an insignificant amount of rent. These tenant rights can be traced back more than fifty years when the poor were guaranteed protection against unfair rental practices. Over the past two generations, the rents of sitting tenants have either remained fixed or increased only nominally. Furthermore, individuals have been able to inherit tenancy rights from their parents. As a result, present-day tenants often pay the astonishingly low sum of 50p to £1 per week for as much as 3,000 square feet of urban living space. Georgian restorationists must carefully weigh the tenant situation before they make the decision to buy. Some prefer to seek a vacant Georgian property and simply avoid the dilemma but this is not always possible. Others boldly buy a Georgian house with as many as thirty tenants and set about the task of finding a viable solution. Tactics vary. Some new owners employ a forceful 'de-tenanting' strategy of threats and bribery, while others allow some tenants to remain. The tactic of bribing tenants to depart is a very common one but it can be quite expensive. The amount offered depends on the financial resources of the owner and the degree of desperation in clearing space for restoration. It is not unusual for an owner to offer tenants several thousand pounds to vacate the premises if the goal is to repossess an especially important section of the house. At present a proposed new owner-tenant law is under study which would dramatically change matters. It is proposed that a rent tribunal be established to set fairer, more realistic rates of rent, thereby granting the owner a reasonable profit on his property. However, the idea of this new law is understandably opposed by groups concerned about the fair treatment for poor tenants who cannot afford to pay appreciably higher fees.

Once a Georgian house is acquired, purist restoration means putting it back into the pristine form of its proper historical period. This means, as An Taisce explicitly recommends, not only that street façades be retained but 'where inappropriate alterations have been made, the original features should be restored whenever opportunity permits', even when it pertains to 'correct window-sashing, doorways, and railing and balcony details'. Such scrupulous attention means taking an eighteenth- or early nineteenth-century house, basically intact, and restoring the façade, interior and remaining backland so as to appear on completion as nearly as possible as it did when originally built, taking particular care to preserve to the greatest extent practicable the patina of age. This is particularly difficult in the poorer north neighbourhoods where generations of tenementation have disfigured and obscured original features. It calls for generous doses of imagination and historical expertise to visualise in necessary detail how the house must have appeared before it suffered such drastic transformation at the hands of multiple owners.

The physical condition of houses bought by restorationists usually varies from poor to appalling. Some are virtually roofless and windowless. Disintegrating brickwork, crumbling chimney-pieces, dry rot, cracked ceilings and walls, and water leakage are commonplace. So dilapidated and primitive is the setting that restorationists often retain another residence during the early stages for living purposes and work on their Georgian property during virtually all non-sleeping hours. Others, however, cannot afford such a luxury and must subsist during the initial months amid what might best be termed a condition of urban encampment without sufficient shelter from the elements, decent heating, and civilized bathroom and cooking facilities. Such conditions of hardship along the urban frontier are better endured during the warmer summer months. Most restorationists follow a common sequence in rehabilitating their Georgian possession. Structural soundness is always the first concern. Usually this means repairing the roof, windows, doorways and exterior brickwork. Owners conduct as much of the work as possible and hire professionals to perform the other tasks. A few restorationists, especially those with an architectural background, manage to carry out full restoration on their own. Where there is a flourishing restorationist community, the communal spirit is conducive to sharing expertise and labour. The co-operative approach to restoration, even if it only applies during the early stages, is important psychologically as well as physically (this will be documented in the following chapter).

The restoration of brickwork must be handled with great care. Bricks used for the Georgian houses have a life expectancy estimated at well over 250 years. But if these structures are to be preserved for future centuries, they have to be refaced or rebuilt periodically. Some exterior brickwork, such as that found along Henrietta Street, is in an advanced state of deterioration with cavities as deep as six inches. Repair and replacement of original bricks should be done by an expert bricklayer, not an ambitious amateur. Actually, modern brick and other materials can be applied effectively if they are used in a discriminating manner by skilled hands. But they should always be used in strict accordance with established Georgian principles. The fact that the Georgian physical environment was the product of so many diverse personalities and materials is conducive to restoration, because it means that the introduction of a new personality or compatible element need not destroy it. Even brickwork crudely covered with plaster can be retrieved, providing that the cleansing process is properly conducted. This is where professional consultation and guidance are important. Even the most highly motivated and skilled restorationists need expert advice on occasion. Most western governments freely dispense such important information to citizens engaged in preservation activities. Since there is no such governmental assistance in Ireland, this advice must be provided

(above) Harold Clarke, one of the 'urban pioneer' restorationists along North Great George's Street; (below and overleaf) two of the magnificently restored rooms in Harold Clarke's house, which has become something of a Dublin showpiece for its exuberant splendour (courtesy of Harold Clarke)

These 'before and after' photographs of a room in Harold Clarke's house show what miracles can be wrought by restoration *(courtesy of the North Great George's Street Preservation Society)*

by the Irish Georgian Society, An Taisce, or architectural scholars or art historians.

Once the house is structurally repaired and made sound, formal restoration can begin. This often means a process of purification in which both exterior and interior must be purged of apocryphal accoutrement. All illegitimate excrescences must be ruthlessly stripped away. Large-pane windows should be replaced with originals or at least respectable replicas; so, too, should altered fanlights, sidelights and doorway features that are not authentic. Any incongruous ironwork, letter-boxes, name-plates or door knockers should likewise be expunged and replaced by originals or copies that sympathetically match the real thing. Admittedly, this sort of puritanical probing for historical 'truth' can sometimes border on the eccentric. For instance, efforts to restore Georgian doors to their original colour have triggered something of a debate among ardent restorationists and architectural historians. Purists scramble through historical archives and painstakingly scrape off layers of paint, much like an archaeologist excavating a miniature 'dig', to discover the original hues. However, some doors bear a veritable geological strata bed of paint layers; thus it is sometimes impossible to decipher the first brush strokes.

Faithfully restoring ornate Georgian interiors is indisputably the most challenging and daunting task. At the outset it often seems almost insurmountable. It is a tedious endeavour which can literally take decades. Indeed, it commonly takes up to three years for a single room to be properly restored. The normal strategy is to attack one room at a time. Few restorationists possess the funds necessary to restore the house in one grand effort. Restoration work is almost always done in stages as money and time become available. This normally demands considerable sacrifice. Georgian restorationists routinely relinquish new cars, clothes, television sets, appliances, entertainment and even holidays to support their project. Psychologically, it is wise to work on a single room or section at a time because, when completed, it serves as a strong impetus to move to the next; it may be compared to writing a book one chapter at a time. To attempt restoration of huge areas in a single effort is unrealistic; it invites demoralization and defeat. A common psychological ploy used by restorationists is to set target dates for completing specific tasks. Usually they aim to finish a favourite room by Christmas, a birthday, an anniversary or holiday time. Every incentive is important. Ordinarily the scheme is first to complete a bedroom, bathroom and perhaps the drawing-room or library. This forms a sort of liveable core from which further restoration efforts can gradually evolve.

Restorationists become accustomed to living in a restricted world of only a few restored rooms while the remainder of the property awaits revival at some propitious date. The discrepant scene may be one in which an elegantly restored room, fully furnished, stands in startling contrast to others still in a dilapidated state with walls in rubble and floorboards torn out. Purists often have to be painfully practical. Although they may abhor the idea of using any part of their house for non-residential purposes, it is financially profitable during the first few years to rehabilitate their basement and rent it on a temporary basis for office or commercial space. This is now common practice because it allows restorationists to generate much-needed additional income for their mission. Two basements along North Great George's Street are currently let for a Kung Fu Centre and a massage parlour—hardly in the classical Georgian tradition but eminently profitable.

Since most north-side Georgian houses have held hordes of poor tenants over the generations, they bear all the marks of abuse, neglect, accumulated filth and extensive tampering. Before serious restoration can commence, the bowels of the building must be cleansed. Debris must be dug out and hauled away. All post-Georgian utilitarian partitions and embellishments must be removed to restore original scale and proportion. Wallpaper, paint and linoleum must be stripped from walls and floors. In some cases this means excavating as many as ten layers of wallpaper, ½in thicknesses of paint and eighteen layers of linoleum. Fireplaces must be unclogged and plasterwork scraped clean. Retrieving delicate plasterwork atop walls and ceilings is probably the most tedious chore. Due to thick coats of paint, dirt and grime, the intricate features are no more than amorphous bulges. Plasterwork must be patiently picked clean with a small knife or screwdriver; it often takes up to five hours per foot to scrape clean and repaint the strips of plasterwork atop Georgian walls. Thus, it can take in excess of 500 hours of eye-straining labour on a ladder just to restore the plasterwork on the walls of a drawing-room. Digging out ornamental plaster designs on ceilings is equally demanding and time consuming. Despite the drudgery, there is often great joy as splendorous revelations appear before the entranced eyes of restorationists as they meticulously remove the house's artificial nineteenth- and twentieth-century 'clothing' to expose the original eighteenth-century essence.

When repainting and redecorating, most restorationists make every effort to adhere to originality. Redecorative colours are often selected from the classical Georgian palette. Compromise is necessary when installing modern lighting, plumbing and electrical fixtures but this is usually accomplished in as unobtrusive a manner as possible so as not to detract from the eighteenth-century theme. A particularly challenging problem for restorationists is the acquisition of original fittings such as fireplaces, ironwork, balconies, banisters, woodwork and plaster panels. In many other Western European countries these components are methodically collected and saved specifically for historic rehabilitation. But in Ireland there is no such system and, as a consequence, an alarming proportion have been lost. Irreplaceable old fixtures have been carelessly destroyed or discarded. Some pieces are sold to tinkers (Ireland's itinerants) by demolition crews as scrap metal. A good number of finer interior pieces have been exported for the British and American antique markets. A handful of Irish architects are engaged in this important retrieval work and the Irish Georgian Society often purchases valuable appurtenances from eighteenth-century houses being razed, but there is a real need for some organized procurement scheme. In the absence of such, restorationists are on their own and must scavenge about to find the right pieces for their house.

By necessity, all restorationists are adept scavengers, always keeping a vigilant eye out for the right fireplace item, chandelier, woodwork, fanlight, plaster section, piece of furniture or modest eighteenth-century memorabilia to legitimize the setting. Word of fertile new territory for scavenging spreads through the restorationist community via the 'bush telegraph'. Scavenging 'raids' are conducted regularly by restorationists and are carefully orchestrated for security and efficiency. They are pursued with all the zeal of a conquistador in quest of Inca treasure. Usually, raids assume the form of collective clandestine searches in derelict Georgian houses on the verge of demolition. As collectors find and remove valuable pieces, friends are posted as sentries at entrances. Co-operative raids are best because of the difficulty in removing large items. Hammers, chisels, and screwdrivers are the basic tools of the trade. Scavenging raids are usually conducted with a mixture of adventure, daring, cunning, bravado and frivolity; but it is serious business. Some scavengers are more discreet than others, prowling only during the cover of darkness; others boldly remove artefacts in full daylight. If interrupted by passers-by or police, restorationists always hasten to explain that they are *rescuing* threatened historical items. The response is almost always sympathetic. Even if a restorationist finds an item for which he has no immediate use he will claim it, store it away and later swap it for a piece he does need. Apart from its purely brazen good fun, scavenging is an absolutely necessary part of the purist restoration process. It is incontestably a functional means of recycling and conserving valuable eighteenth-century artefacts in the city of Dublin, many of which would surely be lost otherwise. Every restored Georgian house in Dublin is liberally festooned with items rescued from crumbling eighteenth-century relatives.

Once restored, every effort is made to furnish rooms with pieces that appropriately match the architectural mood and period. Sometimes original eighteenth-century chairs, beds, tables or chests are affordable, but more often reproductions must do. Restorationists are also normally very attentive to what backland remains behind their house. Rather than paving over the area as a corporate owner in the south may do, restorationists resurrect it for its intended use. The typical surviving plot is only about 50ft in depth but it can be transformed into a charming, private garden. There is considerable variety to be found in recovered Georgian gardens which are often embellished with water fountains, statues, large urns, fishponds, and perfectly manicured hedges, flower-beds and shrubbery. They stand as oases of colour and greenery amid the otherwise pallid north-side environment.

SAVING THE STREET FURNITURE

> A street whose 'wallpaper' of building façades may be architec-
> turally excellent can find its character gained or lost in the design
> of service furniture such as lamp standards, bollards, seats, and
> kerbs.[3]

The resplendent Georgian panorama is more than merely a collection of buildings, backlands and squares. It is also sculpted of certain adjunct elements that contribute saliently to the historical setting. Some of the most important early townscape constituents include lampposts, bollards, post-boxes, boot-scrapers, coal-hole covers, horse-troughs and assorted other paraphernalia. Collectively, these are termed 'street furniture' and may be found along what is aptly known as the 'carpet' of the street. They are not incidental minutiae; indeed, they form an 'essential part of the city's architectural treasure'. The genius of historic districts is always their variety of visual experiences. In this respect, street furniture enhances the variegated detail and dimension of the composite Georgian tapestry. Some items are so subtle that they often miss discovery by those who daily walk by, or literally over, them. But if they are accorded little special attention, it is probably because they fit so naturally, and therefore inconspicuously, into the greater architectural mould. Ironically, many pedestrians would doubtless find them more conspicuous by their sudden absence. To the initiated, the loss of these street pieces is unthinkable—the result would be visual impoverishment. For this reason, protection of the street furniture in the Georgian districts is a vital part of purist restoration.

Dublin fortuitously possesses a remarkable assortment of street furniture in its Georgian neighbourhoods; in fact, one of the most unique collections in all Europe. For the most part, this bountiful heritage has been inadvertently preserved. While most other European cities were replacing old city street fixtures with modern ones, Dublin was forced by economic necessity to retain the originals, converting some to new uses. But owing to carnivorous urban redevelopment, street widening, obsolescence, theft, vandalism and neglect over the past two decades, the wealth of Dublin's street furniture has been alarmingly whittled away. One must examine old photographs of the Georgian streetscapes to appreciate just how much street furniture has actually vanished. Fortunately there are still excellent examples of eighteenth- and nineteenth-century street furniture to be found throughout most parts of the Georgian city, and the Merrion and Fitzwilliam squares district serves as a kind of open museum for such study. Here, street furniture is found in a sensible arrangement and individual items are well balanced in terms of design, configuration, height and size; each element seems to complement others around it. This is also true of North Great George's Street and a few other intact north-side terraces. Especially impressive is the dazzling array of surviving ironwork in the form of railings, balconies, balconettes and gates. Superb samples of wrought iron, some well over two hundred years old, can be found along the older Georgian streets. This wrought, or hand-worked, iron was created by Irish craftsmen with great artistic skills. Iron pieces were heated and hammered into original designs at a forge. Though it was expensive to produce, even at the time, because of the intensity of labour, most builders lavishly embroidered their houses with it. In the second half of the eighteenth century cast, or moulded, ironwork became very popular since it could be produced more cheaply and in greater quantity at an iron foundry. However, even this variety was made in original designs. The present-day Georgian scene reflects a healthy mix of wrought- and cast-iron work. Much of it is still in remarkably good condition owing chiefly to the purity of the metal and early smelting processes. Commonly, the old iron railings are smothered with layers of paint which obscure their original delicacy.

169

Some of Georgiana's best ironwork finery can be seen along forgotten Henrietta Street where exuberant coils and geometrically shaped railings continue to withstand the elements. But along other north Georgian streets there is much evidence of ironwork rusted beyond repair.

Old street lamps are a ubiquitous feature in the street furniture system. Most lamp-standards that typically line Georgian streets actually date from the period 1825 to 1925 but they have become naturally integrated into the Georgian environment. Although a great many were forged in Britain, they were designed specifically for the Irish with the familiar shamrock emblem generally in evidence somewhere. Their lean and curvaceous design lends grace to the unbroken terraces. The old lamp posts have now all been converted to modern lighting systems but they still seem a natural extension of the railings, gates, balconies and other ironwork moulded to most Georgian fronts. Boot-scrapers are a particularly curious relic of a past epoch. Still found beside the entrances of many Georgian houses, they reflect the era of mud streets. A few of Dublin's boot-scrapers are of the cavity-in-the-wall variety but the majority are the free-standing type embedded into the stone. Considering that they served so simple a function, they boast of surprisingly elaborate craftsmanship in the form of fish, flowers and myriad designs. They were rendered archaic by the mid-nineteenth century when streets were paved. Yet they continued to appear into the early twentieth century—their excuse being the presence of the horse. They, too, fit into the native pattern of ironwork and are usually painted to match adjacent railings.

One of the most artistic, albeit often missed, relics of early street furniture are the coal-hole covers implanted regularly along the floor of the streets. The coal-holes were, of course, delivery chutes to the expansive coal cellars below ground. Most are no more than about a foot in diameter, supposedly kept small to prevent burglars from making easy entry into the houses. Although many of the covers have been badly worn down since their casting date (c1760–1830), one may still recognize their elaborate designs. Some covers off the beaten pedestrian track retain fine detail and dimension. But too many have already had their handsome faces eroded into oblivion by infinite pedestrian tramplings. Georgian Dublin once contained a splendid set of coal-hole covers but they are fast disappearing. For the sake of posterity a representative collection of these covers should be removed and securely placed in a museum. But no one seems to be coming to the rescue. In Britain coal-hole covers have attracted ardent devotees who recognize their historic and artistic merits. In fact, one Briton, so smitten by the covers that he produced a small book containing 150 different designs, even coined a term for his obsession, 'opercula', derived from the Latin *operculum* meaning a cover or lid. But in Ireland there seems to be no appreciation for them and they are much endangered.

Passers-by may miss the coal-hole covers but they seldom fail to notice the Georgian door knockers. These famous appurtenances to the eighteenth-century street furniture have gained great fame. Most were originally of iron but brass knockers eventually became more common. Georgian door knockers have greatly diminished in number. During the 1880s and 1890s the student sport of snatching knockers flourished, reaching epidemic proportions. Even today owners have a problem with the theft of brass knockers and other exterior brass fixtures.

It would be a shame if Dublin's bounty of street furniture were allowed gradually to perish from the Georgian scene, because it provides the delicate frill along the greater architectural fabric. Yet this is precisely what is happening—mostly through innocent indifference. At a time when western architects are forced to recreate antique street pieces for their historic quarters at great cost, Dublin needs only to retain those that have survived naturally. In most British cities there are archivists, architects and planning officers who keep a vigilant eye on the welfare of the street furniture. There are even museums which contain a fine collection of street furniture pieces for public examination. Not so in Dublin.

Lastly, it should be noted that the preservation of the furnished streetscape involves more than just holding on to surviving components; it also means protecting the ambience. Planning controls should protect the integrity of the setting by prohibiting the introduction of any foreign elements that damage or detract from the existing street furniture collage. This especially applies to parking meters and large signs. The vile intrusion of the parking meter has wreaked havoc with Georgian Dublin's indigenous mood. Like uniformed columns of mechanized soldiers from some distant galaxy, they have invaded every Georgian row, colliding perceptibly with the eighteenth-century idiom. So dense now is vehicular traffic and parking that one can only really examine and appreciate the Georgian vistas on weekends.

Notes

1 Madden, Aodhan. 'Another Georgian Street in Danger', *Evening Press*, 30 August 1979, p8
2 'Restoration of Things Past', *Newsweek*, 23 March 1981, p86
3 O'Connell, Derry. *The Antique Pavement* (An Taisce, 1975), p7

10

Profiles of Georgian Restorationists on the Urban Frontier

The restoration of Georgian houses on Dublin's urban frontier is, above all else, a matter of sheer dedication and determination. In an age of slick solutions and quick-fix technology, restorationists are indeed a rare breed. They live by patience and ingenuity; the worth of the final reward is seldom questioned. There is no better way to illuminate the trials, tribulations and triumphs of devout restorationists than to take a glimpse into the life of the select few. At the very least, their idealism and enthusiasm are inspirational.

HAROLD CLARKE: URBAN PIONEER

Harold Clarke, a director at Eason and Sons, booksellers, is the archetype of the modern Irish urban pioneer. He was the first of the new settlers along tattered and forgotten North Great George's Street, and through courage and vision effectively blazed a trail in the north city wilderness for others to follow. His background prepared him well for the role. Born in County Roscommon some forty-odd years ago, Clarke attended school in eighteenth-century buildings, went on to historic Trinity College and eventually moved into a Victorian house in Dublin. His dream, however, was to own a splendid Georgian home. Unable to afford a high-priced eighteenth-century property in the fashionable south city, he considered a house in forlorn Mountjoy Square. But the derelict and dormant state of the square in the 1960s proved a major deterrent and the idea was abandoned. Then, one day in 1967 a north-side friend stopped by Eason's for some shopping. In jest, Clarke asked whether he had found him a Georgian house yet. Much to his surprise the friend replied that there was one going in North Great George's Street, to which Clarke queried, 'and where in the dickens is North Great George's Street?' He was soon to find out. Since it was approaching lunchtime it

The John Molloy family of Mountjoy Square. For the past fifteen years they have waged a courageous restoration battle against great odds

was suggested that they go and have a look at the property. Clarke agreed, and it turned out to be a classic case of love at first sight; he bought it the next day. It was not so impulsive an act as it may seem, because he actually had several weeks in which to weigh the wisdom of his decision before the final papers had to be signed. During this period he had an architect's report on the structural condition of the building which happily supported his belief that the house had enormous potential.

Clarke's new home-to-be was built in 1787 and was occupied by relatives of the original family until 1850 when it was turned over to a succession of lawyers through the latter half of the century. Between 1900 and 1910 it served as a hotel. In 1911 it was converted into poor tenements and deteriorated over the next fifty years. By the 'sixties the whole of North Great George's Street had fallen on to hard times. Clarke recalls that when he took up residence, 'it was a very run-down street, nearly all the doors were open—a sign of tenement houses. It had been a well-known street for prostitutes.' Though he firmly believed in the restoration concept, he had serious reservations about life in the 'dreary and depressing' north side with all its unsavoury elements. He admits that 'at first people just did not believe that someone was coming in to restore a house here'. Even friends who lauded the idea of restoring an old house thought him 'mentally unbalanced' for deciding to reside north of the Liffey.

After paying £5,000 for the rambling dwelling, he set about making it habitable. The enormity of the task was immediately apparent. The house was virtually roofless and had been declared a dangerous building by the Dublin Corporation because of some structural damage to the front wall. On the other hand, there were no tenants to contend with, meaning that he could immediately plunge into major repairs. This meant hiring professional labourers to do the reroofing, electrical wiring, plumbing, brickwork repair and assorted other necessities such as treating dry rot—at a total cost of £7,500. To offset the financial burden, he applied for a grant from the Dublin Corporation but received a letter back stating that no grant was available because the 'house was not suitable for the accommodation of the working classes'. Clarke rather caustically muses, 'what their definition of "working class" was, I don't know.' Just as his funds were nearly depleted, he received a welcome

(*opposite*) A bedroom in the home of Michael and Aileen Casey awaiting restoration when the time and money become available (*courtesy of the Irish Architectural Archive*)

grant of £200 from the Irish Georgian Society. Though seemingly a modest amount, Clarke affirms that it provided him at the time with an important incentive for which he will always be grateful.

Once the major structural problems had been remedied, he took over full responsibility for restoration. Every day Clarke and a resident companion would leave their offices and labour faithfully on the house from about 5.30 to 10.30 pm. In the beginning, some of the older residents along the street viewed his intrusion with healthy suspicion. But after witnessing him toiling diligently week after week they gradually came not only to accept but to respect him. On weekends restoration took on a decidedly collective spirit as 'work and wine' parties consisting of ten to twelve friends were organized. Clarke concedes that the value of the unfailing support, both physical and moral, of these friends is inestimable; the house could never have been restored in such a grand manner without their assistance. At first they had to work during the chilling months of winter with little glass in the windows. To keep warm they made bonfires of the eighteen layers of linoleum put down by past tenants. Much of the house had to be physically dismantled before it could be properly restored. Floorboards were torn out, scaffolding erected and crumbling debris strewn about. Because the house was in such a state of utter shambles for the first few months, Clarke had to retain his Victorian residence for living purposes. Thus, the immediate goal was to make two bedrooms and the library habitable as a sort of base-camp from which to embark on further restoration. Dozens of layers of paint which obscured the fine features of the plasterwork had to be painstakingly scraped off. The drawing-room alone took fully two months of communal work to strip clean for painting. Despite the tedious daily routine of restoration, Clarke rarely became discouraged, primarily due to the constant support of friends and also because 'something was always happening under your hands . . . a continual sense of accomplishment and progress . . . the house seemed to respond well to any attention given it'. As the house slowly shed its shabby image and took respectable form, Clarke became even more attached. He describes his growing attraction to the house: 'like having an affair' which gradually developed into 'love and marriage'. Finally, on St Patrick's Day 1968, the house was ready for occupation and he moved in, reflecting that the first few nights in the Georgian setting were 'sheer joy'. Once in full residence he probed every little nook and cranny to learn as much about the house as possible; in return, it revealed some of its past secrets. A small mice-nibbled cache of letters, carefully tucked away beneath the bathroom floorboards, was discovered. They were from a lady in Limerick to a man who had lived in the house around 1850. Clarke treasures them as a part of the house's rich social history.

Now, after fourteen years in residence, Harold Clarke is regarded as a long-established resident of the street and a veteran on the Dublin restoration scene. He obviously exults in enjoying the fruits of his long labour, pointing out with pride to visitors every lovingly restored detail of the eighteenth-century dwelling. His house has become something of a Dublin show-piece portrayed in newspaper and magazine articles. Described as 'unabashedly exuberant', it is beautifully decorated and furnished. For authenticity, he has abided by the original colour scheme as closely as possible. Furnishings include many original period pieces including an Irish Chippendale four-poster bed, fine eighteenth-century chairs, a chest and a large wardrobe. Many of the furniture pieces were bought at bargain prices at country auctions. The rear garden is attractively landscaped and festooned with fountains, statues and large urns which soften the squareness of the setting. It is like a bit of the country in the very heart of the inner city—scarcely one hundred yards removed from bustling O'Connell Street.

As the 'founding father' of the North Great George's Street Preservation Society, he likes to ruminate philosophically about the Georgian world of which he is now so much a part:

> The house is very much a part of my life. It is still a continuing love affair and one feels very wedded to it. When one enters the Georgian world restoration gets into the bloodstream. It takes a lot of faith, believing that you'll win through. There is also the missionary element that you're doing something worthwhile that needs to be done. You are moving into hostile territory in Ireland in restoring an eighteenth-century building because there is no support for what you're doing.

In terms of a healthy blend of social and economic types, he sees his street as a 'microcosm of what Irish society should be . . . the street is not a ghetto in any way, nor is it divided between the élitists and the under-privileged . . . we're all great friends, we're all workers together.'

Despite the obvious devotion to his house and neighbourhood, he is a realist, noting that 'there are frustrations such as the difficulty in parking and the general scruffiness of this area of Dublin. When the time comes for retirement it is not an ideal part of the city. It's a long way to the sea and pollution in Dublin has become a much greater problem. Really, it is the things outside the house that would make me think of moving.' He

177

estimates that his house might bring £80,000 on the current market. But as the street undergoes further revival a figure closer to £200,000 might be commanded in five or ten years. Should he some day have to relinquish his hard-earned niche in the Georgian realm it would be with the deepest sense of sadness and loss. Yet, he would doubtless be comforted by the knowledge that the street's rebirth was due in great part to his early pioneering efforts.

DESIREE SHORTT: TENACIOUS RESTORATIONIST

Desiree Shortt was one of the most loyal of Harold Clarke's coterie of volunteer workers. For eight years she devoutly spent weekends assisting him with restoration. During this period Clarke repeatedly suggested that she buy the Georgian house just across the street. Her firm rebuttal was: 'A twenty-two room house for a single woman, with twenty-seven people living in it—no way.' It was generally considered to be academically one of the finest houses in the street but one of the worst buys because of the congested tenant situation. Inexplicably, after years of coming and going along the street with no real temptation to consider the proposal she awoke one night and said to herself, 'I must have that house'. She thought it quite an extraordinary revelation yet admits, 'I went out and bought it the next day'.

She was well suited from childhood for the unorthodox life of a Georgian restorationist. By her own admission she inherited a rebellious, stubborn character and was taught as a child not to conform—advice faithfully heeded. During her twenties, several years were spent in London and California where she rose through the business ranks to senior account executive with advertising firms. Having succeeded abroad, she returned to Dublin at the age of twenty-six and took a position as executive at a major design studio. Life revolved around a comfortable home in Ballsbridge, fashionable dress and a sparkling social set. But the absence of challenges bred discontent. The prospect of taking on the restoration of a huge Georgian house in a socially disreputable part of the city obviously intrigued her. She bought the house in 1975 for £8,000 and was promptly offered £10,000 for it a few weeks later. But there was no temptation to take the short-term profit; the commitment had been made. She candidly proclaims, 'I bought the house on a dream'.

At the outset, coping with twenty-seven tenants proved the major frustration. Several tenants had resided in the house for thirty-four years yet continued to pay only £1.50 in weekly rent. They clearly regarded

178

the property as their domain. Shortt relates that their attitude toward her new ownership was 'how dare I move in . . . who the hell did I think I was?' Her perceived intrusion was much resented—and resisted. The situation would have been stressful enough under normal circumstances, but to exacerbate matters she had broken her back shortly before moving in and was restricted to bed for most of the day. Furthermore, since the house was already densely populated upon her arrival, she was forced to reside in a small, damp basement room for the first four years. She felt like a prisoner in her own castle. Once a doctor friend paid a visit and was absolutely 'appalled at the cramped living quarters', exhorting her to seek healthier living conditions elsewhere in the house. This was not easily accomplished. Her rebellious nature clashed with the defensive and haughty attitudes of the tenants and a full-fledged 'cold war' developed. Mutual suspicion and antagonism took the form of a series of petty acts in which opposing parties would torment each other. Each would leave 'smart notes' at the other's door. Shortt would disconnect the tenants' doorbells so that visitors could not reach them; in retaliation, they would be verbally abusive, deliberately make noise and litter the property. Several times they smashed down her door during the night, a terrifying experience. Eventually the adversarial relationship subsided and an informal 'truce' was called. Pranks ceased and a state of domestic tranquillity ensued.

Since she was largely bedridden for the first eighteen months, she had to devise some scheme for generating income. Her creative talents allowed her to set up a modest china-restoring business in the basement. A major break came when she was written up in the *Irish Times* and the publicity resulted in a flock of customers at her door with arms full of damaged china. By training several girls in the craft, the business was quickly expanded and showed a good profit. This permitted her to bribe two tenant families for £1,100 each into vacating the premises. It was well worth the investment because it meant securing two major rooms on the ground floor for restoration.

Restoration has been financially burdensome and physically strenuous. Every free minute has been devoted to restoring the large drawing-room. This has meant replacing woodwormed floors, removing up to eight layers of wallpaper, stripping paint, and some days standing on a ladder for up to sixteen hours. Scraping clean the delicate plaster panels has been especially tiresome. But thanks to her experience in restoring fine pieces of china, she has adapted the skill to remoulding lost or damaged fragments of eighteenth-century plasterwork. Finally, after three full

179

years of toiling and an investment of £7,000, the drawing-room has been immaculately retrieved and elegantly furnished. But the sacrifices have been great. As Shortt puts it: 'Everything went by the board—social life, clothes, hair, nails, food, holidays, car, petrol. I'm an extremist. I would work myself into the ground becoming so tired that I could not even get off the ladder, then go to bed totally exhilarated, collapse immediately, get up the next morning to do china and then get back up on the ladder . . . I nearly broke my health.' There were also periods of intense discouragement and depression. She confides that 'there were times when I simply could not stand it and I would ring Harold Clarke in floods of tears (often around midnight) and say to him "Oh, God, I've spent sixteen hours working on the ceiling and I'm so tired that I can't stand it". He was sympathetic because he had been through the same problems . . . he would know what I was talking about.' Though she credits the consolation of Clarke and other restorationists with pulling her through the most traumatic moments, she eschews the idea of defeat, contending that 'I just happen to be Irish and a female and strong'. In her estimation the most fundamental requisites a restorationist must possess are 'a dream, tenacity and cash' (in that order), adding 'tenacity is my most important asset'.

After seven years in residence, the most imposing obstacles have been cleared. All but eight of the tenants have departed (through various persuasive means), the china-restoring business has expanded to a staff of twelve, and a steady income now means that restoration can proceed at a steady pace. Although the final cost of restoration will reach around £55,000, she is supremely confident, exclaiming that 'I can't wait [to get at restoring the next room] . . . I know to the last tone of colour, the last braid of curtain, the last ornament what the room is going to be like.' The vision remains clear. And the rewards have apparently been worth all the frustration and drudgery. As Shortt divulges, 'I love the house, I draw from it and enjoy it . . . it has become a surrogate husband. I sit here at night and say "God, this is so gorgeous" . . . the house has done more for me than anything else could have in terms of consolation. But the house is far more important than I am, it's going to be here long after I go and I must not touch anything important in it [in a destructive way] . . . I am only a caretaker.'

THE MOLLOYS OF MOUNTJOY SQUARE:
AN URBAN OUTPOST FAMILY

John and Ann Molloy have waged perhaps the most heroic struggle on Dublin's restoration front. For fourteen years they have lived in a lonely urban outpost along the decrepit south side of Mountjoy Square, deprived of any community participation and without even the solace of neighbours. They have survived by courage and persistence. Within restorationist circles the Molloys are much respected because they embody the most admirable traits of their Dublin counterparts.

Both grew up in the west of Ireland with some recollection of medieval buildings but no real exposure to Georgian architecture. John's only vivid memory of the Georgian terraces is traced to his college days when he would cycle past Mountjoy Square on the way to Croke Park. It was really only after John and Ann were married and lived for a period in London that they became sensitized to historic architecture. In 1967 they returned to Dublin, moved into a flat and began seeking a house. John was twenty-six years old and Ann a few years younger. Their attention was drawn to Mountjoy Square which at the time was a highly publicized and controversial site because Mrs Desmond Guinness had bought a property in the square and was promoting a scheme for residential revival. By all accounts the square seemed on the brink of urban renewal. The Molloys thought it an ideal opportunity to be among the first wave of residents moving back into the square. They found a house along the south side that appealed to them because of its spaciousness, proportions and pleasing view of the square—seemingly a perfect setting in which to raise a family. When John first inspected the interior, it struck him as dreadful that such fine plasterwork and craftsmanship might be destroyed if the property fell into the hands of developers who were menacingly eyeing the house at the time. From the outset he felt a certain sense of duty to try and retrieve the ageing building.

Typically, the house had its good points and bad points. Ann recalls that 'it was really filthy, having been lived in by an eccentric old woman for twenty or thirty years'. On the other hand, the house was structurally sound, had not been butchered by past occupants and held no tenants to contend with. As an engineer, John was confident of his restorationist ability to make 'order out of chaos'. They decided to secure a twenty-year loan and buy the house for £6,500. It was a major decision because at the time they could have purchased a good house in Ballsbridge for about the same amount. But both agreed that the prospects 'looked very promising . . . that other houses would be bought up by people like ourselves so that you would have a community here'. When they moved in they had two children aged nine months and eighteen months. At this stage the children were naturally confined to the house and there was little thought given to the potential problems of the sterile social environment beyond their door. After all, it was presumed that other families would soon be settling in along both sides of them.

The first few months were brimming with optimism and merriment. Admiring and supportive friends were organized into work parties and a good time was had by all. The Molloys were an exuberant young family who felt as if they were setting out on a great adventure. To enhance the mood of excitement, attention was lavished on them by the news media. They remember 'being treated like celebrities with interviews and all that'. In both press and television coverage they were regaled as urban pioneers. However, there was little realism to temper their idealism and John, in retrospect, believes that all the early attention and publicity tended to 'cloud the problems of the future'. The glamour of restoration soon gave way to tedium and financial sacrifice. And after a few months the curiosity and support of friends and visitors quickly waned. As John reflects, 'they moved off the stage and we were left sitting on our own . . . as the years went on interest in the square vanished and the people who were supposed to buy the houses never materialized; gradually the surrounding houses began to fall down and Mrs Guinness ceased her involvement with the square . . . so we were literally left on our own.' The grim realities of isolation settled upon them. Mountjoy Square not only failed to experience the predicted revival but its downward spiral actually accelerated as houses along the south side decayed further. The badly dilapidated condition of adjoining properties even posed a hazard to their home (the south side fell into such a shocking state of crumbling ruination that in the summer of 1981 a French film company staged an on-location rendition of the World War II London Blitz directly next door to the Molloys' house). Meanwhile, the Molloy family expanded to three boys and a girl. The older boys were reaching the age when they needed contact with friends. The absence of neighbouring children became a major problem. There developed a creeping consciousness of estrangement; declares John, 'we had become hermits'.

To compensate for the unmet social needs of their children in the neighbourhood, John and Ann personally sacrificed to send them to private schools with sprawling grounds. This, of course, put them in contact with well-to-do children residing almost exclusively in the posh suburbs of the south city. Though it enhanced their friendships, it also tended to reinforce the notion that they were somehow different from their friends by virtue of the area from which they came. This created a certain inferiority complex. As Ann confesses, 'my son, Patrick, refuses to invite friends to the house because he is ashamed of it. He says it's a terrible dump.' All his friends live in what she terms 'shiny houses'. Although the Molloys understand that their son's condemnation is really more of a reference to the *area* in which he lives than the house itself, it is a painful revelation and fortifies their sense of growing guilt over raising four children in such an insipid social climate.

The Molloys have now lived on the edge of the urban frontier for fourteen years. Their children are aged between ten and sixteen, very social years. They have considered the possibility of leaving the square but as John laments, 'once we got in, it was practically impossible to get out. The amount of money we would have got for the home would not have bought a hen-house . . . we're in a catch-22 position because we would not have got very much for the house, so where do we go from here? Now we have to wait until this side of the square is restored again.' And their house is still far from fully restored. The financial burden of supporting a family of six has meant that restoration of sections of the house has been delayed. Plaster still needs to be scraped clean, walls painted and rooms carpeted and furnished. Ann points out that the costs of restoration and maintenance have meant that 'we were always in debt because we were always spending on the house' and 'there has been no time for pastimes'. John intones, 'I'm forty years old now and there are times when I say "Jesus, I've had a belly full of this".' Yet, both unmistakably love the house. And it does indeed appear that things are finally changing for the better. A scheme has tentatively been approved by the planning authorities to demolish the crumbling properties along the south side and build offices with Georgian façades on the sites. Though office development is hardly the type of revival the Molloys originally envisaged, it does at least guarantee that their property value will appreciate. This means that they will face some important decisions over the next few years. Already, in 1981, they were offered £50,000 for their house by a developer whose intention was to demolish it and implant an office. It struck John and Ann as abhorrent that their home could be so summarily obliterated to make space for a functional workplace. John concedes that he might be tempted to sell if the price is satisfactory and there is an assurance that the house will be retained. He

183

reasons, quite correctly, that the price of the house will probably be its best safeguard because 'if a developer pays me only £50,000 for the house he can afford to knock it down; if he pays me £200,000 there is no way he can afford to knock it down'. Actually, it is their fervent hope that some day one of their children might take over the house to raise a family; the continuity would be comforting.

Has it all been worth it? The Molloys express mixed sentiments. Both agree that 'from a family point of view the sacrifices have been too great'. And there is an almost palpable sense of having been let down—both by the government which refused to offer them any financial assistance and by those Dubliners who failed to accept the challenges of restoration alongside them. It has been a difficult struggle to raise a family in a forgotten Georgian enclave along a socially deserted row, ignored by greater Irish society. Yet they take immense satisfaction and pride in the knowledge that they have single-handedly saved a fine Georgian house, now destined to survive into another century. As Mountjoy Square's frayed south side prepares to be inundated with office development, the Molloys' home stands as a solitary beacon of family life, its integrity proudly intact. John and Ann rightfully savour this unmitigated victory.

DAVID NORRIS: TRIBAL CHIEF OF THE RESTORATIONIST CLAN

David Norris is a Professor of Literature at Trinity College and a James Joyce scholar; but he is a 'blow-in' along North Great George's Street—meaning that he arrived only recently upon the scene. He has hardly been intimidated by his newcomer status. In only four years he has become the head of the street's preservation society and has emerged as the most flamboyant, popular figure along the terrace. Norris is really a rather unlikely candidate for restorationist. Reared in Ballsbridge, he had scant knowledge of Georgian architecture. In 1975 he noticed a listing in the newspaper for a Georgian house along North Great George's Street. Though curious, he procrastinated for fully one year, apprehensive at the thought of living in Dublin's reputed slum-land. He admits that his preconceptions of the area were that 'only savages and down-and-outs lived in the north city'. But exploring the antiquated Georgian cityscape he found a certain 'romantic attraction about beauty in decline'. Finally in 1976 he went to inspect the property and recalls being 'immediately attracted to the house and determined to buy it by hook or by crook'. Thus, against the well-intentioned advice of friends, he bought the house for £35,000 and rather reluctantly became a north-sider.

184

His 'new' 194-year-old house was structurally intact but needed considerable work and he was not able to move in until 1978. A small building contractor was hired to install modern plumbing and electricity but Norris has done most of the other work himself. Every floor of the property had been converted into flats and one large room divided into two levels; thus he had to dismantle the tangle of partitions in order to return the house to its original proportions. Fireplaces were clogged with accumulated dirt and had to be dug out. By necessity, restoration has been conducted in stages as the money and time have become available. To date, restoration has cost £10,000 and the job is far from completed. He estimates that it might take another ten years to put it into desired form. Always the eternal optimist, he copes better than most with the rigours of restoration and rarely becomes discouraged. He credits this to his 'capacity to live in the future', conjecturing that 'somebody who absolutely lives in the present would be driven to despair . . . it takes the ability to sit in the middle of a room surrounded by dust and rubble and look up at the [unrestored] plasterwork on the ceiling and say, "God, isn't it going to be lovely at Christmas".'

Norris is an invaluable reservoir of confidence for the entire community and he has become a sort of tribal chief for the restorationist clan. By cajoling and consoling, he always seems to elevate the sagging spirits of others during troublesome times. He possesses the rare ability to view poverty-gnawed tenements along the street's lower course and see a reconstituted streetscape in a few years' time. This vision serves the community well for, as the head of the preservation society, he eloquently propounds the potentials of Georgian reclamation before government authorities and other official bodies. Along the street itself he is something of a human dynamo, exhibiting boundless energy and spouting innovative ideas. His current project is the creation of a James Joyce Centre in house number thirty-five which is still in a ramshackle state. But he has specific plans for acquiring the necessary funds for the project and few doubt that he will succeed. Perhaps more important, he has become a real catalyst for the street's population, bridging the sensitive gap between young and old, tenants and owners, and poor and middle-class. He honestly regards everyone as equal, and champions the cause of saving the street in its entirety for *everyone*. He is deeply committed to resurrecting the deteriorated lower segment near Parnell Street so that the elderly residents can live out their lives at home, rather than being forcibly transplanted at some future date by the Corporation.

No one relishes the eighteenth-century setting more than David

Norris. And as a convert to Georgian restoration he is forgivably prone to preaching about its rewards. As he opines, 'there is something refining about living in beautiful surroundings, something immensely satisfying. On a winter's eve, with a good fire roaring in the drawing-room, I lie back on my sofa and look up at the ceiling and get a thrill when looking at the delicacy of the plasterwork and thinking of the craftsmanship that went into it. One becomes addicted to life in spatial elegance and it would be exceedingly difficult to fit back into the typical Irish suburban semi-detached house.' He has even adjusted well to life in the north city, finding it quite safe to walk the streets at all hours without the fear of being molested. And he finds the location so convenient that, upon moving into the street, one of his first acts was to sell his car and buy a bicycle. He takes obvious satisfaction in noting that friends who once called him a lunatic for buying a run-down house in a sordid section of Dublin now visit and, seeing its charm, comment, 'Oh, it is lovely . . . I wish that I could do it'. He especially delights in boasting mischievously that 'the Provost of Trinity has a magnificent eighteenth-century house but even he is only a *tenant*—I actually *own* mine'. He genuinely considers himself 'steeped in luck' to have acquired such a treasure in the midst of modern-day Dublin, professing that he is still 'amazed that the opportunity had been left' to him and 'incredulous at the stupidity of others for not snapping up' the house before him. He foresees the not so distant day when the entire street will be restored and repopulated, the roadway cobbled again, trees planted and all the corroding ironwork replaced. Then, he believes, Dubliners will finally understand what restoration is all about—when the evidence is clearly visible. If this dream is realized, it will be due in part to his energies. He is an indispensable figure in the street's current history.

THE CASEYS OF HENRIETTA STREET:
ARCHITECTURAL ARCHAEOLOGISTS

If north-side Georgian restorationists are a rare breed, the Michael Caseys must be thought of as a truly unique species. They have become something of a novelty on the restoration scene. Michael and Aileen Casey, both aged thirty, are seeking to revive a palatial house along historic Henrietta Street. At present the house is little more than a dilapidated hollow shell and the Caseys subsist amid surroundings that even other seasoned restorationists consider primitive. They face an Homeric challenge. And in contrast to their peers, they have defiantly set out on an independent course.

186

Michael seems born and bred for the role he now plays in restoration. He was raised in a 1720s house along Fishamble Street, one of Dublin's oldest. His family was steeped in Irish heritage, and from childhood he was inculcated with a natural appreciation for history, tradition and things old and held dear. It is unthinkable that he would ever live in a bland, contemporary dwelling. Aileen, by contrast, was brought up in a small but smart modern house in Rathgar. They seemed a curious match. In his early twenties, when a student at the National College of Art studying theatre, film technology and art design, Michael became involved in a project which required him to make some sketches of several houses along Henrietta Street. He became particularly enamoured with number thirteen and when he learned that the house was up for sale he promptly sought the necessary loan from a bank. Financiers scarcely took him seriously. The very notion of an unemployed college student seeking to borrow £13,000 to buy a decrepit 12,000 square-foot mansion along a deserted Georgian row struck them as highly impractical, if not downright absurd. One bank manager openly scoffed at his proposal which only made him more determined. Michael recalls that virtually everyone viewed him as 'very, very eccentric . . . a nutcake'. Undeterred, he finally secured the funds from Desmond Guinness. In 1975, without first consulting his prospective bride, he bought the house—a typical manifestation of his fierce individuality.

The house was built in the early 1730s and is today one of the oldest surviving Georgian structures in Dublin. Like all the houses constructed along the street, it was designed to be ostentatious and meant to be lived in by wealthy, prominent citizens of Dublin's upper-crust society. But after the street fell from fashion, the houses were treated meanly for well over a century by a myriad of owners and tenants. Exteriors were neglected and interiors ravaged by intense tenementation. In the Caseys' house literally every section has been destructively tampered with in some form. Original features had been stripped, partitions added and rooms modified to house the indigent. Michael bought it in what could only be called wretched condition—gaping holes in the roof through which rain freely flowed, floorboards torn out, sections of walls and staircases extracted, wood rotting and bricks crumbling. It reeked of all the squalor of generations of harsh tenement use; rot and decay were pervasive. To exacerbate the situation, when Michael bought the house it held thirty-six tenants, many of whom had for years deliberately hastened the property's decay in the hope that the Dublin Corporation would evict and rehouse them in better quarters.

One evening, without warning, Michael drove Aileen to Henrietta Street, stood her across the way from the house at dusk and blithely proclaimed, 'Well, my dear, here is your future home'. Surveying the gaunt, drab edifice before her, smelling the cooking cabbage emanating from within, and seeing the shadowy figures of tenants moving about, Aileen discloses that she promptly burst into tears 'out of sheer horror and dismay', feeling that she 'can't live here'. The enormity of the structure itself made it appear frightening and unmanageable. But she was persuaded by Michael to give it a chance. At first, Aileen found it an 'expedition' just to move about from one floor to another, so great is the size of the house; the top floor was seldom visited at all. Shortly after the Caseys took possession of the property, the Dublin Corporation declared it 'unfit for human habitation' in terms of health, sanitation and safety standards. The tenants were legally evicted and settled elsewhere.

Once the property had been vacated, the Caseys set about the seemingly impossible task of restoration. Physically, much of the building was in a state of ruination. Thus, they embarked on what they aptly term 'architectural archaeology', a methodical process of excavating the filth, litter and foreign excrescences built up over more than a century. Wallpaper, paint and partitions were stripped away to reveal the true identity of the house. One of the worst jobs was excavating the basement which is more like an ancient catacomb. Rubble heaps 8–9ft high comprised of parts of three cars, twenty-six motor bikes, bricks, stone, timber and indefinable debris had to be dug out one section at a time and hauled away.

After six years of occupation the house has been purged of its wastage deposited by the horde of past tenants. But very little actual restoration has taken place. Unlike most other restorationists, the Caseys feel no urgency to make even a single room comfortable. Instead, Michael believes that years should be spent in getting to know the intrinsic physical and historical character of the structure before any rehabilitation takes place. He argues that 'I would have made huge errors if I had ploughed into major restoration'. As a result, the house remains in what many visitors, including some restorationists, regard as an 'uncivilized' and uninhabitable condition. Rain still flows through apertures in the roof and rotten and open spaces remain in walls and floors. The continuing absence of modern bathroom, heating and lighting facilities alarms many outsiders, some of whom, Michael admits, consider him a bit 'mad'. The barren, cavernous interior with its often crumbling, ashen walls creates a mood of eerie primitiveness. In the minds of some visitors the stark, tomb-like ambience is ghostly and forbidding. The primeval scene seems rather like a set for a Gothic horror film. Indeed, the Caseys' house has been used as a site for several movies. The highly acclaimed *Strumpet City* was filmed, in part, in the stark, sullen chambers, depicting the grim days of Dublin tenementation and poverty. There is also another practical aspect of the house's rawness. Sections of exposed brick and timber throughout the interior have proved valuable to scholars studying eighteenth-century architectural materials and techniques.

Both Michael and Aileen feel an obligation to open their house to any interested strangers who amble up the street, curiously peering through windows. They have even become accustomed to those visitors who, upon witnessing the harshness within, overtly express shock and occasionally make critical comments. Aileen identifies three types of visitors on the basis of their initial reactions: those who say, 'Oh, my God, you're so lucky, look at this place, we'd like to be living here ourselves'; those who comment 'Yes, it'll be lovely when it's finished'; and others who simply blurt out 'Oh, My God'. The last type, says Aileen, 'have no idea why we're here in a wreck like this'. But the Caseys remain unperturbed by outside society's opinion of their alien lifestyle. They have obviously adjusted to their bare-bones existence and seem untroubled at the prospect of raising their four-year-old son in such socially unnatural conditions. They possess meagre funds for restoration. There is a sporadic income from design work, which they both perform, and some supplementary money has flowed in from the film companies allowed to work in their home. Although Michael concedes that at times he has been tempted to 'throw up my eyes and pull out my hair', he rejects the idea of any support or co-operation. He prefers to rely solely on the occasional assistance of an uncle. He estimates that it will take at least £20,000 just to make the basic structural repairs on the house, realizing that restoration could become a lifetime job. Yet, he entertains notions of one day 'being rich' and furnishing the entire house with original period pieces.

Michael views his life in historical terms, noting that ten generations of residents have already filtered through the house, all leaving their special imprint. He confesses that 'I don't intend living totally in the past or trying to recreate the past. This house will be restored but not as a piece of pseudo eighteenth-century art; there will be cracks in the ceiling, the early furniture will actually creak. The real quality of the house is that it is 250 years old. Its position in history is just as important as the fabric of the house . . . I am a part of the history of the house.'

THE KIERNANS: SILENT SETTLERS

The Kiernans moved into North Great George's Street next door to Desiree Shortt in 1976. They are not leaders in the community and prefer to maintain a rather low profile. Patiently and persistently they daily work at the gargantuan task of restoring their Georgian home to its former grace and dignity. But as 'silent settlers' they, and others like them, are the real core of the restoration movement.

Tom and Caitriona, both aged thirty-four, met in the late 'sixties during their college years. He was studying architecture at Bolton College and became involved in the student battle to save the Georgian buildings along Hume Street. Caitriona initially thought Tom's participation in the struggle to be merely 'a passing student fancy'. Only through time did she learn to understand his devotion to architectural preservation. From early childhood he had a fascination with old houses, and during his teens used to explore around Mountjoy Square peeking through fanlights at the exquisite plasterwork. As he tells it, even as a young boy 'I never doubted for a minute that one day I would own a Georgian home'. At nineteen he attended a lecture on Georgian Dublin given by Desmond Guinness to architectural students. This further inspired him to pursue the dream. At first he set his sights on a house in Mountjoy Square but decided that the emergent community along North Great George's Street offered greater security. Thus he and Caitriona decided to buy house number thirty-nine for £32,000, a considerable sum of money by their standards.

From their first day in occupation it was a financial, physical and emotional struggle. Caitriona explains: 'we went through very bad times for the first two years . . . everything seemed to be going wrong.' Most disheartening was their 'absolute miscalculation of the amount of time' required for jobs—combined with the constant financial strain and mounting weariness of it all. Since they were financially unable to hire labourers, Tom had to do literally all the repairs and restoration himself. This included extensive rewiring and plumbing as well as a complete reroofing. Because their friends were also young and busy raising a family, the Kiernans did not have the aid of regular work parties. Tom worked furiously to renovate the two upper floors so that they could be rented as flats to generate additional income. He would routinely return

(*opposite*) A partially restored room in the Casey's palatial Georgian house along Henrietta Street

home from his office around 5.00 pm and work until 10.00 pm before even sitting down for dinner. To save money for restoration they gave up new clothes, concerts, plays and other normal pleasures. At one point they were even financially reduced to selling a treasured silver teapot to raise needed funds. Caitriona was compelled to take a full-time teaching position. At first, she believed this to be only a temporary financial necessity. She soon realized, however, that the financial exigencies of restoration demanded that she continue indefinitely in full employment. This was a major blow because both had always wanted to have four children; this was no longer possible under the circumstances. It was a supreme sacrifice for the sake of the house.

The strain of restoration took a far greater toll on Caitriona than on her husband. During the strenuous second year when everything seemed to be going awry, she began thinking that 'I can no longer bear this, I'm going to have to give it up'. She remembers feeling like being 'in the grips of a big octopus . . . you're just getting off one tentacle and you find that there are two more strangling you somewhere else'. She longed for emancipation from their self-imposed Georgian bondage. This caused considerable mental anguish because she firmly believed that 'Tom was unshakeable, that once having got the house he would be carried out dead or to a mental hospital or to another kind of hospital with an ulcer or something'. In desperation, she contemplated that 'if I broke every window in the house', maybe it would convince him to leave. An additional strain was placed on the marriage because they became slowly estranged from good friends. Since the house was in such a state of disarray during the early years, they did not dare invite friends to visit. Furthermore, there was simply no time for such ordinary leisure pursuits. Regrettably, some of their friends interpreted this as snobbery and social climbing associated with moving into a big Georgian house. Caitriona notes that even when some of her friends would visit they often assumed a condescending attitude, sometimes insensitively remarking: 'I don't know how you can put up with this. I don't know how you can live here in this state of deprivation.' Such demeaning comments hardly bolstered her confidence and self-image. During the pivotal second year, the Kiernans seriously discussed giving it all up. In retrospect, Caitriona believes that she did not succumb to the temptation to concede defeat

Georgian reproductions: (*above*) a copy in Baggot Street; (*below*) a neo-Georgian house in the suburbs of Dublin (*courtesy of Castletown Homes Ltd*)

primarily because of the fear that in future years she might be nagged by the feeling that she had failed to 'give it a fair try'. She was also put off by the thought of a standardized sort of life in the suburbs.

After six years of relentlessly combating debt and scraping plaster-work, the hardship has eased, though by no means ceased. Through it all, Caitriona credits Tom with being absolutely 'unshakeable', a pillar of strength. The major repairs have been completed and it is no longer necessary to let rooms to tenants. There are now two daughters aged four and five and family life is more normalized. All things considered, the Kiernans view the experience as character-building and marriage-strengthening. As Tom proffers, 'if our marriage survived the second year it can survive anything'. Caitriona concurs, adding that 'there are very few things that I would now fear. I wouldn't fear financial or material deprivation because we've sort of scraped the bottom of the barrel and it couldn't get any worse.' For the present, all thoughts of 'giving up' have been put out of mind; the worst tribulations have been survived. Yet, as some problems subside, others arise. Their daughters have now reached the age when they need social contacts and the freedom to play along the street. Like the Molloys, the Kiernans are coming to realize that the north side is not the ideal physical or social environment in which to raise children. There are only a few other children along the street with whom they can play. On the other hand, the Kiernans hope that their daughters might learn much from living in such a socially mixed society (neighbours range from former prostitutes to nuns).

Restoration proceeds at a steady but unfrenzied pace—a welcome relief from the early years. Tom is finally able to utilize his most creative talents, sculpting original delicate plasterwork to frame the fireplace. His minuscule plaster figures and embroidery would even draw the praise of eighteenth-century craftsmen. To be sure, much of the house remains unrestored and in need of painting, carpeting and furnishing but Tom affirms that 'a dream keeps you going'. He cares deeply about the city's vanishing architecture and cannot conceal his disappointment over the government's unwillingness to assist in his honourable enterprise. Caitriona has become a bona fide *aficionado* of Georgiana but she will probably never feel as strongly as Tom whom she describes as a 'committed, rabid Georgian'. Both recognize that they are doing something important by restoring their house and saving a piece of the Georgian inheritance, and Caitriona feels a 'slightly better person' for it. Her only wish is that restorationists could be blessed with 'two lifetimes . . . the first to restore the home and the second to enjoy it'.

11
The Future of Georgian Dublin: Requiem or Revival?

If Dublin is to be saved, it will require nothing less than a reincarnation of the spirit and determination of the Wide Streets Commission—that great body of men who gave the city its 18th century Georgian streets and squares. Their mission was to make Dublin a truly great city, equal in rank to the great European cities of their day, and they succeeded. Since then, however, Dublin has lost its greatness because the authorities have simply been 'muddling through' from one crisis to the next, settling for half-baked solutions which have done more damage than good to the fabric of the city.[1]

If there is not a consciousness among all the people of our common interest in our heritage, if there is not a political will, and, above all, if there is not education to that end, the mere enactment of the most elaborate and rarefied piece of legislation is no good.[2]

Decades have passed since Dubliners were implored to 'let us have sense . . . let us preserve the best of our Georgian environment . . . let us be remembered as a people who valued their finest possessions rather than as having destroyed them in ignorance'. This invocation to save the Georgian heritage has been little heeded. The mindless and licentious destruction goes on as the Georgian stock is steadily whittled away. Indeed, at the time of writing fine eighteenth-century buildings around Mountjoy and Parnell squares and along Baggot, Harcourt and Leeson streets stand perilously close to their demise at the hands of developers. There is a terrible irrationality about it all. How incongruous that a society internationally acclaimed for its love of fine literature, music and art should be so insouciant toward its invaluable architectural heritage. Whatever is to be the fate of the Georgian city?

The survival of the Georgian heritage remains much in jeopardy because the synchronous forces which have conspired against it for the past two decades are still at work: governmental neglect, developer's cupidity and public apathy—the deadly triumvirate. If allowed to persist, they can doom the Georgian terraces; attrition will surely take its toll. But there is still ample time to redress past mistakes and wrongdoings and secure the welfare of the historic architecture. However, this will demand a new realism. As one Irish journalist bluntly asserted, it is hypocritical to talk about preserving Georgian Dublin when, in fact, 'we do absolutely nothing to preserve it'. Either preservation is to be taken seriously or it is not. To be taken seriously preservation requires *commitment*.

A realistic approach to Georgian preservation implies the recognition and acceptance of certain incontrovertible facts:

1 Whether appraised in terms of its intrinsic historic or artistic merits, and judged by either national or international standards of the art, Dublin's Georgian architecture is indisputably unique and worth saving. Protestations to the contrary are stale and limp; they simply will not hold up under objective scrutiny. And the weary argument about 'offensive foreign relics' is anachronistic, an insult to modern progressive Irish thought.

2 The imperilled state of the Georgian architecture cannot justifiably be blamed on any single source. To ascribe fault to a particular group may be expedient, but at this critical stage in the architecture's evolution it is not constructive. In truth, culpability for the sad saga of Georgiana's destruction must be shared by every segment of Irish society. It is important to recognize this fact. Irish officialdom, citizens and urban developers have all contributed in their own ways to the degenerative process. It can be argued fairly that the Georgian terraces would not be so diminished and endangered today if the government had acted more forcefully, if the citizens had expressed greater concern, or if the developers had exhibited more sensitivity and less greed. Urban developers could never have taken such bold liberties with the historic quarters if the government and citizens had not given them tacit licence to do so by failing to exert their own responsibilities and powers. All three groups have conspired, perhaps unwittingly, against the welfare of the city's Georgian architecture. It is the cumulative effect of their actions, or inactions, that has been so harrowing.

3 The government's present policy of preventive controls for preservation has been an unqualified failure. Anyone who seriously doubts this need only take a casual stroll through the north Georgian neighbourhoods or

along Harcourt, Baggot or Lower Leeson streets. The evidence is painfully abundant. The cold fact obtrudes that although Dublin is one of the oldest and finest surviving cities in all Europe, its historic architecture lacks the basic legislative and planning protection now considered *normal* in most other Western European countries. The mere listing of buildings will do absolutely nothing to save them. Noble proclamations about preservation, whether in written or verbal form, are worthless unless buttressed by affirmative legal and planning action. There is no substitute.

4 Essential to all preservation efforts must be the basic conviction that the Georgian architecture can really be saved. As in other Western European countries, preservation success in Ireland must be predicated on two vital ingredients: government commitment, leadership and financial assistance and vigorous public support. The absence of either component will cripple the best-intentioned efforts. There is nothing inherent in Irish society which precludes preservation success. All the necessary resources exist—they must simply be applied in a determined and imaginative manner.

These fundamental presumptions provide a realistic and honest working premise for preservation efforts. The denial or omission of any of these precepts will distort the true preservation picture and impede progress. It may not be easy for some segments of Irish society to accept these verities but it is necessary that they do so. In some instances it will mean exploding old myths and adopting fresh attitudes.

GOVERNMENT LEADERSHIP AND RESPONSIBILITY

There is no escaping the fact that the chief responsibility in the field of Irish preservation must rest with the government, as it does elsewhere in Europe. It is unreasonable to suppose that any other body in Ireland is equipped to assume the burden of so monumental a task. To date, the government has shunned its responsibility. It is really more accurate to state that successive governments have neglected their responsibilities. The principal failure has been the absence of any financial assistance scheme. This omission is remarkable for two reasons (both dealt with in an earlier chapter). First, An Taisce forcefully asserted some fifteen years ago in its widely circulated report that of all the measures applied in the preservation process, *incentive* is the 'most important factor'. Secondly, the Western European preservation experience verifies that governments must play a pivotal role by allocating grants, loans and tax relief to ensure restoration and preservation of a nation's architectural assets. Inexplicably, the Irish Government has ignored this hard evidence, founding its policy on a lethargic system of listing and negative planning controls. The results are evident.

In *Architectural Conservation in Europe,* author Sherban Cantacuzino documents that successful preservation programmes depend in large measure on the 'necessary legislation and the will to use these powers' as well as the 'determination of priorities in allocating money'. Herein lies the real problem. In Dublin there seems to be a reservoir of good will among urban authorities on the personal level toward architectural preservation (it is indeed rare to find anyone openly opposed to the concept), but there is incontestably a distinct 'lack of really decisive official policy about architectural conservation in the city'.[3] Consequently, there is a dire need for a critical, yet constructive, review of the Dublin Corporation's current preservation position. The recurring contention in governmental circles, that modern Ireland is too impoverished a country to contribute financially to preservation, is a frail excuse, subject to serious rebuttal. Ireland may not yet be a wealthy country but it most assuredly possesses sufficient financial resources to assist with preservation. In its 1981 *Annual Review*, An Foras Forbartha stated that the scale of investment necessary to bring Ireland's physical infrastructure (houses, roads, hospitals, schools, telecommunications, etc) to the required level amounts to between £20,000 and £30,000 million over the next decade—apparently not a solitary pound of which is marked for Georgian preservation in the national capital! The financial resources exist—about this there can be little doubt—but they are simply not allocated because the *will* is lacking. Nowhere is this more apparent than in the continuing lack of legislative protection for Georgian interiors. It is appalling to realize that the Corporation has failed to safeguard these antiquated chambers despite their full authority to do so. This libertine attitude, when compared with the protection accorded to similar interiors elsewhere in Europe, honestly amounts to gross negligence towards an invaluable public trust. Benign neglect can no longer be excused—it has already exacted too costly a toll on the city's historic fabric. It is at least encouraging to note that many of the younger urban planners and staff members of the Dublin Corporation seem genuinely sympathetic to the need for rigorous new preservation codes. Unfortunately, it is usually their less-appreciative senior colleagues who make the major policy decisions.

What is perhaps most needed is a fresh philosophical outlook on the part of government towards the entire preservation issue. At present, officialdom is locked into the archaic thinking that private individuals be allowed to exert tremendous control over the nation's historic architecture. This is drastically at odds with prevailing European philosophy, founded on the principle that owners of historic buildings are really caretakers of a national treasure. Governments possess not only the right but the *duty* to protect the public heritage. It is this paramount question of private property rights versus social rights that remains at the 'very heart of the Dublin preservation dilemma'.[4] It cannot be ignored. In the light of Ireland's deeply ingrained and admirable tradition of individual property rights, it is understandable that the government is reluctant to impinge on old freedoms. Nowhere is human attachment to land and property more cherished than in Ireland—for good reason. However, a national heritage belongs to the citizens collectively; there is such a thing as protecting society's rights. This means that custodial owners of valuable, aged buildings cannot be free to alter or blemish them to suit their personal fancy. The government is duty-bound to provide essential protections. This approach implies recognition that owners of Georgian buildings are merely 'temporary custodians for posterity'. Certainly in an age when personal freedoms are continually challenged, government intervention is not viewed kindly. However, in certain spheres of modern society it is not only justified but mandatory for the public good. Preservation of historic architecture is such an area. As proven on the Western European front, governmental intervention to rescue and safeguard the national architectural inheritance is to be welcomed, even applauded. This is preservation realism.

Apart from a philosophical shift, the government might try a new practical tack—namely, co-operation with the business-development sector. The cause of preservation could be well served by a fruitful partnership between the two. Ideally, they might work in concert towards specific preservation objectives, sharing management and costs. There is a sound rationale for collaboration. A city's perceived image can have a strong bearing on its financial welfare. Some cities enjoy a decidedly more positive image than others. Not uncommonly, such imagery is based in part on the attractiveness of the built environment. Cities with special appeal and 'personality' naturally draw tourists, conventions and investment. In this respect, Dublin's business community has much to gain from participating in preservation. In many western cities the historic quarters have become a recognized asset and their preservation a natural part of urban planning. The destruction or impairment of this resource results in economic as well as cultural loss.

Simply stated, architectural preservation is a sound financial investment. This is especially true at present when many once-distinguished cities are fast losing their individuality as massive urban redevelopment shapes them into anonymous entities. Old cities able to retain their dignity and distinctiveness will increasingly profit from their special status.

To date, there has been no appreciable co-operation between government and business in the matter of urban preservation. In fact, private organizations have made more progress in this realm than governmental bodies. An Taisce has had considerable success in bridging the gap between preservationists and the business community. As a consequence, Dublin's business community is gradually coming to realize that 'architectural quality makes sound economic sense'. In the late 1970s, with encouragement from preservationists, a number of major Irish companies launched the Heritage Trust with contributory funds. This is a modest but significant beginning. Under a grant from the Heritage Trust, the Dublin Architectural Study Group was recently formed whose responsibility it is to examine all aspects of Georgian preservation and produce a definitive report. However, there is no guarantee that officialdom will heed the advice contained in this document; it could result in just one more futile exercise. Despite the formation of the Heritage Trust, the business sector has not been satisfactorily tapped as a potential source of financial support for preservation. If properly approached, several conspicuously prosperous Irish companies, among others, might be persuaded to join the preservation battle. Additionally, there are now hundreds of foreign-based industrial firms operating in Ireland under the aegis of the Industrial Development Authority, many of which would perhaps be willing to contribute a fair share to so important a national enterprise. This, of course, presupposes that the Irish Government changes its policy and begins injecting funds into preservation as a model for others to follow. This, hopefully, is preservation realism.

THE QUESTION OF FUTURE FORM AND FUNCTION

What will be the status of Georgian Dublin in the twenty-first century? In answer to this question, multiple scenarios could be contemplated. At worst, the Georgian terraces could ultimately fall victim to obsolescence and demolition, simply eradicated from the cityscape. This is not likely. It is most improbable that Dublin will ever lose all its Georgian houses; some would have to be retained if only as museum pieces. At best, one might envision full restoration and preservation of all surviving Georgian buildings and their glorious return to private residences. This seems equally unlikely. Their destiny doubtless lies somewhere between these two extremes. Whatever Georgian Dublin's future is to be, it must be appraised in terms of function as well as form. It seems reasonable to presume that a good many Georgian buildings will be structurally saved, but what is to be their role in future times? The continuing trend towards conversion of Georgian stock for office and commercial use constitutes a superficial sort of preservation. Although it does not satisfy traditionalists, it is clearly preferable to the outright loss of the terrace houses.

Georgian Dublin's past can serve as an index to its future potential. One thing can be stated with certainty: over its long and turbulent life the Georgian city has endured the vicissitudes of history, both kind and cruel, with remarkable aplomb. Their innate resilience and functional flexibility have allowed the eighteenth-century dwellings to survive. The intrinsic adaptability that has helped to save them to the present day promises to serve equally well in the future. It is when the Georgian structures cease to be functional that they become most vulnerable. For this reason, the utilization of Georgian houses for office, institutional and commercial space, which has become so prevalent since the 1960s, is not entirely to be condemned. This convertibility factor has acted as a practical 'stop-gap' measure; had many buildings not been transformed into new uses, they would surely have met their demise.

The concept of reversing the functional pattern of Georgian terraces deserves serious exploration. It is not unreasonable to imagine that Georgian buildings could experience a gradual occupational reconversion to their original use as private residences. The logical goal would be to return Georgian properties to a *prescribed* level of residential use. This is not so quixotic an idea as it may first appear. It is, in fact, a viable prospect. In Edinburgh, a city often compared with Dublin in terms of architectural heritage, eighteenth-century buildings have been preserved and retained predominantly in residential use; it has been hailed as a 'remarkable example of a living centre'. Of course, preservation in Edinburgh has been generously funded by the government and a large number of grants have been awarded to citizens for historic restoration and maintenance. Such a scheme in Dublin would be perfectly consistent with the avowed goal of the Planning Authority to maintain and expand the population of the inner city. If the government is indeed serious about a strategy for residential renewal, the Georgian terraces could play an important role. Owing to the current scarcity of existing housing and land available for building, it is probable that many properties currently used for non-residential purposes would have to be acquired for housing. The reconversion of Georgian structures to private occupancy could form a natural part of this urban process. After all, the great social virtue of Georgian Dublin was that it embraced a salubriously mixed society—an 'examplar of a satisfactory sort of city life'. The reincarnation of Georgian houses as private homes could contribute to the recreation of a truly living city.

Socio-economic rejuvenation of historic inner-city quarters has become a reality in many western cities. It would seem that the potential for this type of rebirth in Dublin is greater than in most cities. Dublin possesses a formidable stock of potentially habitable Georgian houses advantageously located within close proximity to transport, shops and restaurants. Thus, the nucleus for a living city exists—it simply needs to be resuscitated. Rehabilitation of Georgian terraces as living places would presumably take the form of gentrification in which middle-class or upper-income groups would return to the old historic districts of the city centre. This type of urban resettlement is now a common feature of urban revival in many cities of the western realm. Gentrification of Georgian Dublin could recapture the social vitality once indigenous to the squares and terraces. The reappearance of Dubliners from the more prosperous ranks would have a healthy effect on the city centre, forging a more natural, heterogeneous social milieu. And certainly there is much to be said for returning Georgian houses to individuals who would love them and take care of them. One notable advantage enjoyed by Dublin is that, unlike many other western cities, its centre is not plagued by crime and violence. Dublin remains relatively free from serious predatory crimes which might dissuade prospective residents.

Residential renewal of the Georgian districts cannot occur without incentives and ingenuity. Typically, the impetus for urban regeneration comes from the government or business sector, sometimes both. In Dublin, strong governmental sponsorship would be indispensable. In short, what is needed is a government plan that would make the Georgian terraces less attractive as office and commercial space and more appealing as residential districts. Ideally, perhaps 50–80 per cent of all Georgian houses might eventually revert to some residential use. The remainder would be used for offices and commercial purposes compatible with the social order. Such a functional reordering of the Georgian sections would contribute to a 'normalization' of the area and the new balance would more closely reflect the original residential-occupational patterns of the city. As a first effort, the Planning Authority might promote, in co-operation with the business sector, the development of new alternative office nodes in other desirable parts of the city or urban fringe. These would have to be well provided with amenities and services for the work-force. There is, of course, no guarantee that non-residential occupants at present along the terraces could be lured away *en masse*. One can reasonably assume that a number of Georgian buildings would remain securely in the hands of doctors and lawyers as their prestigious offices. But certainly most offices now used by government bodies and private firms could be returned to living quarters if enticing alternatives were offered.

Even if a good portion of Georgian buildings were purged of their alien element and made available again for private residence, it would not likely become a reality without government assistance. Georgian houses are too costly for most Dubliners to purchase, restore and maintain. Georgian resettlement could be triggered only with the proper inducements. Gentrification would have to be made economically feasible. This could be accomplished if the Irish Government would follow the example set by other European countries and provide grants, loans and tax relief for residents of older historic districts. These residents, in their capacity as caretakers of the public's inheritance, would be deserving of government financial assistance. This is an integral part of the stewardship philosophy adopted by most Western European governments toward their national architectural heritage. Some may sceptically view the concept of residential repopulation of the Georgian city as little more than a fanciful vision. But the North Great George's Street community, with no support from the government, stands as a proud exemplar of what can be accomplished.

PUBLIC EDUCATION AND PARTICIPATION

> Architectural heritage will survive only if it is appreciated by the public and in particular by the younger generation. (1975 Declaration of Amsterdam)

In the final analysis, successful architectural preservation depends on the 'right climate of public opinion'. No seasoned preservationist would question the veracity of this contention. Public apathy has clearly abetted the decline of Georgian Dublin in the past. In the future, public attitudes will continue to play a vital role in the preservation issue—but hopefully in a positive rather than negative manner. Having witnessed the litany of destruction about them for the past twenty years, Dubliners now seem genuinely more sensitive to the loss. They have certainly shed much of their naïvety about urban redevelopment and developers; but the lessons learned have been costly. The dramatic public protests in recent years over the destruction of the Wood Quay archaeological site are strong testimony to a growing public conscience. As a consequence, it is most unlikely that public sentiment would permit the ESB débâcle to occur today. Much of this nascent awareness of the architecture can be attributed to the tireless activities of preservationists who have managed to keep important issues before the public eye. But despite heightened public awareness about preservation, there is still a pressing need for more enlightened thinking and action before Georgian Dublin is secured from further destruction.

Dubliners may well be better informed than in the past but they are still fundamentally passive about protection of the historic architecture. The proverbial 'silent majority' remains essentially unresponsive to Georgiana's peril. This is a serious failing because citizens must make their will known to city officials. This is an age in which officialdom is highly susceptible to public pressure. Citizens can wield enormous political clout when they focus their energies on a particular problem. But social change results from sustained public pressure, not a single Wood Quay-type protest march, admirable though it may be. In Dublin the problem seems to be a lack of organization and leadership. Addressing the topic of public attitudes toward national heritage, an *Irish Times* editorial posited that 'Dublin is in dire need of general leadership . . . people will respond if they are given a lead . . . Dubliners do care'. But simply 'caring' is not sufficient. Public concern must be translated into messages meaningful to decision-makers. The raw power of public opinion, vigorously expressed in the proper forums, seems to have little hold on the imagination of Dubliners. It may be that many Dubliners are so habituated to being manipulated by the bureaucratic forces that they do not believe it possible to exert influence over public issues. The notion still prevails that the 'ordinary people of Dublin have little hope of fighting these speculative developers'. One distressed citizen recently lamented that the Irish have in Dublin a city equal to Amsterdam, Venice or Warsaw in terms of architectural character—yet it is being destroyed before their very eyes. He theorizes that this loss might be attributed in part to a 'feeling of inferiority in ordinary people'.

His point may well be a valid one. There does indeed seem to be an almost palpable sense of defeatism and impotence among Dublin's citizens when it comes to challenging the powers at work on the city. Dubliners even seem to devalue their capital instinctively, further suggesting an inferiority complex of sorts. The average Dubliner exhibits little detectable pride in his city. Indeed, he is often prone to express genuine surprise when Dublin is praised by foreigners. He seems curiously uncomfortable with the compliment.

It is regrettable that many Dubliners apparently labour under the misconception that they cannot induce positive change. For in Ireland urban preservation can succeed only if the general public have both the 'political strength and emotional persuasion' to ensure that policies are formulated and vigorously enforced.[5] This is precisely the problem in Dublin. Dubliners indisputably possess the political power to bring about preservation change—they simply have not chosen to use it. Whether or not they have the emotional persuasion remains uncertain. If the people of Dublin clamoured loudly for the protection of *their* Georgian inheritance, government authorities would not dare to ignore them—they could ill afford to do so. Conversely, in the absence of such public concern and pressure one can hardly blame officials for perpetuating their tradition of benign neglect; it is just human nature.

So far, the preservation battle has been waged by a relatively small band of conscientious Dubliners. It would be incorrect to believe that they could indefinitely carry the burden for greater society. Even the most energetic and determined proponents of preservation have their limits of endurance. As the giant wheels of bureaucracy relentlessly turn and the 'officials win' time after time, it is easy to become dispirited and demoralized. Each defeat at the hands of the bureaucrats or developers takes a certain psychological and emotional toll on front-line preservationists. And it is difficult to maintain a high level of morale and stamina in the midst of widespread public apathy. In Dublin, preservation can seem a lonely and hopeless cause. Wider-based public support is desperately needed. Only public education can accomplish this.

Underlying all public attitudes is education—or lack of it. Public education is fundamental to any preservation movement but in Ireland, where there is no real tradition of urban architectural protection, it assumes special importance. The Irish are nurtured on fine literature and music; in these areas they are well advanced and much envied. But their exposure to the architectural art form is woefully lacking. Public appreciation for architecture has never been a strong feature of Irish life.

In Ireland, architecture of any style or period is not instinctively valued; appreciation must be *learned*. Since the surviving Georgian buildings are under intense pressure, the need for educating public opinion has never been greater. Only education can ensure a future for Dublin's past.

Preservation education is needed at all levels of Irish society but especially in the primary schools where young fertile minds are not cluttered with bias and misconceptions. Noting this need in its 1967 report, An Taisce suggested talks and presentations in schools. This is a constructive idea providing that it is handled imaginatively. Drab lectures and abstract sermons will hardly ignite the passions of children to appreciate and defend old buildings. To be most effective, the subject of preservation must be enlivened. Since the responsibility for motivating students toward a positive preservation outlook rests with teachers, they must realistically be won over first. At present there are probably few teachers capable of intelligently discussing urban preservation with their students. This could be remedied by a series of seminars or special courses in which teachers at different levels could be instructed about the subject. The funding for such programmes, which would not be prohibitive, could logically be provided by some government body, private industry, or, if necessary, perhaps An Taisce. Awards could be granted to teachers for developing imaginative ideas to involve their students in preservation-oriented projects.

Direct involvement is the key to student preservation projects. Innovative field trips that take children into different Georgian neighbourhoods so that they can witness the processes of decay and restoration would be likely to have a potent impact on their thinking. There are doubtless many suburban children who have had scant acquaintance with the older Georgian sections of their city. Walking the historic streetscapes could prove quite a revelation—for students and teachers alike. Preservationists would surely be willing to contribute their time and talents in developing serious student excursions along such streets as North Great George's or Henrietta. Once students have been exposed to the Georgian heritage they should be encouraged to question its evolution. Most effective would be the problem-solving approach in which they are asked to make creative and critical judgements about the architectural scene. What do they think about the loss of such dignified old structures? What does this reveal about contemporary Irish society? Why might Georgian buildings be worth saving? How might this be accomplished? What are the alternatives? The topic of Georgian preservation is conducive to discussion in several disciplines, most notably history, geography and civics. Different strategies might be developed to elicit thought and creativity. Study projects could be devised which encourage students to involve their parents or relatives. They could be asked to sample adult opinions on the subject. Involvement of adults would be particularly productive because it could lead to dialogue between generations and awareness of the issue. This would cultivate fresh thought on the subject across a wider spectrum of Irish society. Students could be asked to compare in written or art form finely restored eighteenth-century interiors with modern dwellings—a natural comparative study in contrasting forms and functions. A city-wide essay contest, perhaps sponsored by the Department of the Environment or Bord Failte, on the subject of Georgian preservation could promote widespread interest. This might be strategically correlated with the declaration of a 'National Preservation Week'. The government's sponsorship of the annual Tidy Town competition sets a convenient precedent for such environmental involvement. To support the effort, Irish newspapers could be coaxed into running special series of articles to coincide with other events. Ideally, such articles would place the preservation of Georgian Dublin within the larger European context, thereby alerting readers to the Irish dilemma. By these and numerous other means, Irish youth could gradually learn to recognize and accept their architectural surroundings from an early age. The bedevilling myth that preservation in Ireland is a purely 'middle-class luxury' could finally be dispelled. Dubliners would learn to perceive preservation as an egalitarian ideal, not an élitist crusade. This is vital because preservation is most successful when it is championed by all classes of society. It must be thought of as a shared cause.

Dubliners should be mindful of one paramount fact. In many western cities the once-charming historic core has been so disembowelled and disfigured that the original character is utterly beyond redemption. But Dublin rather miraculously retains much of its enchanting eighteenth-century persona and eccentricity. This Georgian ethos still lingers perceptibly along the reticent squares and terraces. It is an irretrievable heritage—once lost, it is gone for all time. But Dubliners still have a *choice*. Major decisions are yet to be made. For good or ill, this generation of Irishmen is blessed (or cursed as the case may be) with the responsibility for making these important decisions. The human perspective should be kept always in mind. Modern urban man is often adrift in a sea of sleek structures, functionalism and efficiency. It can be an impersonal and disorienting vacuum. He needs identifiable links with the past—cultural anchors. Kindly old buildings offer emotional and psychological comfort. They are therapeutic for the human spirit. They are meant to be visually stroked and mentally assimilated. Dubliners would surely be impoverished by their absence. They deserve to be saved and savoured by Dubliners yet to come. To deny still unborn populations the sheer personal joys of relishing Georgiana's antiquities would be a legacy of shame. It ought to be the nation's duty to see that the Georgian architecture is not allowed to perish. To the query, 'are there not more important things on which to spend public money than on archaeological remains and old buildings?', an *Irish Times* editorial affirmatively retorts—'there is nothing more important than our self-respect'.

Future generations of Dubliners may one day have to ponder with dismay why their forbears allowed such a rich inheritance to be frittered away. Why was there no concerted effort to grasp it from the clutches of extinction? Sadly, some day Georgian Dublin may be recalled only in lamentful ballads and melancholic poetic verse—most visible traces having vanished from view. *It need not be so.*

Notes

1   McDonald, Frank. 'Dublin—What Went Wrong?', *Irish Times*, 15 November 1979, p14
2   'Heritage and All That', *Irish Times*, 23 October 1980, p9
3   Nowlan, Kevin B. 'Conservation and Development', *Dublin's Future: The European Challenge* (A Conservation Report for An Taisce, published by *Country Life* Magazine, 1980), p10
4   Sewell, Leslie. 'Viewpoint', *Taisce Journal*, 5 no 2 (1981), p9
5   Shaffrey, Patrick. *The Irish Town: An Approach to Survival* (O'Brien Press, 1975), p144

Bibliography

Aalen, F. H. A. *Man and Landscape in Ireland* (Academic Press, 1978)

Abercrombie, Patrick, Kelly, Sydney, and Kelly, Arthur. *Dublin of the Future* (Hodder & Stoughton, 1922)

Agena, Kathleen. 'Historic Preservation: A Matter of Dollars and Sense', *Ekistics*, March 1975, pp177–80

An Foras Forbartha. *Annual Review, 1980/81* (An Foras Forbartha, 1981)

An Foras Forbartha. *The Protection of the National Heritage* (An Foras Forbartha, 1969)

An Taisce. *Amenity Study of Dublin and Dun Laoghaire* (An Taisce, 1967)

Ashbee, Felicity. 'Balconettes—A Forgotten Aspect of Cast Iron', *The Connoisseur*, 179 no 721 (1972), pp188–91

Ashe, F. A. 'Mountjoy Square', *Dublin Historical Record*, III (1940–41), pp 98–115

Bannon, Michael J. 'Growth of Office-Type Employment in the Republic of Ireland', *Irish Geography*, 7 (1974), pp111–15

Bannon, Michael J. 'The Changing Centre of Gravity of Office Establishments Within Central Dublin, 1940 to 1970', *Irish Geography*, 6 (1972), pp480–4

Barrington, Sir Jonah. *Historic Memoirs of Ireland* (Henry Colburn, 1833, two volumes)

Barrington, Sir Jonah. *Personal Sketches of His Own Times* (Henry Colburn, 1827, two volumes, and 1832, one volume)

Barry, Francis. 'Reproduction: For and Against', *Dublin: A City in Crisis* (The Royal Institute of the Architects of Ireland, 1975), pp52–6

Barry, T. B. 'The Destruction of Irish Archaeological Monuments', *Irish Geography*, 12 (1979), pp111–13

Beckett, J. C. *The Anglo-Irish Tradition* (Faber & Faber, 1976)

Biddle, James. 'Historic Preservation', *Journal of Housing* (May 1971), pp219–27

Bord Failte. 'Eighteenth Century Dublin', *Ireland Information Sheet Number 7* (Bord Failte, 1980)

Bord Failte. 'Eighteenth Century Dublin', *Ireland of the Welcomes*, 8 no 6 (1960), pp17–22

Butler, Eleanor. 'The Georgian Squares of Dublin—I', *Country Life* (25 October 1946), pp756–9

Butler, Eleanor. 'The Georgian Squares of Dublin—II', *Country Life* (1 November 1946), pp810–12

Butler, R. M. 'Dublin: Past and Present', *Dublin Civic Week Official Handbook* (Civic Week Council, 1927), pp28–31

Butler, R. M. 'Georgian Dublin', *Centenary Conference Handbook* (The Royal Institute of the Architects of Ireland, 1939), pp27–46

Cantacuzino, Sherban. *Architectural Conservation in Europe* (Watson-Guptill Publications, 1975)

Clarke, Desmond. *Dublin* (B. T. Batsford, 1977)

Clarke, Harold. *Georgian Dublin* (Eason & Son, 1976)

Cloncurry, Lord Valentine. *Personal Recollections of His Life and Times* (James McGlashan, 1849)

Connery, Donald S. *The Irish*, (Eyre & Spottiswoode, 1968)

Costello, John. 'Streets, Streetscapes, and Traffic', *Dublin: A City in Crisis* (The Royal Institute of the Architects of Ireland, 1975), pp57–60

Costonis, John J. *Space Adrift: Saving Urban Landmarks Through the Chicago Plan* (University of Chicago Press, 1974)

Craig, Maurice. 'An Irishman's Diary', *Irish Times*, 16 January 1980

Craig, Maurice. 'Attitudes in Context', *Architectural Conservation: an Irish Viewpoint* (Architectural Association of Ireland, 1974), pp9–21

Craig, Maurice. *Dublin 1660–1860* (Cresset Press, 1952)

Craig, Maurice. 'Dublin Doorways', *Ireland of the Welcomes*, 21 no 4 (1972), pp19–26

Craig, Maurice. 'Unknown Dublin', *The Antique Collector*, August 1974, pp53–60

Cuffe, Luan. 'Indicators', *Architectural Conservation: An Irish Viewpoint* (Architectural Association of Ireland, 1974), pp72–8

Curran, C. P. 'Ceasar Ripa and the Dublin Stuccodores', *Studies: an Irish Quarterly Review*, XXVIII (1939), pp237–48

Curran, C. P. *Dublin Decorative Plasterwork of the Seventeenth and Eighteenth Centuries* (Alec Tiranti, 1967)

Curran, C. P. 'Dublin Plasterwork', *The Journal of the Royal Society of Antiquaries of Ireland*, LXX (1940), pp1–16

Curran, C. P. 'Michael Stapleton: Dublin Stuccodore', *Studies: An Irish Quarterly Review*, XXVIII (1939), pp439–49

Dale, Anthony. 'Listing and Preserving Historic Buildings: The European Picture', *The Architectural Review*, August 1965, pp97–104

D'Arcy, Peter. 'Infill Policy in Existing Streets', *Dublin: A City in Crisis* (The Royal Institute of the Architects of Ireland, 1975), pp46–51

Delany, Patrick. 'The Streets Where You Live', *Irish Times* (Special Supplement entitled 'Dublin: Impressions and Observations'), 18 May 1976

Dillon, William. 'The Tailors' Hall, Back Lane', *Quarterly Bulletin of the Irish Georgian Society*, III no 2 (1960), pp9–12

Downes, J. Neil. 'The Georgian Architecture of Dublin—Action Now Can Save Heritage', *Irish Independent*, 27 February 1962, p6

Downes, J. Neil. 'The Georgian Architecture of Dublin—A Knotty Problem for the E.S.B.', *Irish Independent*, 26 February 1962, p6

Downes, J. Neil. 'The Georgian Architecture of Dublin—Change As Renaissance Developed', *Irish Independent*, 13 February 1962, p6

Downes, J. Neil. 'The Georgian Architecture of Dublin—Dublin Has a Unique Distinction', *Irish Independent*, 19 February 1962, p12

Downes, J. Neil. 'The Georgian Architecture of Dublin—Genius Not Confined by Rules', *Irish Independent*, 14 February 1962, p6

Downes, J. Neil. 'The Georgian Architecture of Dublin—Preservation Work is Still Possible', *Irish Independent*, 28 February 1962, p6

Downes, J. Neil. 'The Georgian Architecture of Dublin—"Spec-Builders" Who Wrought Miracles', *Irish Independent*, 20 February 1962, p6

Downes, J. Neil. 'The Georgian Architecture of Dublin—The Best of Both Worlds', *Irish Independent*, 26 February 1962, p6

Downes, J. Neil. 'The Georgian Architecture of Dublin—The Summerson Report is Assailed', *Irish Independent*, 1 March 1962, p6

Downes, J. Neil. 'The Georgian Architecture of Dublin—Three Courses Are Open to the E.S.B.', *Irish Independent*, 2 March 1962, p6

Downes, J. Neil. 'The Georgian Architecture of Dublin—What Are We Trying to Preserve?', *Irish Independent*, 12 February 1962, p6

Downes, J. Neil. 'The Georgian Architecture of Dublin—Where The Real Magic is Found', *Irish Independent*, 22 February 1962, p6

Downes, J. Neil. 'The Georgian Architecture of Dublin—Vista That is the Finest in the World', *Irish Independent*, 23 February 1962, p6

'Dropping the Pilot?', *The Architectural Review*, December 1970, pp341–6

Dublin—A Living City? (Publication of the Dublin Living City Group, no date cited)

'Dublin City's Falling Down', *City Views*, no 12, (1980), p1

Dublin City Development Plan—1971 (Government Stationery Office, 1971)

Dublin City Development Plan—1976 (Government Stationery Office, 1976)

Dublin Development: Preservation and Change (A Draft Interim Report prepared by Llewelyn-Davies, Weeks, Forestier-Walker and Bor for the Dublin Corporation, January 1967)

'European Conservation Year', *The Architectural Review*, December 1970, pp333–6

European Heritage (Phoebus Publishing Company, 1974), a special magazine produced for the European Architectural Heritage Campaign by the Council of Europe

Evans, E. Estyn. *The Personality of Ireland* (Cambridge University Press, 1973)

Evening Press, 'Plan to Save North Great George's Street', 12 December 1980

Evening Herald, 'Return to an Age of Elegance', 22 October 1980, p8

Feilden, B. M. 'Training for Restoration', *The Architectural Review*, November 1970, pp301–2

Fennell, Desmond. 'The Irish Cultural Prospect', *Social Studies*, 1 no 6 (1972), pp682–9

Ffolliott, Rosemary. 'The New Culture: Domestic Life and the Arts, 1680–1830', *The Irish World: The History and Cultural Achievement of the Irish People*, ed Brian DeBrefeny (Thames and Hudson, 1977)

Fitzpatrick, William J. *Ireland Before the Union* (W. B. Kelly, 1867)

Fitzgerald, Brian. *The Anglo-Irish* (Staples Press, 1952)

'Fitzwilliam Fiasco', *Taisce Journal*, 3 nos 2 and 3 (one issue, 1979) p21

Fletcher, Sir Banister. *A History of Architecture* (The Athlone Press, 1975)

Flood, Donal T. 'Eighteenth Century Dublin', *Dublin Historical Record*, XXXIII no 3 (1980), pp109–10

Flood, Donal T. 'The Decay of Georgian Dublin', *Dublin Historical Record*, XXVII no 3 (1974), pp78–100

Ford, Larry R. 'Continuity and Change in Historic Cities: Bath, Chester, and Norwich', *The Geographical Review*, 68 no 3 (1978), pp253–73

Fox, Kevin. 'European Perspective', *Architectural Conservation: An Irish Viewpoint* (Architectural Association of Ireland, 1974) pp64–71

Fraser, James. *A Handbook for Travellers in Ireland* (William Curry, 1845)

Frondorf, Anne F., McCarthy, Michael M. and Zube, Ervin H. 'Quality Landscapes: Preserving the National Heritage', *Landscape*, 24 no 1 (1980), pp17–21

Froude, James Anthony. *The English in Ireland in the Eighteenth Century* (Longman, Green, 1881, three volumes)

Gamble, John. *Sketches of History, Politics, and Manners in Dublin* (Baldwin, Cradock and Joy, 1826)

Geoghegan, Joseph A. 'Notes on 18th Century Houses', *Dublin Historical Record*, VII no 2 (1945), pp41–53

Georgian Architecture in Northern Ireland (Booklet published by the Council for the Encouragement of Music and the Arts, 1948)

Gilbert, J. T. *A History of the City of Dublin* (James McGlashan, 1854, one volume, and 1859, two volumes)

Goodison, Nicholas. 'The Door Furniture at Ely House', *Quarterly Bulletin of the Irish Georgian Society*, XIII April–September 1970, pp45–8

Gray, Tony. *The Irish Answer* (Heinemann, 1966)

Griffin, David. 'Eighteenth Century Architecture', *Dublin Handbook*, ed Tom Kennedy (Albertine Kennedy, 1979), pp7–8

Guinness, Desmond. 'Decorative Plasterwork in Ireland', *Apollo Magazine*, October 1966, pp290–7

Guinness, Desmond. *Georgian Dublin* (B. T. Batsford, 1979)

Guinness, Desmond. 'Irish Georgian Society', *Quarterly Bulletin of the Irish Georgian Society*, II no 1 (1960), p2

Guinness, Desmond. 'Irish Georgian Society', *Quarterly Bulletin of the Irish Georgian Society*, VI no 1 (1968), p14

Guinness, Desmond. 'Irish Georgian Society', *Quarterly Bulletin of the Irish Georgian Society*, XIII no 1 (1970), p1

Guinness, Desmond. 'Irish Georgian Society', *Quarterly Bulletin of the Irish Georgian Society*, XIV nos 1 and 2 (1971), p3

Guinness, Desmond. 'Irish Rococo Plasterwork', *Ireland of the Welcomes*, 10 no 6 (1962), pp18–22

Guinness, Desmond. 'Robert West: Architect and Stuccodore', *Ireland of the Welcomes*, 12 no 6 (1964), pp20–4

Guinness, Desmond. 'The E.S.B. Buildings: Will They Survive?', *Quarterly Bulletin of the Irish Georgian Society*, IV nos 3 and 4 (1961), pp29–30

Handbook for Delegates to the Annual Conference at Dublin (The Royal Institute of British Architects, 1931)

Hanna, Denis O'D. 'Ulster Georgian', *Quarterly Bulletin of the Irish Georgian Society*, no 3 (July–September, 1958), pp36–40

Harris, Walter. *The History and Antiquities of the City of Dublin* (John Knox, 1766)

Harvey, John. *Dublin—A Study in Environment* (B. T. Batsford, 1949)

Houghton, Joseph P. 'The Social Geography of Dublin', *The Geographical Review*, XXXIX no 2 (1949), pp257–77

Hibernia, 'Behind the Rotten Façades in Mountjoy Square', 2 October 1980, p9

Hibernia, 'Dereliction Reigns Supreme in Mountjoy Square', 5 June 1980, p6

Hibernia, 'George Moore Georgian', 2 October 1980, p13

Hosmer, Charles B. *Presence of the Past: A History of the Preservation Movement in the United States* (G. P. Putnam, 1965)

Houses of Distinction (A special study conducted by the Dublin Architectural Study Group for An Taisce, 1981)

Humphreys, Alexander J. *New Dubliners* (Routledge & Kegan Paul, 1966)

Image, 'Revitalized, Renewed—North Great George's Street', March 1980, pp8–11

Irish Architecture—A Future for our Heritage (National Committee for European Architectural Heritage Year, 1975)

Irish Independent, 'Dublin's Changed—But They're Terrible Changes', 31 August 1980, p5

Irish Independent, 'The Rape of Harcourt Terrace', 17 February 1981

Irish Times, 'A Past Under Attack', 28 April 1981 (Special Supplement entitled 'Developing Dublin')

Irish Times, 'Heartbreak City', 17 November 1979, p13

Irish Times, 'Heritage and All That', 23 October 1980, p9

Irish Times, 'Conservation is Keynote to Powerscourt Plan', 22 August 1980, p20

Irish Times, 'Property Development in Ireland', 29 May 1968, p1 of Special Supplement

Irish Times, 'What England Left Behind', 18 May 1978, p iv of Special Supplement

Jacobs, Stephen W. 'Architectural Preservation in Europe: French and English Contributions', *Curator*, 9 no 3 (1966), pp196–215

Johnson, Denis. 'In Search of Irish Identity', *Irish Times*, 29 October 1977, p10

Johnson, Edith Mary. *Ireland in the Eighteenth Century* (Gill and MacMillan, 1974)

Kearns, Kevin C. 'Industrialization and Regional Development in Ireland, 1958–1972', *American Journal of Economics and Sociology*, 33 no 3 (1974), pp299–316

Kearns, Kevin C. 'Ireland: A New Image for the "Ould Sod" '. *Focus*, XXVI no 2 (1975), pp1–8

Kearns, Kevin C. 'Resuscitation of the Irish Gaeltacht', *The Geographical Review*, LXIV no 1 (1974), pp82–110

Kee, Robert. *The Most Distressful Country* (Quartet Books, 1976)

Kelly, Deirdre. *Hands off Dublin* (The O'Brien Press, 1976)

Kelsall, Moultrie R. and Harris Stuart. *A Future for the Past* (Oliver and Boyd, 1961)

Kennealy, Ginnie. 'Desiree Has the Georgian Touch', *Sunday Press*, 14 September 1980

Kennedy, Tom. 'Dublin's Ironwork', *Ireland of the Welcomes*, 18 no 5 (1970), pp8–12

Kennedy, Tom (ed). 'Walking through Dublin', *Dublin Handbook* (Albertine Kennedy, 1979)

Kerr, Robert J. 'Historic Preservation—A Pragmatic Approach', *American Institute of Architects Journal*, 41 no 14 (1964), pp36–8

Lecky, William E. H. *A History of Ireland in the Eighteenth Century* (Longman, Green, 1892, five volumes)

LeHane, Brendan. *Dublin* (Time-Life International, 1978)

Lewis, Pierce F. 'The Future of the Past: Our Clouded Vision of Historic Preservation', *Pioneer America*, VII no 2 (1975), pp1–20

Lewis, R. *The Dublin Guide* (Correcting Office, 1787)

Liddle, Laurence H. *A Valuation Approach to the Conservation of Georgian Buildings* (An Foras Forbartha, 1972)

Local Government (Planning and Development) Act, 1963 (Government Stationary Office, 1963)

Local Government (Planning and Development) Act, 1976 (Government Stationary Office, 1976)

Longford, Christine. *A Biography of Dublin* (Methuen, 1936)

Lowenthal, David. 'Past Time, Present Place: Landscape and Memory', *The Geographical Review*, LXV no 1 (1975), pp1–36

Lowenthal, David. 'The Bicentennial Landscape: A Mirror Held Up to the Past', *The Geographical Review*, LXVII no 3, (1977), pp252–67

'Lower Fitzwilliam Street', *Quarterly Bulletin of the Irish Georgian Society*, V no 1 (1962), pp1–2

Lynch, Paula. 'A Dublin Street: North Great George's Street', *Dublin Historical Record*, XXXI no 1 (1977), pp14–21

MacLaughlin, Adrian. *Guide to Historic Dublin* (Gill and MacMillan, 1979)

Madden, Aodhan. 'Another Georgian Street in Danger', *Evening Press*, 30 August 1979, p8

Malcomson, A. P. W. *John Foster—The Politics of the Anglo-Irish Ascendancy* (Oxford University Press, 1978)

Malton, James. *A Picturesque and Descriptive View of the City of Dublin* (London 1792–99)

Martin, Seamus. 'A Street of Hope', *The Sunday Tribune*, 21 June 1981, p20

Maxwell, Constantia. *Dublin Under the Georges: 1714–1830* (Faber & Faber, 1936)

McCullough, Joseph. 'Conservation Struggle in Dublin', *Town and Country Planning*, 1970 November, pp473–7

McDermott, Matthew J. *Ireland's Architectural Heritage* (Folens and Co, 1975)

McDonald, Frank. 'Battle to Save One of City's Finest Streets', *Irish Times*, 12 November 1980, p10

McDonald, Frank. 'Dublin—What Went Wrong?', *Irish Times*, 12 November 1979, p10

McDonald, Frank. 'Dublin—What Went Wrong?', *Irish Times*, 15 November 1979, p14

McDonald, Frank. 'Dublin—What Went Wrong?', *Irish Times*, 4 December 1979, p11

McDowell, Robert B. *Irish Public Opinion, 1750–1800* (Greenwood Press, 1975)

McGovern, Sean. '18th Century and the Present', *Irish Times*, 22 October 1976, p10

McGrath, Raymond. 'Dublin Panorama', *The Bell*, 2 no 5 (1941), pp35–48

McGregor, John J. *New Picture of Dublin* (Johnson and Deas, 1821)

McParland, Edward. 'The Case Against Neo-Georgian', *Irish Times*, 14 August 1974, p10

McParland, Edward. 'The Wide Streets Commissioners: Their Importance for Dublin Architecture in the Late 18th–Early 19th Century', *Quarterly Bulletin of the Irish Georgian Society*, XV no 1 (1972), pp1–29

Melvin, Peter. 'Conservation and the Built Environment', *Progressive Architecture*, 53 (November, 1972), pp86–91

Middleton, Michael. 'Conservation Conspectus', *The Architectural Review*, December 1970, pp374–5

Miner, Ralph W. *Conservation of Historical and Cultural Resources* (American Society of Planning Officials, 1969)

Montgomery, Niall. 'Irish Perspective', *Architectural Conservation: An Irish Viewpoint* (Architectural Association of Ireland, 1974), pp55–63

Mulcahy, Rosemarie. 'Dublin's Loss—How Many More?', *An Taisce*, 2 no 3 (1978), p25

Mulcahy, Rosemarie. 'Viewpoint', *Taisce Journal*, 3 no 1 (1979), p11

Murphey, Michael W. *Education in Ireland: Now and the Future* (The Mercier Press, 1970)

Murtagh, Tommy. 'Going Through An Identity Crisis', *Irish Times*, 29 October 1977, p10

National Trust for Historic Preservation, *A Guide to Delineating Edges of Historic Districts* (Washington, D.C.: The Preservation Press, 1976)

National Trust for Historic Preservation, *Historic Districts: Identification, Social Aspects and Preservation* (Washington D.C.: National Trust for Historic Preservation, 1975)

National Trust for Historic Preservation, *Historic Preservation Today* (Charlottesville: University of Virginia Press, 1966)

National Trust for Historic Preservation, *Information: From the National Trust for Historic Preservation, Information Sheet Number 20* (Washington D.C.: National Trust for Historic Preservation, 1979)

Newsweek, 'The Restoration of Things Past', 23 March 1981, pp84–8

Norris, David. 'Plea For An Exciting Extra-Mural Venture', *Trinity College Gazette*, 16 no 3 (1980), pp1–2

Nowlan, Kevin B., 'Conservation and Development', *Dublin's Future: The European Challenge* (A Conservation Report for An Taisce, published by *Country Life* Magazine, 1980), pp8–13

Nowlan, Kevin B. 'Dublin Since 1916', *Dublin Handbook*, ed Tom Kennedy (Albertine Kennedy, 1979), pp12–13

Nowlan, Kevin B. 'Growth of Public Interest', *Architectural Conservation: an Irish Viewpoint* (Architectural Association of Ireland, 1974), pp95–9

O'Brien, Michael. 'Preservation of Historic Areas in Dublin' (Paper presented before the International Federation for Housing and Planning Conference in Dublin, May 1969)

O'Connell, Derry. *The Antique Pavement* (An Taisce, 1975)

O'Connor, Deirdre. *Housing in Dublin's Inner City* (Housing Research Unit, University College, Dublin, 1969)

O'Faolain, Sean. 'Fair Dublin', *Holiday*, April 1963, pp73–80

O'Faolain, Sean. *The Irish* (Penguin, 1980)

O'Hanlon, Thomas J. *The Irish*, (Harper and Row, 1975)

O'Rourke, Madeline. 'Urban Decay and Renewal', *Taisce Journal*, 4 no 4 (1980), pp4–5

Orme, A. R. *Ireland* (Aldine Publishing, 1970)

Peter, A. *Dublin Fragments: Social and Historic* (Hodges and Figgis, 1925)

Peter, A. *Sketches of Old Dublin* (Sealy, Bryers and Walker, 1907)

Prince, Hugh C. 'A Future for the City's Past', *Geographical Magazine*, May 1978, pp529–32

Robertson, Edward G. and Robertson, Joan. *Cast Iron Decoration: A World Survey* (Watson-Guptill, 1977)

Robertson, Manning. 'Old and Future Dublin', *Centenary Conference Handbook* (Royal Institute of the Architects of Ireland, 1939), pp27–46

Robinson, Nicholas. 'What is to be Done?', *Dublin's Future: The European Challenge* (A Conservation Report for An Taisce, published by *Country Life* Magazine, 1980), pp14–16

Roth, Frederick L. and O'Connell, Merrilyn Rogers. (editors) *Historic Preservation* (American Association for State and Local History, 1975)

Rothery, Sean. *Everyday Buildings of Ireland* (Department of Architecture, College of Technology, 1975)

Rowan, Alistair. 'The Historic City', *Dublin's Future: The European Challenge* (A Conservation Report for An Taisce, published by *Country Life* Magazine, 1980), pp2–7

Scully, Seamus. 'Around Dominick Street', *Dublin Historical Record*, XXXIII no 3 (1980), pp82–92

Sewell, Leslie. 'Viewpoint', *Taisce Journal*, 5 no 2 (1981), p9

Shaffrey, Patrick (editor). *Irish Architecture: A Future For Our Heritage* (National Committee for European Architectural Heritage Year, 1974)

Shaffrey, Patrick. *The Irish Town: An Approach to Survival* (The O'Brien Press, 1975)

Sheaff, Nicholas. *Iveagh House: An Historical Description* (Department of Foreign Affairs, 1978)

Sheehy, Jeanne. 'Contribution of History II', *Architectural Conservation: An Irish Viewpoint* (Architectural Association of Ireland, 1974), pp32–6

Simms, J. G. 'Dublin in 1776', *Dublin Historical Record*, XXXI no 1 (1977), pp2–13

Somerville-Large, Peter. *Dublin* (Hamish Hamilton, 1979)

Sunday Press, 'Georgian Dublin: The Fight Goes On', 21 December 1980

The Dublin Civic Survey Report (The Dublin Civic Survey Committee, 1925)

'The E.S.B. Buildings: Will They Survive?', *Quarterly Bulletin of the Irish Georgian Society*, IV, nos 3 and 4 (1961), p29

The Knight of Glin, *Irish Furniture* (Eason and Son, 1978)

The Restoration of North Great George's Street (North Great George's Street Preservation Society, 1980)

'Twenty-Five Years of Listing', *The Architectural Review*, November 1970, pp308–9

Viney, Michael. 'Prestige Office Use Could Preserve Georgian Houses', *Irish Times*, 2 July 1975

217

Wallace, Martin. *The Irish: How They Live and Work* (David & Charles, 1972)

Walsh, John E. *Rakes and Ruffians: The Underworld of Georgian Dublin* (Four Courts Press, 1979)

Warburton, J., Whitelaw, J., and Walsh, Robert. *History of the City of Dublin* (T. Cadell and W. Davies, 1818, two volumes)

Warren, Geoffrey. *Vanishing Street Furniture* (David & Charles, 1978)

Whitelaw, Rev James. *An Essay on the Population of Dublin* (Graisberry and Campbell, 1805)

Winks, Robin. 'Conservation in America: National Character as Revealed by Preservation', Jane Fawcett (editor) *The Future of the Past* (Watson-Guptill, 1976)

Woodham-Smith, Cecil. *The Great Hunger* (New English Library, 1975)

Wright, Lance, and Browne, Kenneth. *A Future for Dublin* (The Architectural Press, 1974)

Ziegler, Arthur P. *Historic Preservation in Inner City Areas* (The Allegheny Press, 1971)

Acknowledgements

This book is the product of three years' labour, including two summer field research trips to Dublin. Owing to the inherently sensitive and often controversial nature of this subject in Irish society, it was, from the very outset, a most challenging undertaking. Such a forthright treatise could never have been written without the generous assistance and co-operation of a multitude of people to whom I am deeply indebted.

Because I have endeavoured to place this relevant subject in a social/humanistic perspective, rather than in a cold clinical framework, the views and experiences of Irish preservationists at all levels comprise a vital part of my research. Personal accounts were gleaned from a host of concerned, involved and knowledgeable individuals who spoke with me most candidly and at great length about every imaginable aspect of the Irish architectural preservation dilemma. If I have in any way been successful in breathing new life into this topic, it is due in large measure to their provocative insights and shared experiences. I am most thankful to those special few who, during the most difficult stages of research and writing, continually assured me that this work was 'most important and long overdue'; their abiding faith in this project has been of inestimable value.

Particular appreciation is extended to the following individuals for their important contributions to this study: Professor Maurice Craig for his constructive criticism of some historical sections; the Honourable Desmond Guinness for his unfailing support and guidance; Professor Kevin B. Nowlan, Uinseann MacEoin and Deirdre Kelly who shared their unique views on the Irish preservation scene; Nicholas Sheaff and his devoted staff at the National Trust Archive for making available their wealth of archival data on Georgian architecture; I wish also to recognize the kind assistance of Lewis Clohessy, Director of An Taisce; George Bagnall, a director of Bord Failte Eireann, Bernard Muckley, Michael Gough and Michael Hughes of the Dublin Corporation; Professor Alistair Rowan; Professor Edward McParland; M. D. Burke; Rosemarie

Mulcahy; and Tom Kennedy. Thanks also go to Alan Farmer for his cartographic expertise and to Patrick 'Lucky' Duffy for his illuminating recollections of life along a Georgian street some fifty years ago; and I wish to credit the personnel of the *Irish Times* library and the staff at the Gilbert Collection, Pearse Street Library, for their valuable archival assistance. The photographs reproduced by courtesy of the American Geographical Society were taken by the author but appeared earlier in an article published in the *Geographical Review*, Vol. 72, 1982.

I owe a great debt of gratitude to the following Georgian restorationists who opened their homes to me, took me into their confidence and shared with me their personal trials, tribulations and triumphs: Harold Clarke, Desiree Shortt, David Norris, Brendan and Josephine O'Connell, Tom and Caitriona Kiernan, Michael and Aileen Casey, and John and Ann Molloy. Special thanks are extended to Kathleen Ann Bohlen for indefatigable efforts in trekking the Georgian streets in quest of research data. And I am deeply beholden to my wife, Enita, without whose patience, selflessness and unwavering support this book would never have seen the light of day. Lastly, it is important to note that, in part, the research for this book was funded by grants from the American Philosophical Society and the University of Northern Colorado Research and Publications Committee. It is fervently hoped that their investment in this project proves a judicious one.

Index